HEALTHY LIVING

HEALTHY LIVING

volume

2

health care systems
health care careers
preventive care
over-the-counter drugs
alternative medicine

Caroline M. Levchuck
Michele Drohan
Jane Kelly Kosek

Allison McNeill, Editor

AN IMPRINT OF THE GALE GROUP

DETROIT · SAN FRANCISCO · LONDON
BOSTON · WOODBRIDGE, CT

Healthy Living

Caroline M. Levchuck, Michele Drohan, Jane Kelly Kosek

STAFF

Allison McNeill, *U•X•L Senior Editor*
Carol DeKane Nagel, *U•X•L Managing Editor*
Thomas L. Romig, *U•X•L Publisher*

Margaret A. Chamberlain, *Permissions Specialist (Pictures)*

Rita Wimberley, *Senior Buyer*
Evi Seoud, *Assistant Production Manager*
Dorothy Maki, *Manufacturing Manager*
Mary Beth Trimper, *Production Director*

Michelle DiMercurio, *Senior Art Director*
Cynthia Baldwin, *Product Design Manager*

Pamela Reed, *Imaging Coordinator*
Robert Duncan, *Imaging Specialist*
Randy Bassett, *Image Database Supervisor*
Barbara Yarrow, *Graphic Services Manager*

GGS Information Services, Inc., *Typesetting*

Cover illustration by Kevin Ewing Illustrations

Library of Congress Cataloging-in-Publication Data
Levchuck, Caroline M.
   Healthy living/Caroline Levchuck, Michele Drohan.
      p. cm.
   Contents: v. 1. Nutrition, exercise, and environmental health —v.2. Medicine and healthcare —v. 3. Mental health and self-esteem.
   Includes bibliographical references and index.
   ISBN 0-7876-3918-4 (set) —ISBN 0-7876-3919-2 (v.1) —ISBN 0-7876-3920-6 (v.2) —ISBN 0-7876-3921-4 (v.3)
   1. Health–Juvenile literature. 2. Mental health–Juvenile literature. 3. Medical care–Juvenile literature. [1. Health. 2. Mental health. 3. Medical care.] I. Drohan, Michele Ingber. II. Title.
RA777.L475 2000
613–dc21   99-053258

Contents

Reader's Guide

Healthy Living covers a wide range of health-related topics and lifestyle issues in fifteen chapters spread over three volumes. Each chapter is devoted to a specific health-related topic:

- Nutrition
- Personal Care and Hygiene
- Sexuality
- Physical Fitness
- Environmental Health
- Health Care Systems
- Health Care Careers
- Preventive Care
- Over-the-Counter Drugs
- Alternative Medicine
- Mental Health
- Mental Illness
- Eating Disorders
- Habits and Behaviors
- Mental Health Therapies

Each chapter begins with a brief overview to introduce readers to the topic at hand. Paired with the overview is a chapter-specific table of contents that outlines the main sections presented within the chapter.

A "Words to Know" box included at the beginning of each chapter provides definitions of words and terms used in that chapter. At the end of each chapter, under the heading "For More Information," appears a list of books and web sites that provides students with further information about that particular topic.

Health and safety tips, historical events, and other interesting facts relating to a particular topic are presented in sidebar boxes sprinkled throughout each chapter. More than 150 photos and illustrations enhance the text.

Each volume of *Healthy Living* includes a comprehensive glossary collected from all the "Words to Know" boxes in the fifteen chapters, and ends with a general bibliography section. The offerings in the bibliography provide more general health-related sources for further information. A cumulative index providing access to all major terms and topics covered throughout *Healthy Living* concludes each volume.

Related Reference Sources

Healthy Living is only one component of the three-part U•X•L Complete Health Resource. Other titles in this library include:

- *Sick! Diseases and Disorders, Injuries and Infections.* This four-volume set contains 140 alphabetically arranged entries on diseases, disorders, and injuries, including information on their causes, symptoms, diagnoses, tests and treatments, and prognoses. Each entry, four to seven pages long, includes sidebars on related people and topics, as well as a list of sources for further research. Each volume contains a 16-page color insert. *Sick* also features more than 240 black-and-white photographs and a cumulative subject index.
- *Body by Design: From the Digestive System to the Skeleton.* This two-volume set presents the anatomy (structure) and physiology (function) of the human body in twelve chapters. Each chapter is devoted to one of the eleven organ systems that make up the body. The last chapter focuses on the special senses, which allow humans to connect with the real world. Sidebar boxes present historical discoveries, recent medical advances, short biographies of scientists, and other interesting facts. More than 100 photos, many of them in color, illustrate the text. *Body by Design* also features a cumulative index.

Acknowledgements

A note of appreciation is extended to the *Healthy Living* advisors, who provided invaluable suggestions when this work was in its formative stages:

Carole Branson
Seminar Science Teacher
Wilson Middle School
San Diego, California

Bonnie L. Raasch
Media Specialist
Vernon Middle School
Marion, Iowa

Doris J. Ranke
Science Teacher
West Bloomfield High School
West Bloomfield, Michigan

Gracious thanks to Allison McNeill, Tom Romig, and Christine Slovey as well as the rest of the U•X•L team for their patience and first-rate editorial direction. Thanks also to Leslie Levchuck, R.D., Laura Wheeldreyer, Helen Packard, Stefanie Weiss, Kristin Ward, Lynda Beauregard, Robin Mayhall, Sean G. Levchuck, M.D., and Rosemarie Rich for their expertise and contributions to this project.

Comments and Suggestions

We welcome your comments on *Healthy Living*. Please write: Editors, *Healthy Living,* U•X•L, 27500 Drake Rd., Farmington Hills, Michigan, 48331–3535; call toll free: 1–800–877–4253; fax: 248–414–5043; or send e-mail via http://www.galegroup.com.

Please Read: Important Information

Healthy Living is a medical reference product designed to inform and educate readers about health and lifestyle issues. U•X•L believes this product to be comprehensive, but not necessarily definitive. While U•X•L has made substantial efforts to provide information that is accurate and up to date, U•X•L makes no representations or warranties of any kind, including without limitation, warranties of merchantability or fitness for a particular purpose, nor does it guarantee the accuracy, comprehensiveness, or timeliness of the information contained in this product.

Readers should be aware that the universe of medical knowledge is constantly growing and changing, and that differences of medical opinion exist among authorities. They are also advised to seek professional diagnosis and treatment for any medical condition, and to discuss information obtained from this book with their health care provider.

Words to Know

A

Abscess: When pus from a tooth infection spreads to the gums.

Abstinence: Voluntary, self-denial of sexual intercourse.

Accredit: To recognize an educational institution for having the standards that allows graduates to practice in a certain field.

Acetaminophen: A generic name for a compound that affects the brain and spinal cord, altering the perception of pain and lessening it.

Acid rain: Rain with a high content of sulfuric acid.

Acupuncture: A form of alternative medicine that involves stimulating certain points, referred to as acupoints, on a person's body to relieve pain and promote healing and overall well-being.

Adaptive behavior: Things a person does to adjust to new situations.

Addiction: The state of needing to compulsively repeat a behavior.

Adrenaline: A hormone that is released during times of high pressure, stress or fear; also a chemical that blocks the histamine response in an allergic reaction.

Advocate: A person who supports or defends a cause or a proposal.

Aerobic: Something that occurs in the presence of oxygen.

Affect: An individual's emotional response and demeanor.

Affectations: Artificial attitudes or behaviors.

Allergy: A chronic condition in which an allergic reaction occurs when the immune system responds aggressively to a certain foreign substance.

Allopath: A kind of doctor who advocates the conventional system of medical practice, which makes use of all measures that have proved to be effective in the treatment of disease.

Allopathic: The system of medical practice making use of all measures that have proved to be effective in the treatment of disease.

Altered consciousness: A state of awareness that is different from typical, waking consciousness; often induced with the use of drugs and alcohol.

Alternative medicine: Medical practices that fall outside the spectrum of conventional allopathic medicine.

Alzheimer's Disease: A degenerative disease of the brain that causes people to forget things, including thought, memory, language, and the people in their lives, and which eventually leads to death. Predominantly affects the elderly.

Amenorrhea: The absence of menstrual cycles.

Anaerobic: Something that occurs without oxygen because a person is using energy to do activities at a faster rate than the body is producing it.

Analgesic: A drug that alleviates pain without affecting consciousness.

Anemia: The condition of low iron in the blood.

Anhedonia: The inability to experience pleasure.

Anorexia nervosa: A term meaning "lack of appetite"; an eating disorder marked by a person's refusal to maintain a healthy body weight through restricting food intake or other means.

Antacids: A medication used to neutralize up to 99 percent of stomach acid.

Anti-inflammatory: Chemical that counteracts inflammation.

Antibiotics: Drugs used to treat bacterial infections.

Antibodies: A substance made in the body that protects the body against germs or viruses.

Antihistamine: The drugs most commonly used to treat allergies.

Antioxidants: Powerful molecules found in certain foods and vitamins that help neutralize free radicals, which are damaging molecules.

Antipsychotic drugs: Drugs that reduce psychotic behavior, often having negative long-term side-effects.

Antiseptic: A substance that prevents the growth of germs and bacteria.

Antitussive: A type of cough medication that calms the part of the brain that controls the coughing reflex.

Anus: An opening in the body through which solid waste is expelled.

Anxiety: An abnormal and overwhelming sense of worry and fear that is often accompanied by physical reaction.

Appeal: To take a court's decision and have another higher court review it to either uphold or overturn the first decision.

Archetypes: Universally known images or symbols that predispose an individual to have a specific feeling or thought about that image.

Aromatherapy: A branch of herbal medicine that uses medicinal properties found in the essential oils of certain plants.

Art therapy: The use of art forms and craft activities to treat emotional, mental and physical disabilities.

Arthritis: Chronic inflammation of the joints; the condition causes pain and swelling.

Artificial: Human-made; not found in nature.

Asbestos: A mineral fiber.

Associate's degree: Degree granted from two-year college institutions.

Astringent: Topical solution that tightens the skin.

Attention-Deficit/Hyperactivity Disorder (ADHD): A disorder that involves difficulty in concentrating and overall inattentiveness.

Autism: A developmental disorder marked by the inability to relate socially to others and by severe withdrawal from reality. Language limitations and the extreme desire for things to remain the same are common symptoms.

Autonomy: Being in charge of oneself; independent.

B

Bachelor's degree: A four-year college degree.

Bacteria: Single-celled micro-organisms, which can be either beneficial or harmful.

Bedside manner: A physician's ability to put a patient at ease and communicate effectively.

Behavior Therapy: A form of therapy that has its history in the experimental psychology and learning processes of humans and animals. Its main focus is to change certain behaviors instead of uncovering unconscious conflicts or problems.

Behavioral Medicine: Also known as health psychology, it is another developing mental health therapy technique in the field of medicine; the interdisciplinary study of ideas and knowledge taken from medicine and behavior science.

Behaviorism: Focuses on the study of observable behavior instead of on consciousness.

Benign: Harmless; also, non-cancerous.

Binge-eating disorder: An eating disorder that involves repetitive episodes of binge eating in a restricted period of time over several months.

Bingeing: When an individual eats, in a particular period of time, an abnormally large amount of food.

Bioenergetics: Body/mind therapy that stresses the body and the mind being freed of negative actions.

Biofeedback: The technique of making unconscious or involuntary bodily processes (as heartbeats or brain waves) perceptible in order to manipulate them by conscious mental control.

Bladder: An organ that holds urine.

Blood pressure: Pressure of blood against the walls of blood vessels.

Blood vessel: Vessel through which blood flows.

Body set-point theory: Theory of weight control that claims that the body will defend a certain weight regardless of factors such as calorie intake and exercise.

Bonding: Attaching a material to the surface of a tooth for cosmetic purposes.

Brief Therapy: Also called brief psychodynamic therapy, this form of therapy involves holding therapy sessions for a briefer period of time than the classic analytical form; brief therapy focuses on the specific situations that are causing patients upset

Bulimia nervosa: A term that means literally "ox hunger"; an eating disorder characterized by a repeated cycle of bingeing and purging.

Byproduct: Something other than the main product that is produced in a chemical or biological process.

C

Caffeine: An organic compound that has a stimulating effect on the central nervous system, heart, blood vessels, and kidneys.

Calcium: A mineral in the body that makes up much of the bones and teeth, helps nerve and muscle function, as well as the body's ability to convert food into energy.

Calorie: A unit of energy contained in the food and liquids that people consume.

Capitation: An agreement between doctor and managed health care organization wherein the doctor is paid per person.

Carbohydrate: The body's primary energy source, carbohydrates are the body's fuel.

Carbon monoxide: A highly toxic, colorless, odorless gas that is produced whenever something is burned incompletely or in a closed environment.

Carcinogenic: Cancer-causing.

Carcinogens: Substance that produces cancer.

Cardiovascular fitness: How efficiently the heart and lungs can pump blood (which holds oxygen) to muscles that are being worked.

Carve out: Medical services, such as substance abuse treatment, that are separated from the rest of the services within a health care plan.

Cervix: Narrow outer end of the uterus.

Chiropractic: A way of treating certain health conditions by manipulating and adjusting the spine.

Cholera: Any of several diseases of humans and domestic animals usually marked by severe gastrointestinal symptoms.

Cholesterol: A cousin to fat, is a steroid found only in foods that come from animals, such as egg yolks, organ meats, and cheese.

Chronic condition: A condition that lasts a long time or occurs frequently (e.g., asthma). Chronic conditions can be treated but not cured.

Circumcision: The removal of the foreskin from the glans of the penis.

Classical conditioning: Learning involving an automatic response to a certain stimulus that is acquired and reinforced through association.

Clinical trial: A study that evaluates how well a new drug works, positive effects, negative side effects, and how it is best used.

Clitoris: Small erectile organ in females at front part of the vulva.

Coexisting: Existing, or occurring, at the same time.

Cognition: The grouping of the mental processes of perception, recognition, conception, judgment, and reason.

Collagen: Fibrous protein found in connective tissues such as the skin and ligaments.

Collective unconscious: According to Karl Jung, the storage area for all the experiences that all people have had over the centuries. Also present in the collective unconscious are instincts, or strong motivations that are present from birth, and archetypes.

Compulsion: Habitual behaviors or mental acts an individual is driven to perform in order to reduce stress and anxiety brought on by obsessive thoughts.

Compulsive behavior: Behavior that is repeated over and over again, uncontrollably.

Conception: Also called fertilization. The formation of a cell capable of developing into a new being, such as when a man's sperm fertilizes a woman's egg creating a human embryo.

Congenital: Existing at birth.

Conscious: According to Karl Jung, the only level of which a person is directly aware.

Contaminate: To infect something or make something unsafe for use.

Continuing education: Formal schooling above and beyond any degree that is often required of medical professionals in order to keep practicing in their specific field.

Contraception: A birth control tool that prevents conception.

Convergent thinking: Thinking that is driven by knowledge and logic (opposite of divergent thinking).

Copayment: A fixed amount of money that patients pay for each doctor's visit and for each prescription.

Correlation: The relation of two or more things that is not naturally expected.

Cortisone: A hormone from the steroid family that originates in the adrenal cortex and is known for its antiinflammatory properties.

Cosmic: Relating to the universe in contrast to Earth.

Cowper's glands: Two small glands on either side of the male urethra, below the prostate gland, that produce a clear, sticky fluid that is thought to coat the urethra for passage of sperm.

Crash(ing): Coming down from being high on drugs or alcohol.

Creativity: One's capacity to think and solve problems in a unique way.

Credentials: Proof that a person is qualified to do a job.

Cruciform: The term for certain vegetables with long stems and branching tops, such as broccoli and cauliflower.

Cunnilingus: Oral stimulation of the female genitalia (vulva or clitoris).

Cut: The practice of mixing illegal drugs with another substance to produce a greater quantity of that substance.

Cuticle: The skin surrounding the nail.

D

Dance therapy: The use of dance and movement to treat or alleviate symptoms associated with mental or physical illness.

Date rape: Also called acquaintance rape; forced sexual intercourse between a person and someone she or he is acquainted with, is friends with, or is dating.

Decongestant: A compound that relieves a stuffy nose by limiting the production of mucus and reducing the swelling in the mucous membrane by constricting the blood vessels in the nose, opening the airways and promoting drainage.

Deductible: The amount of money a patient must pay for services covered by the insurance company before the plan will pay for any medical bills.

Defense mechanism: The ego's unconscious way of warding off a confrontation with anxiety.

Delirium: Mental disturbance marked by confusion, disordered speech, and even hallucinations.

Delusions: False, often illogical, beliefs that an individual holds in spite of proof that his or her beliefs are untrue.

Dependent: A reliance on something or someone.

Depression: Common psychological disorder characterized by intense and prolonged feelings of sadness, hopelessness, and irritability, as well as a lack of pleasure in activities.

Detoxification: The process of freeing an individual of an intoxicating or addictive substance in the body or to free from dependence.

Diagnostic: Used to recognize a disease or an illness.

Diarrhea: An increase in the frequency, volume, or wateriness of bowel movements.

Dissertation: An in-depth research paper.

Diuretic: A drug that expels water from the body through urination.

Divergent thinking: Thinking driven by creativity (opposite of convergent thinking).

Down syndrome: A form of mental retardation due to an extra chromosome present at birth, often accompanied by physical characteristics, such as sloped eyes.

Dream analysis: A technique of Freudian therapy that involves looking closely at a patient's dreams for symbolism and significance of themes and/or repressed thoughts.

Dysfunction: The inability to function properly.

Dyslexia: A reading disorder that centers on difficulties with word recognition.

E

Echinacea: A plant (also known as purple coneflower) that herbalists believe bolsters the immune system and treats certain ailments.

Edema: Swelling.

Ego: The part of one's personality that balances the drives of the id and the exterior world that is the center of the superego.

Eidetic memory: Also known as photographic memory; the ability to take a mental picture of information and use that picture later to retrieve the information.

Ejaculation: Sudden discharge of fluid (from penis).

Electrologist: A professional trained to perform electrolysis, or the removal of hair using electric currents.

Electromagnetic: Magnetism developed by a current of electricity.

Emergency: The unexpected onset of a serious medical condition or life-threatening injury that requires immediate attention.

Emission: Substances released into the air.

Empathy: Understanding of another's situation and feelings.

Emphysema: A chronic lung disease usually caused by smoking that produces shortness of breath and relentless coughing.

Enamel: The hard outer surface of the tooth.

Endocrine disrupter: Manmade chemical that looks and acts like a naturally-occurring hormone but which disturb the functioning of the naturally-occurring hormone.

Endometrial: Referring to mucous membrane lining the uterus.

Endorphin: Any of a group of natural proteins in the brain known as natural painkillers that make people feel good after exercising and act as the body's natural pain reliever.

Endurance: A person's ability to continue doing a stressful activity for an extended period of time.

Enema: A process that expels waste from the body by injecting liquid into the anus.

Enuresis: The inability to control one's bladder while sleeping at night; commonly known as bed-wetting.

Environmental tobacco smoke (ETS): The mixture of the smoke from a lit cigarette, pipe, or cigar and the smoke exhaled by the person smoking; commonly known as secondhand smoke or passive smoking.

Enzyme: A complex protein found in the cells that acts as a catalyst for chemical reactions in the body.

Ephedra: A type of plant (also known as Ma Huang) used to treat ailments, including bronchial problems, and as a decongestant.

Epidemic: The rapid spreading of a disease to many people at the same time.

Epidemiology: The study of disease in a population.

Epididymis: System of ducts leading from the testes that holds sperm.

Esophagus: The muscular tube that connects the throat with the stomach.

Estrogen: Hormone that stimulates female secondary sex characteristics.

Euphoric: Having the feeling of well-being or elation (extreme happiness).

Exercise: A subset of physical activity, which is an activity that is structured and planned.

Exercise addiction: Also known as compulsive exercise, a condition in which participation in exercise activities is taken to an extreme; an individual exercises to the detriment of all other things in his or her life.

Existential therapy: Therapy that stresses the importance of existence and urges patients to take responsibility for their psychological existence and well-being.

Expectorant: A type of cough medication that helps clear the lungs and chest of phlegm.

Extrovert: Being outgoing and social.

F

Fallopian tubes: Pair of tubes that conducts the egg from the ovary to the uterus .

Fat: Part of every cell membrane and the most concentrated source of energy in one's diet, fat is used by the body to insulate, cushion, and support vital organs.

Fee-for-service: When a doctor or hospital is paid for each service performed.

Fellatio: Oral stimulation of the male genitalia.

Fellowship: Advanced study and research that usually follows a medical residency.

Feverfew: An herb used to treat migraines.

Fluoride: A chemical compound that is added to toothpaste and drinking water to help prevent tooth decay.

Formulary: A list of prescription drugs preferred by a health plan for its members.

Free radicals: Harmful molecules in the body that damage normal cells and can cause cancer and other disorders.

Fungus: An organism of plant origin that lacks chlorophyll; some fungi cause irritation or disease (a mold is a kind of fungus).

G

Gallstone: Stones made up of cholesterol or calcium that form in the gallbladder.

Generic drug: A drug that is approved by the Food and Drug Administration but does not go by a specific brand name and therefore is less expensive than a brand name drug.

Genetic: Something present in the genes that is inherited from a person's biological parents; hereditary.

Genetic predisposition: To be susceptible to something because of genes.

Genitalia: The reproductive organs.

Geriatric: Elderly.

Gestalt therapy: A humanistic therapy that urges individuals to satisfy growing needs, acknowledge previously unexpressed feelings, and reclaim facets of their personalities that have been denied.

Gingivitis: An inflammation of the gums that is the first stage of gum disease.

Ginkgo biloba: A tree (the oldest living kind of tree, in fact) whose leaves are believed to have medicinal value, particularly in aiding memory and treating dizziness, headaches, and even anxiety.

Ginseng: An herb used as a kind of cureall, with benefits to the immune system and aiding the body in coping with stress. Some also believe it aids concentration.

Gland: A part of the body that makes a fluid that is either used or excreted by the body; glands make sweat and bile.

H

Habit: A behavior or routine that is repeated.

Halitosis: Chronic bad breath caused by poor oral hygiene, illness, or another condition.

Hallucination: The illusion of seeing or hearing something that does not really exist; can occur because of nervous system disorders or in response to drugs.

Hangnail: Loose skin near the base of the nail.

Hangover: The syndrome that occurs after being high on drugs or drinking alcohol, often including nausea, headache, dizziness, and fuzzy-mindedness.

Health Maintenance Organization (HMO): A health plan that generally covers preventive care, such as yearly checkups and immunizations. Care must be provided by a primary care physician and services must be approved by the plan in order to be covered.

Heart disease: When arteries become clogged with a fatty buildup; this can cause a heart attack or a stroke.

Heat stroke: A serious condition that causes the body to stop sweating and overheat dangerously.

Hemoglobin: A protein found in red blood cells, needed to carry oxygen to the body's many tissues.

Hemorrhoids: A form of varicose veins that occurs when the veins around the anus become swollen or irritated.

Hepatitis: One of several severe liver-damaging diseases specified by the letters A, B, C and D.

Herbicide: A chemical agent used to kill damaging plants, such as weeds.

Histamines: Chemicals released in an allergic reaction that cause swelling of body tissues.

Holistic: Of or relating to the whole rather than its parts; holistic medicine tries to treat both the mind and the body.

Homeopathy: A kind of alternative medicine that employs natural remedies.

Hormone: Substances found in the body's glands that control some of the body's functions, such as growth.

Humane: Marked by compassion or sympathy for other people or creatures.

Humanistic: A philosophy that places importance on human interests and dignity, stressing the individual over the religious or spiritual.

Hymen: Fold of mucous membrane partly closing the orifice of the vagina.

Hypertension: High blood pressure.

Hypnosis: A trance-like state of consciousness brought about by suggestions of relaxation, which is marked by increased suggestibility.

Hypoallergenic: Unlikely to cause an allergic reaction.

Hypothesize: To make a tentative assumption or educated guess in order to draw out and test its logical or observable consequences.

I

Ibuprofen: The generic name for a type of analgesic that works in the same manner as aspirin but can be used in instances when aspirin cannot.

Id: According to Sigmund Freud, the biological instincts that revolve around pleasure, especially sexual and aggressive impulses.

Identical twins: Also called monozygotic twins; twins born from the same egg and sperm.

Immune system: The body's own natural defenses against germs and other infectious agents; protects the body against illness.

Immunization: The introduction of disease-causing compounds into the body in very small amounts in order to allow the body to form antigens against the disease.

Incinerator: A machine that burns waste materials.

Indemnity plan: A plan in which the insurance company sets a standard amount that it will pay for specific medical services.

Indigenous: Occurring naturally in an environment.

Industrial: Relating to a company that manufactures a product.

Inert: A chemical agent lacking in active properties.

Infection: A disease that is caused by bacteria.

Infinitesimals: Immeasurably small quantity or variable.

Inhalants: Substances that people sniff to get high.

Inherent: Belonging to the essential nature of something.

Innate: Inborn; something (a characteristic) a person is born with.

Insight therapy: A group of different therapy techniques that assume that a person's behavior, thoughts, and emotions become disordered as a result of the individual's lack of understanding as to what motivates him or her.

Insomnia: Chronic sleeplessness or sleep disturbances.

Insulin: The substance in the body that regulates blood sugar levels.

Intelligence: The ability and capacity to understand.

Intelligence Quotient (IQ): A standardized measure of a person's mental ability as compared to those in his or her age group.

Interaction: When two drugs influence the effects of each other.

Internalized: To incorporate something into one's self.

Internship: Supervised practical experience.

Intestinal: Having to do with the intestine, the part of the body that digests food.

Introvert: Being quiet and soft-spoken.

Iridology: The study of the iris of the eye in order to diagnose illness or disease.

Iron-deficiency anemia: When the body is lacking in the right amount of red blood cells, caused by a deficiency of iron.

Irrational: Lacking reason or understanding.

K

Keratin: A tough protein produced by the body that forms the hair and nails.

Kidney stone: Stones made of calcium or other minerals that form in the kidney or the ureter, which leads to the bladder.

Kinesiology: The study of anatomy in relation to movement of the body.

Kleptomania: Habitual stealing or shoplifting.

L

Labia majora: Outer fatty folds of the vulva (big lips).

Labia minora: Inner connective folds of the vulva (little lips).

Lanugo: Fine hair that grows all over the body to keep it warm when the body lacks enough fat to accomplish this.

Larynx: The voice box.

Laxatives: Drugs that induces bowel movements and alleviate constipation, or the inability to have a bowel movement.

Leaching: The process of dissolving outward by the action of a permeable substance.

Lead: A heavy, flexible, metallic element that is often used in pipes and batteries.

Learning: Modifying behavior and acquiring new information or skills.

Learning disorders: Developmental problems relating to speech, academic, or language skills that are not linked to a physical disorder or mental retardation.

Licensed: Authorization to practice a certain occupation.

M

Mantra: A phrase repeated during meditation to center the mind.

Manual: Involving the hands.

Massage therapy: The manipulation of soft tissue in the body with the aim of relieving and preventing pain, stress, and muscle spasms.

Master's degree: A college degree that ranks above a four-year bachelor's degree.

Masturbation: Erotic stimulation of one's own genitals.

Maturation: Process of becoming mature; developing, growing up.

Medicaid: The joint state-federal health care program for low-income people.

Medicare: The federal health insurance program for senior citizens.

Medigap: Private insurance that helps pay for some of the costs involved in Medicare.

Meditation: The act of focusing on one's own thoughts for the purpose of relaxation.

Memory: The ability to acquire, store, and retrieve information.

Menstruation: Monthly discharge of blood and tissue debris from the uterus.

Metabolism: The rate at which the body uses energy.

Microscopic: Invisible without the use of a microscope, an instrument that enlarges images of tiny objects.

Mineral: A nutrient that helps regulate cell function and provides structure for cells.

Modeling: Learning based on modeling one's behavior on that of another person with whom an individual strongly identifies.

Monosodium glutamate (MSG): A substance that enhances flavor but causes food intolerance in some people.

Mortality: The number of deaths in a given time or place.

Mucous membranes: The lining of the nose and sinus passages that helps shield the body from allergens and germs.

Mucus: A slippery secretion that is produced by mucous membranes, which it moistens and protects.

Musculoskeletal: Relating to the muscles and bones.

Music therapy: The use of music to treat or alleviate symptoms associated with certain mental or physical illnesses.

N

National health care system: A system in which the government provides medical care to all its citizens.

Nature: The biological or genetic makeup of a person.

Naturopathy: A kind of alternative medicine that focuses on the body's inherent healing powers and works with those powers to restore and maintain overall health.

Neurons: Nerve cells that receive chemical-electrical impulses from the brain.

Neurosis: An emotional disorder that produces fear and anxiety.

Neurotransmitters: A substance that transmits nerve impulses.

Nicotine: An organic compound in tobacco leaves that has addictive properties.

Nitrogen dioxide: A gas that cannot be seen or smelled. It irritates the eyes, ears, nose, and throat.

Noninvasive: Not involving penetration of the skin.

Nonproductive cough: A dry and hacking cough.

Nurture: How a person is raised, by whom, and in what environment.

Nutrient: Food substances that nourish the body.

O

Obesity: The condition of being very overweight.

Observational learning: Learning by observing the behavior of others.

Obsessions: Repeating thoughts, impulses, or mental images that are irrational and which an individual cannot control.

Off-label drug: A drug that is not formally approved by the Food and Drug Administration but is approved for legal use in some medical treatments.

Operant conditioning: Learning involving voluntary response to a certain stimuli based on positive or negative consequences resulting from the response.

Oral sex: Sexual activity involving the mouth.

Organic: Occurring naturally.

Orgasm: The peak or climax of sexual excitment.

Osteopathy: A system of medical practice based on the theory that disease is due chiefly to mechanical misalignment of bones or body parts.

Osteoporosis: A degenerative bone disease involving a decrease in bone mass, making bones more fragile.

Ova: Female reproductive cells; also called eggs.

Ovaries: Female reproductive organs that produce eggs and female sex hormones.

Overdose: A dangerous, often deadly, reaction to taking too much of a certain drug.

Ovulation: Discharge of mature ovum from the ovary.

Ozone layer: The atmospheric shield that protects the planet from harmful ultraviolet radiation.

P

Palpitation: Rapid, irregular heartbeat.

Panacea: A cure-all.

Parasites: Any plant or animal that lives on or in another plant or animal and gets food from it at the expense of its host.

Parkinson's disease: A progressive disease that causes slowing and stiffening of muscular activity, trembling hands, and a difficulty in speaking and walking.

Particle: A microscopic pollutant released when fuel does not burn completely.

Penis: Male sex organ and channel by which urine and ejaculate leave the body.

Perception: One's consciousness and way of observing things.

Periodontal disease: Gum disease, the first stage of which is gingivitis.

Person-Centered Therapy: A form of therapy put forth by Carl Rogers that looks at assumptions made about human nature and how we can try to understand them. It posits that people should be responsible for themselves, even when they are troubled.

Personal unconscious: According to Karl Jung, the landing area of the brain for the thoughts, feelings, experiences, and perceptions that are not picked up by the ego.

Personality: All the traits and characteristics that make people unique.

Pesticide: A chemical agent used to kill insects and other pests.

Pharmacotherapy: The use of medication to treat emotional and mental problems.

Phenylpropanolamine (PPA): A chemical that disrupts the hunger signals being sent by the brain; it is often used in weight loss aids.

Phlegm: Sticky mucus present in the nose, throat, and lungs.

Phobia: A form of an anxiety disorder that involves intense and illogical fear of an object or situation.

Physical activity: Any movement that spends energy.

Physiological: Relating to the functions and activities of life on a biological level.

Physiology: A branch of science that focuses on the functions of the body.

Pinna: Outer part of the ear; part of the ear that is visible.

Plaque: A sticky film of bacteria that grows around the teeth.

Plaster: A medicated or protective dressing that consists of a film (as of cloth or plastic) usually spread with a medicated substance.

Point of service (POS): A health plan in which members can see the doctor of their choosing at the time they need to see a doctor.

Pores: Small openings in the skin.

Post-Traumatic Stress Disorder (PTSD): Reliving trauma and anxiety related to an event that occurred earlier.

Potassium: A chemical element that is a silver-white, soft metal occurring in nature.

Predisposition: To be susceptible to something.

Preferred provider organization (PPO): A health plan in which members have their health care paid for only when they choose from a network of doctors and hospitals.

Premium: Fee paid for a contract of insurance.

Preventive care: Medical care that helps to maintain one's health, such as regular checkups.

Primary care physician: The doctor who is responsible for the total care of a patient and has the ability to refer patients to other doctors or specialists.

Pro-choice: Supports a woman's choice in regard to abortion.

Productive cough: A cough that brings up phlegm.

Prohibition: An era in the 1920s when alcohol was made illegal.

Prostaglandin: A hormonelike substance that affects blood vessels and the functions of blood platelets, and sensitizes nerve endings to pain.

Prostate gland: A muscular glandular body situated at the base of the male urethra.

Protein: An organic substance made of amino acids that are necessary for human life.

Protozoan: One-celled organism that can cause disease in humans.

Psychiatry: The branch of medicine that relates to the study and treatment of mental illness.

Psychoactive: Something that affects brain function, mood and behavior.

Psychoanalysis: A theory of psychotherapy, based on the work of Sigmund Freud, involving dream analysis, free association, and different facets of the self (id, ego, superego).

Psychodrama: A therapy that involves a patient enacting or reenacting life situations in order to gain insight and alter behavior. The patient is the actor while the therapist is the director.

Psychodynamics: The forces (emotional and mental) that develop in early childhood and how they affect behavior and mental well-being.

Psychological vulnerability: Used to describe individuals who are potential candidates for drug addiction because of prior experiences or other influences.

Psychology: The scientific study of mental processes and behaviors.

Psychophysical energy: Energy made up of energy from the body and the mind.

Psychotherapy: The general term of an interaction in which a trained mental health professional tries to help a patient resolve emotional and mental distress.

Puberty: The onset of sexual maturation in young adults; usually between the ages of 13 and 16 in males and 12 and 15 in females.

Purging: When a person gets rid of the food that she has eaten by vomiting, taking an excessive amount of laxatives, diuretics, or enemas or engaging in fasting and/or excessive exercise.

Pyromania: Habitual need to start fires.

Q

Qi (or Chi): Life energy vital to an individual's well-being.

R

Radiation: Energy or rays emitted when certain changes occur in the atoms or molecules of an object or substance.

Radon: A colorless, odorless, radioactive gas produced by the naturally occurring breakdown of the chemical element uranium in soil or rocks.

RapidEye Movement (REM) sleep: A deep stage of sleep during which time people dream.

Rational-emotive behavior therapy: Therapy that seeks to identify a patient's irrational beliefs as the key to changing behavior rather than examining the cause of the conflict itself.

Rationing: The process of limiting certain products or services because of a shortage.

Reality therapy: A therapy that empowers people to make choices and control their own destinies.

Referral: Permission from the primary care physician to see another doctor.

Reflexology: A type of alternative medicine that involves applying pressure to certain points, referred to as reflex points, on the foot.

Registered: To complete the standards of education issued by a state government to practice a certain profession.

Rehabilitation: To restore or improve a condition of health or useful activity.

Reimbursement plan: A plan where a patient must pay for medical services up front and then get paid back from the insurance company.

Reinforcement: Making something stronger by adding extra support.

Remorse: Ill feelings stemming from guilt over past actions.

Residency: Advanced training in a medical specialty that includes or follows a physician's internship.

Residential treatment: Treatment that takes place in a facility in which patients reside.

Right-to-life: Supports anti-abortion (with possible exceptions for incest and rape) movement.

Ritual: Observances or ceremonies that mark change, renewal, or other events.

Russell's sign: Calluses, cuts, and sores on the knuckles from repeated self-induced vomiting.

S

St. John's Wort: An herb used as an antiinflammatory drug, to treat depression, and as an analgesic.

Saturated fat: Fat that is solid at room temperature.

Savant: A person with extensive knowledge in a very specific area.

Schizophrenia: A chronic psychological disorder marked by scattered, disorganized thoughts, confusion, and delusions.

Scrotum: External pouch that contains the testes.

Sebum: An oily substance that lubricates the hair shaft.

Secondhand smoke: Also known as environmental tobacco smoke (ETS). The mixture of the smoke from a lit cigarette, pipe, or cigar and the smoke exhaled by the person smoking.

Sectarian medicine: Medical practices not based on scientific experience; also known as alternative medicine.

Self-esteem: How an individual feels about her or himself.

Self-medicate: When a person treats an ailment, mental or physical, with alcohol or drugs rather than seeing a physician or mental health professional.

Sexual abuse: All levels of sexual contact against anyone's will, including inappropriate touching, kissing, and intercourse.

Sexual harassment: All unwanted and unsolicited sexual advances, talk, and behavior.

Sexual intercourse: Involves genital contact between individuals.

Side effect: A secondary (and usually negative) reaction to a drug.

Smegma: Cheesy sebaceous matter that collects between the penis and the foreskin.

Social Security: A government program that provides economic security to senior citizens and the disabled.

Social norms: Things that are standard practices for the larger part of society.

Somatogenesis: Having origins from within the body, as opposed to the mind.

Specialist: A doctor who concentrates on only one area of medicine, such as a dermatologist (skin specialist).

Specialize: To work in a special branch of a certain profession.

Sperm: Male reproductive cell.

Sterilization: A process that makes something free of living bacteria.

Stimulant: Substance that excites the nervous system and may produce a temporary increase in ability.

Stimulus: Something that causes action or activity.

Stressor: Something (for example, an event) that causes stress.

Stroke: A sudden loss of consciousness, feeling, and voluntary movement caused by a blood clot in the brain.

Subatomic: Relating to particles smaller than atoms.

Suicide: Taking one's own life.

Sulfur dioxide: A toxic gas that can also be converted to a colorless liquid.

Superego: According to Sigmund Freud, the part of one's personality that is concerned with social values and rules.

Suppress: To stop the development or growth of something.

Symptom: Something that indicates the presence of an illness or bodily disorder.

Synapse: Gaps between nerves; the connections between neurons that allow people to make mental connections.

Synthetic: Human-made; not found in nature.

T

Temperament: How a person behaves.

Tendinitis: Inflammation of a tendon.

Testicles: Male reproductive gland that produces sperm.

Testosterone: Hormone produced by testes.

Thyroid: A gland that controls the growth of the body

Tic: A quirk of behavior or speech that happens frequently.

Tolerance: The build-up of resistance to the effects of a substance.

Topical: Designed for application on the body.

Tourette's Disorder: A disorder marked by the presence of multiple motor tics and at least one vocal tic, as well as compulsions and hyperactivity.

Toxic: Relating to or caused by a poison

Toxins: Poisonous substances.

Transference: A patient's responses to an analyst that are not in keeping with the analyst-patient relationship but seem instead to resemble ways of behaving toward significant people in the patient's past.

Transient: Passes quickly into and out of existence.

U

Ultrasound: The use of high-frequency sound waves that forms an image to detect a problem in the body.

Unsaturated fat: Fat that is liquid at room temperature, like vegetable oil.

Uranium: A chemical element that is a silver-white, hard metal and is radioactive.

Urethra: The tube from the bladder to outside the body through which urine is expelled.

Uterus: Womb; female organ that contains and nourishes an embryo/fetus.

V

Vaccine: A substance made up of weak bacteria and put into the body to help prevent disease.

Vagina: The female canal that leads from the cervix (or opening of the uterus) to the vulva (or the external female genitalia).

Vas deferens: Spermatic duct connected to the epididymis and seminal vesicle.

Vasoconstrictor: A drug that constricts the blood vessels to affect the blood pressure.

Vegan: A strict vegetarian who doesn't eat any animal by-products or any dairy.

Vegetarian: A person who lives on a diet free of meat products; some vegetarians will eat eggs or dairy products, while others will not.

Veneer: A covering, often made of porcelain, that is placed over a tooth that is damaged or for cosmetic reasons.

Vertebra: A bony piece of the spinal column fitting together with other vertebrae to allow flexible movement of the body. (The spinal cord runs through the middle of each vertebra.)

Virus: A tiny organism that causes disease.

Vitamin: A nutrient that enables the body to use fat, protein, and carbohydrates effectively.

Volatile organic compound (VOC): An airborne chemical that contains carbon.

W

Withdrawal: The phase of removal of drugs or alcohol from the system of the user.

Y

Yeast infection: A common infection of a woman's vagina caused by overgrowth of the yeast Candida Albicans.

Yoga: A form of exercise and a system of health that involves yoga postures to promote well-being of body and mind through regulated breathing, concentration, and flexibility.

HEALTHY LIVING

6

Health Care Systems

The issue of health care and health care reform is a topic of growing debate in the United States. Health care touches everyone. There are families who worry about their children and aging relatives; employers who must provide health insurance to their employees and the employees who need the benefits. In addition, there are the government officials and politicians who are concerned about the rising cost of health care; and, of course, the hospitals and doctors who are responsible for delivering health care.

Having adequate health care is extremely important to people. Even successful medical treatment can involve pain, anxiety, risk, and, inevitably, lots of money. The last thing a patient in a hospital wants to think about is "how am I going to pay for all of this?" Ideally, instead of worrying about money, a patient should be concentrating on getting well. However, the whole subject of health insurance can be mystifying. Very often people do not fully understand their health insurance plans, and many people have run into problems because of their lack of understanding.

This chapter is a starting point for becoming an informed health care consumer by providing valuable information to be used in making health care decisions. When confronted with choices about doctors, specialists, health care plans, and hospitals, a consumer needs to be empowered with the information to make affordable and effective decisions.

This chapter will cover the basics of health care, including information about the health care system in America and in other countries; the different kinds of health insurance; Medicare and Medicaid; and how to navigate the world of health insurance under many different conditions, in sickness and in health.

WHAT IS A HEALTH CARE SYSTEM?

The United States health care system encompasses everyone and everything from the individual who is sick and in need of care, the clinic doctor who sees homeless people and families with no health insurance, to the hospital surgeon who performs state-of-the-art surgeries for thousands of dollars. It also includes executives and other business people who make decisions about health care that influence millions of people, and government officials who are desperate to reform (improve) health care. Health care is as small as the most personal and intimate choices people make about their own health and as big as multi-million-dollar business decisions and local, state, and federal policy-making. The U.S. health care system includes everyone who needs health care and everyone who delivers health care, which means that everyone is affected by health care.

The United States has the most advanced medical care in the world. Most Americans receive health care that is adequate, or even excellent, under the current system. However, there are many problems with the health care system in the United States. For those Americans who are insured because they can afford private health insurance or they receive health insurance through their employers, the current health care system usually works. However, more than thirty-seven million Americans do not have health insurance. Some of the uninsured people work for companies that do not provide health insurance, and some are denied medical insurance because they suffer from previous medical conditions. Others are unemployed or cannot afford private insurance, but they may not be poor enough to qualify for government assistance.

WORDS TO KNOW

Advocate: A person who supports or defends a cause or a proposal.

Appeal: To take a court's decision and have another higher court review it to either uphold or overturn the first decision.

Capitation: An agreement between doctor and managed care organization wherein the doctor is paid per person.

Carve out: Medical services, such as substance abuse treatment, that are separated from the rest of the services within a health care plan.

Chronic condition: A condition that lasts a long time or occurs over and over again. Chronic conditions can be treated but not cured.

Clinical trial: An investigation into new treatment methods for a specific disease or condition.

Copayment: A fixed amount of money that patients pay for each doctor's visit and for each prescription.

Credentials: Proof that a person is qualified to do a job.

Deductible: The amount of money a patient must pay for services covered by the insurance company before the plan will pay for any medical bills.

Detoxification: A process in which doctors use medication to reduce or eliminate drugs or alcohol from a person's body.

Emergency: The unexpected onset of a serious medical condition or life-threatening injury that requires immediate attention.

Fee-for-service: When a doctor or hospital is paid for each service performed.

Formulary: A list of prescription drugs preferred by the health plan for its members.

Generic drug: Drugs that are approved by the Food and Drug Administration but do not go by specific brand names and therefore are less expensive than brand name drugs.

Indemnity plan: A plan in which the insurance company sets a standard amount that it will pay for specific medical services.

Most people without health insurance cannot afford preventative care—such as regular physicals or immunizations—which helps maintain one's health. As a result, small health problems can develop into big health problems, and many of the uninsured are left with no choice but to seek treatment in hospital emergency rooms, which is extremely costly for hospitals. If patients cannot pay for their care, the hospitals must either absorb the loss or pass the cost on to paying patients as costs rise for everything from doctors' services to aspirin. Sometimes hospitals turn away uninsured patients to avoid the expense of treating them. (When there is a medical emergency, however, it is illegal for hospitals to turn away uninsured patients.)

WHEN HEALTH INSURANCE WAS CREATED IN THE MID TO LATE 1800S, ITS PURPOSE WAS NOT TO HELP PEOPLE PAY FOR THE CARE THEY NEEDED BUT TO MAKE SURE THAT HOSPITALS DID NOT GET LEFT WITH UNPAID BILLS.

In recent years, health insurance has become big business and competition between health care providers is fierce. As a result, the price of health insurance has gone up, even while the coverage of services and treatments has become more limited and restricted. The costs for health care in America are the highest in the world. Most Americans agree that health care costs must be controlled, but few agree on how to control the costs.

Medicaid: The joint state-federal health care program for low-income people.

Medicare: The federal health insurance program for senior citizens.

Medigap: Private insurance that helps pay for some of the costs involved in Medicare.

National health care system: A system in which the government provides medical care to all its citizens.

Off-label drug: A drug that is not formally approved by the Food and Drug Administration but is approved for legal use in some medical treatments.

Point of service: A health plan in which members can see the doctor of their choosing at the time they need to see a doctor.

Preferred provider organization: A health plan in which members have their health care paid for only when they choose from a network of doctors and hospitals.

Premium: Consideration paid for a contract of insurance.

Preventative care: Medical care that helps to maintain one's health, such as regular checkups.

Primary care physician: The doctor who is responsible for the total care of a patient and has the ability to refer patients to other doctors or specialists.

Rationing: The process of limiting certain products or services because of a shortage.

Referral: Permission from the primary care physician to see another doctor.

Reimbursement plan: A plan where a patient must pay for medical services up front and then get paid back from the insurance company.

Social Security: A government program that provides economic security to people.

Specialist: A doctor who concentrates on only one area of medicine, such as a dermatologist (skin specialist).

Many reforms have been proposed, from minor improvements to broad sweeping changes. Health insurance and health care are at the center of a nationwide debate: how can America make health care more widely available to everyone and also control costs?

U.S. VS. FOREIGN HEALTH CARE SYSTEMS

A common misconception surrounding the health care debate in the United States is that many other countries have already figured out the answers, and that all America has to do is replicate a foreign health care system and the problems will be solved. There are accounts of how everyone in Canada gets top quality medical care at reasonable costs. Germany and Britain are held up as examples of countries with effective health care systems. How is it that America spends more on health care than every other country and still does not manage to provide coverage for all its citizens?

There is no question that the United States can learn from the experiences of other countries, but there are no easy answers. Building a national health policy is tied closely to the values and priorities of the nation.

Canada, for example, has a national health system called Medicare, which covers all of its citizens. The Canadian government finances Medicare by raising people's taxes. All medical bills go to the government for reimbursement, so much of the paperwork is eliminated. Canada's health system is the second most expensive in the world, after the United States. Canadians pay about ten percent of their income for this universal insurance. People can choose their own doctors and see any specialists needed. The range of services is broad and fair because every person—rich or poor—is treated the same.

Canada makes this system work by imposing price controls on doctors and hospitals and keeping to a strict budget. The Canadian system is fair, but is it working? Business leaders say that the high tax rates are negatively affecting economic growth and employment rates in Canada. The tight budget also means that patients often have a lengthy wait for the care they need. Minor procedures and operations are often not available until the problem has become serious or even life threatening. As a result of these problems, benefits are starting to be reduced, and doctors are spending less time with patients (thirty percent less than American doctors). Even as American politicians are arguing that we should reform the U.S. health care system to be more like Canada's, Canadian politicians are urging the adoption of some of America's health care policies.

There are characteristics about foreign health systems to admire: universal coverage, lower costs, and free medical education. Every benefit, however, is balanced by a compromise, such as the limiting of choice and the rationing of services. Higher taxes, for example, help to pay for health care in countries like Germany.

Other countries have also pointed out that one reason for their lower health care costs is that the United States must treat different social problems that can become medical problems. For example, Americans pay for the high rates of teenage pregnancy, drug abuse, and violence. America also has a greater elderly population than many other countries. Both of these factors serve to increase costs for health care in the United States. It is hoped that the national debate over health care will help Americans decide what is right for the people.

MANAGED HEALTH CARE VS. FEE-FOR-SERVICE

Modern managed health care grew out of a desire to reform the traditional health care system, or the fee-for-service method of charging for health care.

Fee-for-Service

Under the fee-for-service method, doctors and hospitals got paid for each service they performed. There were no limits on their treatment decisions; doctors or hospitals could order as many tests as they felt necessary, for example. Doctors and hospitals made a lot of money under this system because they decided the prices charged for every visit. However, patients did not always benefit because their insurance companies would often only pay a percentage of the fees being charged. For example, if a doctor charged $100 for a checkup, but the insurance company felt that $80 was a fair price, the patient would have to pay the extra $20, until a certain deductible was met. (A deductible is the amount of money, as determined by the health care plan, a patient must pay for services before the health care plan will pay for any medical bills.)

The different types of fee-for-service include indemnity plans and reimbursement plans. In an indemnity plan, the insurer sets an amount that it will pay for a specific medical service. In a reimbursement plan, the patient must pay all fees up front and then file claims to be reimbursed by the insurer. Fee-for-service health care is no longer widely in use. Most people today have some kind of managed care insurance.

Managed Care

There are many kinds of managed care organizations, but there are some common characteristics among them. All managed care organizations supervise the financing of medical care delivered to members. They all are concerned with cost-effectiveness, or saving money. By buying services in bulk, for many members at a time, managed care organizations can get lower prices

CAPITATION

Sometimes doctors reach an agreement with a managed care organization called capitation, wherein the doctor is paid per person. Under this agreement, doctors accept members of the plan for a certain set price per member, no matter how often the member sees the doctor. For example, the doctor may be paid $20.00 per member every month and that amount doesn't change if the member comes in for five appointments that month or none.

with doctors and hospitals. Managed care organizations also reduce costs by limiting choice, which means providing members with a list of doctors from which to choose and lists of labs where tests can be performed. Even doctors are provided with lists of medicines from which to choose. Different plans have different restrictions on choice. Many people feel that limited choices are the downside of managed care. Generally, a member can expand the possible choices if he or she is willing to pay more.

At the same time, managed care organizations take care of the delivery system for their members. For example, they manage who provides the health care, where it is provided, and the different kinds of doctors in their particular system. Nurses, doctors, therapists, pharmacists, and hospitals are all a part of the delivery system.

The Referral Process

Understanding the referral process is critical to navigating the managed care organization. Managed care organizations require patients to get a referral from the primary care physician (the doctor responsible for a patient's total health care) in order to see a specialist. A referral is like a permission slip from the primary care physician. It allows patients to seek treatment from a specialist when the primary care physician is unable to treat the patient's problem. This is one way to keep insurance costs down. Without a referral, the patient may be charged full price for any medical care received by a specialist. Plans deal with referrals in different ways. Certain regular health visits may not require a referral. For example, women can often see a gynecologist (doctors who specialize in treating the female reproductive system) without getting a referral from the primary care physician. The complexities of the referral process may be a factor in the choice of an insurance plan.

FINDING THE PERFECT MATCH

Managed care organizations make the primary care physician the core of health care delivery. Choosing a primary care physician is one of the most important choices in any managed care plan. The primary care physician is responsible for the total care of a member and may also act as a gatekeeper to additional medical services, which means the primary care physician is responsible for referring the patient to other doctors, or specialists. A specialist is a doctor who concentrates on only one area of medicine, such as a dermatologist (skin specialist) or cardiologist (heart specialist).

The first step in choosing a primary care physician is to look at the plan's list of approved physicians. Choosing just any doctor won't do; it is important to find a doctor whose style and approach to health care matches that of the patient. It's recommended that a person ask family and friends about doctors they have seen in the past and would recommend. They may be able to provide important information about how long it takes to get an appointment with a specific doctor or whether the doctor is understanding and easy to talk to. It is also appropriate to ask the insurance plan about the doctor's credentials and whether the plan has received any feedback on the doctor from patient surveys.

Types of Managed Health Care Plans

Managed health care is an alphabet soup of confusing abbreviations: HMOs, PPOs, POS. What do they all mean? Surprisingly, many people do not know.

HEALTH MAINTENANCE ORGANIZATIONS (HMO). HMOs were designed to provide one-stop-shopping for patients: everything a patient might need with no hidden costs. An individual or an employer pays for health coverage in advance by paying the health coverage premium (the amount paid for an insurance policy). Provided a patient stays within the plan, there will not be any additional costs except for copayments, if applicable.

Health maintenance organizations are called such because HMOs generally cover preventative care, such as yearly checkups and immunizations. HMOs have a self-interest in keeping people healthy because healthy people don't spend a lot of money on health care. HMOs want to promote preventive health care so problems are caught or stopped before they can start. HMOs also control the quality of health care for members. The majority of services must be pre-approved by the primary care physician. The referral process allows all service to be reviewed by the HMO for necessity, appropriateness, and cost.

Of course, there are good parts and bad parts of this system. Good HMOs use referrals to screen out bad or inappropriate medical practices. However, bad HMOs can use referrals to limit care that is really necessary for the health of the patient. One criticism of HMOs is that decisions about the necessity or appropriateness of care are made not by doctors but by business people who may care more about cost than quality of care.

In making the final decision there are some other questions to consider:

- Is the location of the doctor's office convenient?

- What are the office hours? Does the office open early? Does the doctor make appointments after 5 P.M.? Does the doctor have Saturday hours?

- Is the office clean and orderly? Is the office staff friendly and polite?

- How do patients communicate with the doctor? Does the doctor have an answering service or voice mail where a patient can leave a message? Will a nurse return calls? Will someone return the call within twenty-four hours?

Making an interview appointment is one way to question the doctor. A phone interview can be sufficient if there is not time to make an appointment. If a patient has a chronic (frequently recurring) condition or special health care concerns, it is even more important to find a doctor with a similar approach to treatment and with experience in treating the specific condition.

Choosing a primary care physician is not a permanent choice. Patients can consult their plan handbook for instructions about how to change doctors. Some plans will limit the number of times one can change doctors within a year. Make sure to alert both the insurance plan and the doctor's office (so that patient records can be transferred) if changing doctors.

There are several different kinds of HMOs. The two most common are staff model HMOs and independent practice associations (IPAs). The staff model HMO is the best example of the one-stop-shopping approach. The doctors, medical records, labs, and pharmacy are all housed within one location. Sometimes services may be off-site from the central location. Patients may have to go to another location to see a specialist, but the specialist must still work for the same HMO system.

IPAs are made up of doctors, both primary care physicians and specialists, who see plan members in their own offices, instead of under one roof. Doctors may participate in several different IPAs. One advantage to IPAs is that there may be a larger selection of doctors and specialists from which to choose than in a staff model HMO. It's necessary to weigh these advantages

Spending time on the phone with a health insurance provider—seeking a referral or clearing up a bill—can be a frustrating part of managed health care. (Photograph by Robert J. Huffman. Field Mark Publications. Reproduced by permission.)

against the convenience of the staff model HMO to make the best choice for oneself. Some people will have more choices than others. They will either ask their insurance company what kind of HMOs are available for them depending on what they can afford, or they will have to pick whatever their employers offer them.

There are several more types of HMOs, but the major difference among the types is in the details of the agreement made between the managed care organization and the doctors, such as patient access to doctors, referrals, and payment arrangements.

PREFERRED PROVIDER ORGANIZATION (PPO). A preferred provider organization is another kind of health plan in which members have their health care paid for only when they choose from a network of doctors and hospitals. The network is a group of health care providers who have contracts with the PPO. The health care providers agree to offer a discount rate to PPO members. The PPO coordinates referrals and reviews treatment recommendations from participating doctors. A PPO can offer more choice and flexibility in choosing a doctor than an HMO. However, if a member sees a doctor outside of the network, the member will be required to pay part, or all, of the fee.

POINT OF SERVICE (POS). A point of service plan offers the most choice to the individual by combining HMOs, PPOs, and more traditional health care plans. The member can choose at the time of each visit, or what's referred to as "the point of service," which doctor to see. For example, while a patient may choose to use a primary care physician from an HMO for a regular checkup, he or she may later decide to go out of network for another service, such as to a cardiologist, or heart specialist. Therefore, the patient chooses, each time there is a need for a doctor, who he or she is going to see. A POS plan has different levels of cost to the member. For example, a member can see a doctor in the HMO for no extra cost, a doctor in the PPO network for some out-of-pocket cost, or even go to a doctor outside of the HMO or PPO for a higher out-of-pocket cost. The PPO may still require referrals from a primary care physician. Since plans vary, members should fully understand the costs and restrictions before visiting a doctor.

MANAGED INDEMNITY. The managed indemnity is the final option for patients choosing

CARVE OUTS

Carve outs are medical services that are separated from the rest of the services within a health care plan. These services are contracted for separately from all other medical services. Carve outs often include mental health and substance abuse treatment, dental and vision care, and pharmacy benefits. Some plans offer these services as a piece of their regular coverage while other plans "carve out" the services, and members choose whether or not the coverage is desired, for an additional premium cost. Specialty HMOs can be set up for one set of medical services, such as dental services. Specialty HMOs operate just like regular HMOs but may have different rules about referrals, so it's important to check out the requirements for making use of these benefits. Check out the fees for seeing specialty providers and the process for getting referrals. There may also be separate lists for participating physicians in specialty areas like counselors, therapists, and dentists.

fee-for-service plans. A member of a managed indemnity plan can choose to see any doctor. However, members must get prior approval for outpatient procedures and hospitalizations. Managed indemnity plans do not always cover preventative health care visits, and members sometimes have to file claim forms for certain services.

There are many kinds of managed health care organizations. Every managed care plan has rules for using its services, especially for referrals. These rules can be complicated but are important for an individual to understand when choosing a health care plan. The trick is to assess one's needs for health care and match those needs with the most accommodating managed care plan. A little homework early on can make for a productive relationship with the managed care organization.

MEDICARE

Medicare is the federal health insurance program for senior citizens and for some younger individuals who are disabled. Nearly all Americans age sixty-five or older are covered under Medicare. Medicare is a component of the Social Security program, and anyone who is eligible for Social Security benefits will be automatically enrolled. (Social Security is a government program that provides financial assistance to senior citizens, the unemployed, or the disabled. Money is funneled into the program by a tax on employers and employees.)

This is not to say that health care choices become simpler for senior citizens. While Medicare has a great deal to offer, it does not cover all the medical care an individual will generally need.

Medicare has two parts. Medicare Part A is hospital insurance and applies to hospital costs, nursing facilities, psychiatric hospitals, and hospice care (care for the terminally ill). If an individual qualifies for Medicare, Part A is free of cost. If an individual does not automatically qualify for Medicare, Part A can be purchased for a monthly fee.

Medicare Part B is medical insurance that covers certain doctors' fees, lab tests, X rays, many outpatient services, home health care, and in-home use of medical equipment. Individuals who qualify for Medicare are automatically en-

FOR LOW-INCOME SENIORS

Medicare offers two programs for low-income people over age sixty-five and for the disabled. Under the Qualified Medicare Beneficiaries Program (QMB), people with incomes at or below the federal poverty level do not have to pay the standard Medicare copayments and deductibles. The poverty level varies by the size of the household and is updated every year. Savings and assets cannot exceed four thousand dollars for one person and six thousand dollars for a couple. The state picks up the Medicare costs for those individuals who qualify for QMB.

The Specified Low Income Medicare Beneficiary (SLMB) Program assists people with incomes at or near the poverty level. The SLMB program covers the costs for Medicare Part B.

For more information on these programs, contact the local Department of Social Services or Area Agency on Aging or call the Medicare Hotline at 1-800-683-6833.

rolled in Part B unless it is declined. Part B has a monthly cost that will be deducted from a person's Social Security check.

Medicare pays for many health care expenses but not all of them. In particular, Medicare does not cover most nursing home care, long-term care in the home, routine foot care, most dental care or dentures, most immunization shots (except flu shots), most routine checkups and related tests, or prescription drugs outside the hospital. Many senior citizens will require services that Medicare does not cover. Medicare also requires copayments and deductibles for covered services, and these costs can add up over time.

To limit the risk of having to pay for medical services, a person should first always ask doctors if they accept Medicare. It's also important to ask if the doctors accept Medicare assignment. Medicare assignment is the amount of money that Medicare has designated for certain services. If the doctor does not agree with the amount of the Medicare assignment, then the doctor will bill the patients, who must then make up the difference with their own money. Finally, patients should ask their doctors if Medicare covers the services planned for their visits.

Medigap

Medigap is private insurance that people buy to supplement Medicare. Medigap literally fills in the gap when Medicare doesn't pay for something, such as prescription drugs not used in a hospital. It also helps to pay for some of the extra costs that Medicare requires, such as copayments. Medigap should be seriously considered if the individual can afford the cost. In most states, there are ten Medigap programs from which to choose, labeled A through J. All insurers offering Medigap insurance are minimally required to offer plan A and can offer other plans at their discretion.

MEDIGAP CAN BE PURCHASED WITHIN SIX MONTHS OF QUALIFYING FOR MEDICARE. DURING THIS PERIOD, INSURANCE COMPANIES CANNOT DENY COVERAGE BASED ON ONE'S MEDICAL HISTORY.

The ten Medigap plans vary significantly in their coverage of services and in their costs. As with all insurance, individuals should choose the plan that most fits their health care needs. In selecting a Medigap plan, one must remember that Medicare pays only for services determined to be medically necessary and only the amount determined to be reasonable. If Medicare won't pay for a specific service, chances are that Medigap won't either. As explained above, Medigap helps pay for outpatient prescription drugs or the copayments that go along with Medicare. It may not cover services that are not covered by Medicare, but it will help lessen the total costs of health care. The Medigap premium will depend either on an age-entry rating or an attained-age rating. Using an age-entry rating, the premium will be higher the older one is upon entering the plan, but does not change as one ages. Using an attained-age rating, the premium will increase every year.

Medicare and HMOs

Medicare normally operates on a fee-for-service basis. Patients are billed for each visit to a health care provider. In a growing number of places, though, HMOs are available to Medicare enrollees as well.

HMO coverage can be more comprehensive, and thus preferable, to a fee-for-service plan. However, HMOs require that members see only providers within the HMO network. A member who sees a doctor outside of the network is likely to pay more money.

HMOs provide many benefits to complement Medicare coverage: costs are low, there is no paperwork, and primary care physicians coordinate the care. On the downside, HMOs may limit services due to cost, members must get a referral in order to see a specialist, members must see doctors from a plan-approved list, and the health care is confined to a specific location. Senior citizens who spend the winter months away from home, for example, might find an HMO unsuitable because the plan does not cover their health care costs during that time.

BECAUSE THEY ARE WARDS OF THE STATE, MEDICAID COVERS FOSTER CHILDREN.

SPEAK UP!

Sometimes the rules for a managed care plan are difficult for people receiving Medicaid. For example, one plan required all appointments to be made by phone. This would be a problem if a person didn't have a phone, or if a person spoke a different language and could not communicate over the phone. If people have problems with Medicaid or the managed care plan, they can and should make the complaints known to both the plan's members services department and the local or state social services department. Unless people speak up, those who are making the decisions may not even be aware that there's a problem.

Some states are now extending Medicaid benefits to low-income people who work and are not eligible for welfare. Many of these efforts are aimed at insuring children whose parents work but still cannot afford private insurance. Medicaid managed care is an option being offered to families around the country.

MEDICAID

While the health care system in the United States is considered among the best in the world, the number of people who do not have health care is still a major problem facing the country. One in every six people under the age of sixty-five, including many children, is uninsured. Medicaid is the joint state-federal health care program for low-income people. Medicaid also covers people who are chronically sick or disabled. Over thirty-six million people rely on Medicaid for health care.

Many states are adopting managed care, instead of fee-for-service, for Medicaid recipients. Roughly one in three people on Medicaid are in a managed care program. Medicaid is different in every state and the District of Columbia. The federal government dictates the rules by which states must run their Medicaid programs.

Having health care coverage under Medicaid does not automatically mean easy access to health care. Many low-income Medicaid recipients have had difficulty in finding local providers, because low-income neighborhoods are often underserved by the medical community. Because Medicaid also limits the amount it will pay for services and often pays below market rates, many doctors won't accept Medicaid patients. Medicaid patients traditionally are forced to rely on emergency rooms for primary care treatment.

Managed care can correct some of these problems for Medicaid beneficiaries. Once a person is enrolled in a managed care program through Medicaid, the act of searching for a provider is unnecessary. The managed care plan will provide a list of approved providers. Access to preventive care is increased through the use of a primary care physician. Managed care has also improved the range of benefits for Medicaid recipients in some states. Despite these benefits, Medicaid managed care is not without problems. Sometimes people get very little time to choose a managed care plan, and/or sometimes the state does not send out a list of providers when it is time to pick a managed care plan. If a person does not choose right away, he or she will be automatically enrolled in a plan. As a result, the providers could be far away and not accessible by public transportation. Also, if a person already has a relationship with a doctor, and the doctor is not a part of the managed care plan network, the continuity of care is interrupted. The transition to managed care for many Medicaid recipients has been less than smooth.

WHAT HAPPENS WHEN THERE IS AN EMERGENCY?

The key to handling emergencies smoothly is advance preparation. Whether a person has a raging fever in the middle of the night or falls and breaks an arm, some knowledge in advance will help ease a stressful situation.

It doesn't matter which health insurance plan a person chooses, reading the materials and familiarizing oneself with emergency procedures is a smart idea. Emergency care is often listed in a separate section in the member's handbook and will explain what to do in case of an emergency. Emergency situations often call for quick action. The more a person has done in advance, the more quickly decisions can be made.

Emergency Preparation

The following checklist includes some things to do to prepare for emergencies:

- Leave a set of clear and simple instructions for emergencies and important telephone numbers near the phone for babysitters and family members.
- Program the telephone speed dial with 911 and the health plan's advice line and urgent care line numbers.
- Check out the health plan's policies for out of town or out of service area emergency care

Healthy Living **151**

- Check into how to notify the health care plan in the event of hospitalization.
- Keep the health care plan ID card close by, in a wallet or purse.

Emergency Care or Urgent Care?

A big part of the health insurance reform that led to managed care was the need to keep people from using the emergency room for everything except true emergency care. Treatment in the emergency room at a hospital is extremely costly. Managed care does not want members to use emergency rooms for non-emergency situations, such as the flu or an earache.

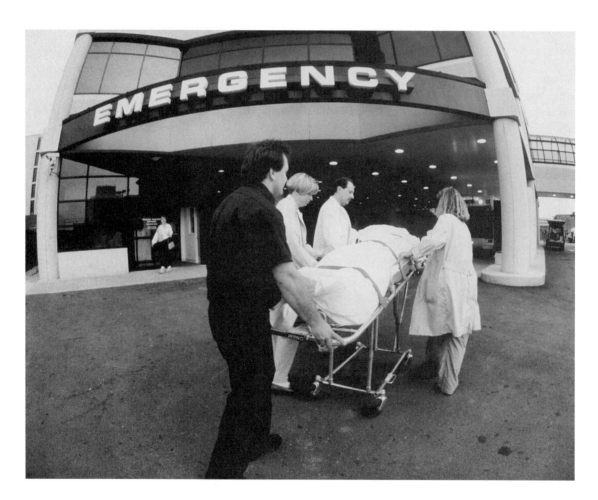

Hospital emergency rooms serve patients with immediate life-threatening conditions. (Photograph © 1999 Kevin Beebe. Custom Medical Stock Photo. Reproduced by permission.)

An emergency is defined as the unexpected onset of a serious condition or life-threatening injury that requires immediate medical treatment. An urgent condition needs treatment within twenty-four hours, in contrast with the immediacy of an emergency. An urgent condition can be treated by a primary care physician or at an urgent care clinic, if available. It is not always clear, however, whether a health problem is an emergency or an urgent care situation. Some managed care plans will cover only emergency care, if it turns out to have truly been an emergency. Whether or not the patient believed it was an emergency does not matter. Other managed care plans use the prudent lay person standard: the decision to seek emergency care will be covered if it is one that an average person with average medical knowledge would

MedStop is an example of a walk-in urgent care facility. It is meant to serve patients with urgent, but non-life-threatening, conditions. (Photograph by Robert J. Huffman. Field Mark Publications. Reproduced by permission.)

make at the time. The decision of whether a condition is an emergency, urgent, or can wait for a regular appointment rests solely on the individual. Common sense is a good guide when all else fails.

If it's obviously an emergency, the person should call 911 (or other emergency numbers). If it is less clear and there is time, the person should call the plan's advice line, or urgent care line. When calling 911, the person should be prepared to describe:

- ABCs: airways, breathing, and circulation. If any airways are obstructed, if breathing is abnormal or there is no breathing, and if a body part has gone numb or the person is turning blue.
- Symptoms: where it hurts, how often, and if the person's temperature is abnormally high or low.
- Chronology: when the symptoms started or when the accident occurred.
- Vital extras: age of the patient, any medications being taken or allergies, chronic illnesses, and any special circumstances (such as what the person ate).

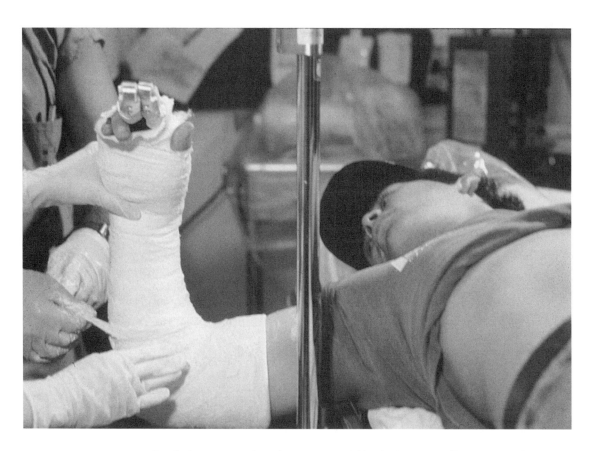

Is a broken arm considered an emergency? Health plans may differ on their definition of an "emergency." (Custom Medical Stock Photo. Reproduced by permission.)

Generally, managed care plans will pay for treatment of emergencies at the nearest hospital. If a person does not have time to notify the plan in advance of hospitalization, it is important to call the plan on the following day or within twenty-four to forty-eight hours, depending on the plan.

If a person seeks emergency treatment and the plan denies coverage, the person can appeal that decision. In that case, the person should gather copies of documents and medical records from the hospital. If there were any other people present at the onset of the illness or when the accident occurred, the person appealing should get statements from these people.

WHAT HAPPENS WHEN FACING A CHRONIC CONDITION?

Most people consider themselves healthy. However, the federal government has data to show that the average American has 1.7 conditions. This may sound surprising, but chronic conditions include hay fever, migraine headaches, and astigmatism that requires eyeglasses. Most people only consider more serious conditions to be chronic, like asthma, diabetes, arthritis, and heart problems. A chronic condition is any health problem that lasts a long time or recurs frequently. A chronic condition can be treated but cannot be completely cured.

STATISTICS SHOW THAT SEVEN DISEASES ACCOUNT FOR NEARLY HALF OF ALL THE MONEY SPENT ON HEALTH CARE IN THE UNITED STATES: HEART DISEASE, CARDIOVASCULAR DISEASE, DIABETES, CANCER, ARTHRITIS, DEPRESSION, AND OSTEOPOROSIS.

The first step to ensuring excellent health care is to fully understand the chronic condition: When do attacks occur? How long do they last? What are minor symptoms vs. intense symptoms? What are successful treatments for the condition? Are there preventative measures that can be effective?

The second step is to find a health care plan that provides all the options and services to successfully treat the condition. Under managed care, a primary care physician and a specialist will care for a person with a chronic condition. The primary care physician will coordinate the overall treatment and is responsible for giving the patient the needed referrals to see the specialists. It is important to pick a primary care physician who is knowledgeable about the chronic condition and is easy to talk to.

GET A SECOND OPINION

If a person is confronted with bad health news, it is imperative to get a second opinion on both the diagnosis of the health problem and the suggested course of treatment. Most conditions can wait for a patient to get a second, or even a third, opinion. The patient should choose an expert for the second opinion and should not be afraid to consider alternative options, especially when surgery is recommended as a part of the treatment. In fact, some health plans will require a second opinion before approving surgery. Plans may cover the expense of a second opinion if the patient uses another doctor within the same network. If the person feels strongly about seeing a doctor outside of the network, the expense may be worth it for one's peace of mind and well-being.

Treating a chronic condition successfully, and quickly, can depend on the managed care organization's rules for seeing a specialist. Sometimes the rules and restrictions for seeing a specialist can be complicated, time-consuming, and frustrating. It is important to follow these rules, however, to ensure the highest amount of coverage from the health plan.

People need to ask some hard questions of their health care plan about their own specific chronic conditions. For example, fill in the blank with the name of the chronic condition:

- Does the plan contract with doctors, hospitals, and community-based health care providers with a track record of serving _____ patients?
- Can a physician with experience in _____ be the primary care physician?
- Does the plan have a drug formulary (a list of drugs and classes of drugs preferred by the health care plan for use by its members)?
- If so, are off-label drugs and new drugs for _____ included in the formulary?

Other questions to ask when dealing with a chronic condition include (adapted from AIDS Action Foundation, Medicaid Reform and Managed Care, undated):

- How and how often is the formulary revised to include new and more effective drugs as they become available?
- What information does the plan have on the health outcomes of chronically ill people, including those with _____?
- What are the plan's policies on specialist referrals?
- What are the plan's policies on new drugs, new treatment rules, and participation in clinical trials?
- Many plans have consumer boards or advisory committees. If the plan has one, are people with _____ and providers with _____ expertise included?

OFF-LABEL DRUGS

An off-label drug is one that has not been formally approved by the Food and Drug Administration. The drugs have been approved for legal use but have not been approved to treat specific conditions. Off-label use is common in cancer treatment, for example. Off-label is not to be confused with generic drugs. Generic drugs are approved by the Food and Drug Administration for specific conditions, but do not go by specific brand names, which makes them less expensive for the consumer.

Referrals with Chronic Conditions

Referrals are the most complicated factor in dealing with chronic conditions and managed care. The process and rules for referrals vary from plan to plan. Some questions to ask the health care plan are:

- How does one get a referral, and for how long can it be used?
- How often can the referral be used before having to get another one? Is it one referral per specialist visit or does one referral cover a series of visits?

Referrals cover not only specialist visits but laboratory tests. Unless a patient has a condition that is life-threatening, the tests may not be performed on the same day as the doctor visit.

Prescription Drugs and Chronic Conditions

Some chronic conditions require no medication while other conditions require medication only during flare-ups, or when the condition is actively bothering the patient. Still other conditions require the long-term use of a prescribed medication. All health care consumers should understand the terms formularies, generic substitution, and therapeutic substitution.

FORMULARIES. Formularies are lists of prescription drugs preferred by the HMO for its members and are common in managed care. Plans develop the formularies on the basis of drug safety, effectiveness, cost, and cost-effectiveness. Formularies can be restrictive and can potentially impact the care a person receives. Managed care has been criticized for taking improper savings on drug use at the expense of consumers' health, even to the extent that illnesses and deaths could have been prevented.

People with chronic conditions need to pay special attention to their health plan's formularies. A doctor's knowledge of formularies is not dependable because a doctor may deal with numerous health care plans. In an open formulary, a patient should be able to get any drug, with some drugs requiring an additional co-payment. In a closed formulary, a patient who wants a specific drug may have to wait for the doctor to seek prior authorization, or approval, if the drug is not on the approved formulary list. If authorization for the nonformulary drug is not granted, the patient can file an appeal or even explore legal action.

GENERIC SUBSTITUTION. Generic substitution is the substitution of one medication with another drug that contains the same active ingredients in the same amount and dosage, but sold by a different company. Generic drugs are common because they cost much less than brand-name drugs. In changing from a brand-name drug to a generic drug, or vice versa, a patient may experience some side effects.

THERAPEUTIC SUBSTITUTION. Therapeutic substitution is the replacement of a prescribed drug with an entirely different drug in the same pharmacological or therapeutic class. These substitutions can pose more danger to the patient than generic substitutions. Different drugs, even those in the same class, can have significantly different effects on people. Pharmacists or hospitals should inform the doctor of any therapeutic substitutions, but they do not always do so. Consumers should check any differences between what was prescribed and what was received.

Emergencies and Chronic Conditions

Sometimes chronic conditions can be so severe that hospitalization is required. It is the patient's responsibility to learn about the chronic condition, including how to know when an episode is mild or serious and what to do about it. The primary care physician or the specialist can provide a list of symptoms, including recommendations for when a patient will need to go to the emergency room.

Disease Management

Some health care plans have disease management programs for people who suffer from chronic conditions like asthma, diabetes, or arthritis. A call to the plan's advice line or member services department will provide information about what is available. These programs focus on care for the whole patient, not just the symptoms or conditions associated with the disease. The disease management program may include patient education or behavior modification (a change in habits and lifestyle) classes, long-term monitored drug use, or the assignment to a case manager, who can recommend treatments and services that might not normally be covered under the plan. The case manager will coordinate the overall care of the patient.

BE SMART! ANYONE WITH A CHRONIC CONDITION THAT CAN CAUSE UNCONSCIOUSNESS SHOULD WEAR A MEDIC ALERT BRACELET AT ALL TIMES. MEDIC ALERT BRACELETS CAN BE FOUND AT A LOCAL PHARMACY.

WHAT HAPPENS WHEN THERE IS A NEED FOR ALTERNATIVE CARE?

Chiropractors, massage therapists, naturopaths and acupuncturists used to be considered alternative health care providers. Today these services are no longer thought of as alternatives to mainstream medicine. Instead they are considered complementary services. These services can be used alone or in conjunction with conventional treatments. As alternative medicine is more widely accepted, more health care plans are covering the alternative services for their patients. [*See also* Chapter 7: Health Care Careers and Chapter 10: Alternative Medicine for more information on alternative medicine.]

Some alternative clinicians are licensed by states and recognized as providers by health care plans. However, alternative treatments are often covered only for specific conditions. For example, a health care plan may cover acupuncture treatment for chronic pain management for one patient. Another patient who wants to use acupuncture for a knee injury may be denied coverage by the same health plan. If a consumer is interested in alternative care, it is important to find out what kinds of treatments are covered and for what conditions.

There remains a lack of mainstream research about alternative medicine and its effectiveness. As a result, managed care organizations will only cover treatments with clear outcomes and evidence. Some alternative practices may not meet these strict guidelines.

Once again, communication with the primary care physician is critical. A patient who decides to pursue alternative treatment should inform and consult with the primary care physician to ensure coordination of all health services. At the same time, a patient should always inform the alternative provider of treatments and medications prescribed by the physician. A patient will get the most effective care when all providers are working with the same information and for the same purposes.

Chiropractic

Chiropractic is the oldest alternative clinical practice in the United States and the most widely licensed. All fifty states and the District of Columbia license chiropractors.

Chiropractors, or doctors of chiropractic, regularly treat lower back pain, headaches, and problems with the neck, the upper back, and the nervous system through spinal manipulation.

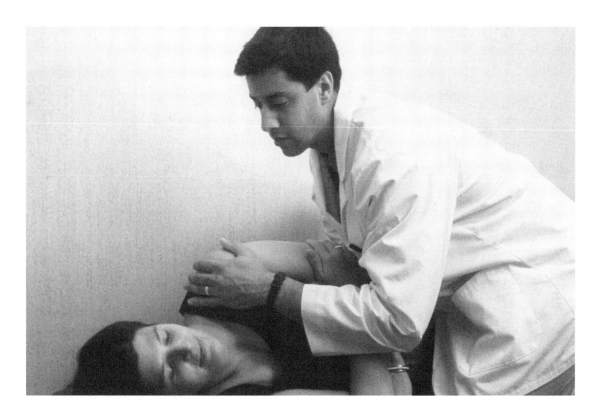

Chiropractic treatments are not always covered by health insurance. If unsure, check with your plan before making an appointment. (Custom Medical Stock Photo. Reproduced by permission.)

Managed care plans vary in their coverage of chiropractic treatment. Some HMOs have chiropractors as part of the network of providers. If patients think chiropractic treatments would be beneficial, they should review the health plan's materials and call member services for more information.

Acupuncture

Acupuncture is an ancient Asian medical practice that involves using very thin needles to pierce different parts of the body to treat certain conditions or relieve pain. Acupuncturists are licensed in twenty-four states and the District of Columbia.

Managed care plans vary widely in their coverage for acupuncture therapy. Some plans do not cover acupuncture at all. Other plans will cover acupuncture for use as an anesthesia (pain blocker) during surgery. If patients think acupuncture treatments would be beneficial, they should review the health plan's materials and call member services for more information. The patient should be prepared to offer evidence that the acupuncture treatment is medically necessary.

Naturopathy

Doctors of naturopathy, or naturopaths, believe in treating illnesses without the use of medications or surgeries, relying instead on natural elements for healing. Some states license naturopaths, but many naturopaths practice without a license in a physician's office or independently. If the naturopath practices in conjunction with a physician, and the doctor prescribes the treatments, the chances of getting health care reimbursement or coverage are greater.

Managed care plans want to do whatever it takes to keep members healthy. Not only is the practice of alternative medicine spreading, health care plans have started to offer complimentary extras to members that focus on member wellness. For example, most health plans have newsletters that contain information about healthy habits and preventive care, self-care and self-help practices, and member services such as exercise classes, yoga, meditation, nutrition education, help to stop smoking, and weight management. There may also be support groups or classes for people suffering from serious illnesses.

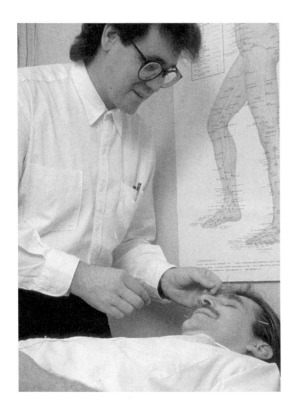

Managed care plans vary widely in their coverage for acupuncture therapy. (Custom Medical Stock Photo. Reproduced by permission.)

WHAT HAPPENS WHEN THERE IS A MENTAL HEALTH OR SUBSTANCE ABUSE PROBLEM?

Coverage of mental health and substance abuse problems varies widely from plan to plan. Just because the information booklet of a health care plan lists mental health and substance abuse care as covered expenses does not mean a consumer won't encounter difficulty. Some plans are more restrictive in reality than they are on paper and may involve a lot of out-of-pocket costs.

Mental health and substance abuse are often carve outs (see page 147) from the rest of the health plan. The care may actually come from a different company with a whole other set of phone numbers and addresses, and another set of rules to learn. These plans decide which kind of medical professional will treat the patient, what medicine or testing is required and approved, whether the treatment will be inpatient or outpatient, and how many sessions are needed and allowed.

Managed care organizations require that all mental health or substance abuse treatments, like all medical treatments, meet the test of medical necessity. There is the very real possibility that, in order to control costs, the managed care plan will first approve treatment that may not be sufficient for the patient. Health care consumers must be their own advocates. However, in cases of mental health or substance abuse problems, the instability caused by the condition may make this more difficult. If individuals cannot advocate for themselves, a family member may need to step in to ensure that the individual gets the care needed for recovery.

EXPERIMENTAL VS. ALTERNATIVE

Experimental treatment is different from alternative treatment. Experimental or investigational treatments may very well be effective but are not yet considered standard treatment in the medical community. A practice could be termed experimental because

- there is inadequate scientific evidence to support the treatment's effectiveness;

- the treatment has not been found to be as safe or effective as the standard treatment; or

- in the case of a prescription drug, the Food and Drug Administration has not yet approved the product.

If a patient has not succeeded with standard treatment, or no standard treatment is available, it could be worthwhile to investigate participating in a clinical trial. A clinical trial is an investigation into new treatment methods, materials, or procedures for a specific disease or condition. Clinical trials can give a patient access to state-of-the-art care before it is widely available. The treatment may not always be effective, but many patients who are suffering from serious conditions are willing to experiment.

Most health plans do not cover experimental treatments. The primary care physician or specialist supervising the treatment can help by submitting documentation to support the need for the experimental treatment. If the plan still denies coverage, the patient can submit a formal appeal.

Sometimes consumers do not meet the requirements for medical necessity of mental health or substance abuse treatment. This means that the problems of some patients may not be viewed as worthy of treatment by their health care providers. For example, a person who is experiencing stress or grief may wish to seek counseling, but the health care plan may only provide for a few sessions. Other times, the consumer has to wait to be referred for services. Both can be frustrating scenarios when a person is in need. The smartest way to avoid these situations is to evaluate a health plan for mental health and substance abuse treatment coverage before it is needed.

Some questions to keep in mind when evaluating a health care plan for coverage of mental health issues:

- Who are the mental health providers, and what are their qualifications?
- How does one get information on mental health providers?
- How many visits are covered by the plan? How many initial visits are allowed before the mental health provider must make the case that further treatment is medically necessary?
- How does one schedule an appointment? Is a referral needed in advance? If so, who gives the referral, the primary care physician or someone else?
- Does the plan offer rehabilitation coverage? What about substance abuse detoxification?
- Does the plan have enough mental health providers so that waiting for an appointment is not an issue?
- How much are the copayments and deductibles?

Mental health care is no different from the rest of managed care. There are many complex rules for getting care, and many of the rules center around the referral process. Not understanding the referral process in advance can add even more stress to a stressful situation. The referral will allow a certain number of visits or a certain length of time during which the referral is valid. If the referral runs out, a patient may have to work with the mental health provider and primary care physician to request extended treatment.

Choosing a mental health provider is as serious as choosing a primary care physician. A patient may be choosing from psychiatrists, psychologists, marriage and family therapists, clinical social workers, psychiatric nurses, and licensed professional counselors. The mental health provider devises a treatment plan and submits it to the managed care organization for approval. This is when it will be determined if mental health treatment is medically necessary.

Outpatient Care

Most mental health and substance abuse treatment will be delivered through outpatient care. Outpatient means that a patient will receive treatment during the day but will not live at the treatment center. As stated ear-

lier, once a provider has been chosen, a treatment plan will be developed. A patient will be authorized for a certain number of visits in a specific length of time.

If therapists think patients need more time or more visits, they will complete the Patient Evaluation and Treatment plan before the authorized time runs out. Another decision will then be made by the managed care organization about whether to extend the treatment for more time or more visits.

Inpatient Care

Inpatient care, or hospitalization, is a difficult subject in managed care. Therapists may see that because the patient lives at the treatment center, inpatient care provides the best opportunity for treatment. The patient and family members may also believe that the hospital provides the safest environment for the patient. However, managed care organizations will generally push for outpatient care because it is less expensive. If inpatient care is approved, it will be approved for only a short amount of time in most cases.

If a patient and therapist feel strongly about having inpatient care, the therapist will have to fight for the patient to receive inpatient care, especially inpatient care beyond the initially approved time period. The outpatient therapist may be a different person from the inpatient therapist, but either can push the limits of the health plan to get the best treatment for the patient.

Common complaints about mental health treatment are:

- denial of care;
- excessive demands for personal patient information from the managed care organization;
- untrained employees following rigid rules in denying treatment;
- interruption of treatment; and
- unclear, or even deceptive, statements about mental health benefits by the managed care organization.

Some plans have very limited mental health benefits. When changing plans, continuity of care can become a problem. A patient may have been seeing a therapist for a period of time but, under a new plan, the therapist is not a part of the approved provider list. Sometimes the patient can continue with the therapist for a higher out-of-pocket cost. Sometimes the patient will be forced to change therapists.

CHALLENGING THE SYSTEM

It's not uncommon to disagree with a decision made by a health care plan. The complexities and restrictions of managed care call for people to learn how to advocate (support) for themselves. A person can challenge any bill or service problem. Problems can occur even when the rules and procedures are followed exactly. The first step is to file a grievance, or complaint. Grievance proceedings can be slow and long. A member's handbook will give information on how to file a grievance. The most important thing is for people to know their rights when it comes to their personal health care.

Books

Castro, Janice. *The American Way of Health*. New York: Little, Brown and Company, 1994.

Horowitz, David and Dana Shilling. *The Fight Back Guide to Health Insurance*. New York: Dell Publishing, 1993.

Kerczyk, Sophie M. and Hazel A. Witte. *The Complete Idiot's Guide to Managed Health Care*. New York: Alpha Books, 1998.

Miller, Marc S., ed. *Health Care Choices for Today's Consumers*. Washington, DC: Living Planet Press, 1995.

Wekesser, Carol, ed. *Health Care in America, Opposing Viewpoints*. San Diego, Calif.: Greenhaven Press, Inc, 1994.

Web sites

Agency for Health Care Policy and Research. [Online] http://www.ahcpr.gov/consumer (Accessed September 27, 1999).

American Association of Health Plans. [Online] http://www.aahp.org (Accessed September 26, 1999).

Families USA. [Online] http://www.epn.org/families (Accessed September 27, 1999).

Health Care Financing Administration. [Online] http://www.hcfa.gov (Accessed September 27, 1999).

Health Pages. [Online] http://www.thehealthpages.com (Accessed September 26, 1999).

Healthfinders. [Online] http://www.healthfinder.gov (Accessed September 27, 1999).

National Association of Insurance Commissioners. [Online] http://www.naic.org (Accessed September 27, 1999).

National Committee on Quality Assurance. [Online] http://www.ncqa.org (Accessed September 27, 1999).

National Conference of State Legislatures. [Online] http://www.ncsl.org (Accessed September 26, 1999).

7

Health Care Careers

A big part of healthy living includes health care, be it from traditional health care providers such as physicians or alternative care providers such as acupuncturists. With people living longer and the world's population increasing, the need for health care professionals continues to grow. In fact, some of the fastest-growing professions that offer the highest pay and lowest unemployment rates are in the health care field, such as physician, physical therapist, and registered nurse.

Also contributing to this growth is the use of new medical technologies to diagnose and/or treat patients. These technologies will require specialists to operate and administer them, creating more jobs in the health care arena.

In addition to diagnosing and treating illnesses, most health care professionals now focus on wellness and prevention. Wellness is the state of being in constant good health while prevention means stopping illness before it starts. More and more, physicians are encouraging patients to adopt healthy habits, including eating well and exercising. Additionally, physicians and other health care providers are looking more closely at patients' lifestyles and emotional well-being to determine whether or not these may be contributing factors in their illnesses.

Understanding exactly what a health care professional does can help an individual decide what type of caregiver he or she should see for a particular ailment. This information can also bring a greater understanding of the vast network of health care professionals who work together to keep people healthy and well.

This chapter will look at professionals in health care that focus on the body—physicians, registered nurses, physical therapists, emergency medical technicians—as well as the mind—art therapists and psychologists, and even alternative practices, such as acupuncture.

Acupuncturist

Art Therapist

Chiropractor

Dentist

Dietitian

Emergency Medical Technician (EMT)

Health Services Administrator

Mental Health Counselor

Occupational Therapist

Optometrist

Pharmacist

Physical Therapist

Physician

Psychologist

Radiological Technologist

Registered Nurse (R.N.)

Social Worker

Speech-Language Pathologist

ACUPUNCTURIST

Through the use of a Chinese medicine called acupuncture, acupuncturists diagnose, treat, and help prevent illness or disease. They also offer relief for chronic pain, drug addiction, nausea, and emotional problems. Some people who quit drinking or smoking seek acupuncture for help in stemming the cravings. More than two thousand years old, acupuncture involves the stimulation of certain points on the body. The stimulation is usually achieved by inserting fine needles into the skin. Other ways of stimulating acupuncture points include applying heat, electrical stimulation (when electricity is used to massage deep tissue or to relieve swelling), pressure, which is called acupressure, friction, or suction.

According to traditional Chinese medicine, every person has vital energy, called Qi (also referred to as chi; both are pronounced "chee"), flowing through his or her body. This invisible energy, which travels along twelve major pathways called meridians, can become imbalanced, creating areas of deficient (less) and excess (more) Qi. It is thought that imbalanced Qi can cause illness. Acupuncture works to restore the balance of Qi by stimulating cer-

WORDS TO KNOW

Accredit: To recognize an educational institution for having the standards that allows graduates to practice in a certain field.

Advocate: A person who defends the cause of another.

Allopathic: The system of medical practice making use of all measures that have proved to be effective in the treatment of disease.

Associate's degree: Degree granted from two-year college institutions.

Bachelor's degree: A four-year college degree.

Bedside manner: A physician's ability to put a patient at ease and communicate effectively.

Congenital: Existing at birth.

Continuing education: Formal schooling above and beyond any degree that is often required of medical professionals in order to keep practicing in their specific field.

Diagnostic: Used to recognize a disease or an illness.

Dissertation: An in-depth research paper.

Fellowship: Advanced study and research that usually follows a medical residency.

Geriatric: Elderly.

Holistic: Treating both the body and the mind.

Internship: Supervised practical experience.

Licensed: Authorization to practice a certain occupation

Master's degree: A college degree that ranks above a four-year bachelor's degree.

Manual: Involving the hands.

Musculoskeletal: Relating to the muscles and bones.

Osteopathy: A system of medical practice based on the theory that disease is due chiefly to mechanical misalignment of bones or body parts.

Radiation: The energy sent out when changes occur in the atoms of an object.

Registered: To complete the standards of education issued by a state government to practice a certain profession.

Residency: Advanced training in a medical specialty that includes or follows a physician's internship.

Specialize: To work in a special branch of a certain profession.

Ultrasound: The use of high-frequency sound waves that forms an image to detect a problem in the body.

tain points on the body that affect the flow of Qi. As a result, Qi is sent to areas of deficiency and removed from areas of excess, which allows the body to function at its best.

During a session, an acupuncturist will first talk with patients about any physical or emotional problems they may be experiencing and will also observe the patients' movements, examine their bodies, and check pulse rates at different points on the wrists. This helps the acupuncturist to make a diagnosis. The acupuncturist will then stimulate certain points on the body, usually with the needles. Some acupuncturists will stay at the patient's side during the whole session in almost continuous contact with the patient. Others will insert the needles and leave the room, allowing the patient to rest.

An acupuncturist, who typically works in a health spa or private practice, must be familiar with all of the acupuncture points (more than 365) on the body and which parts of the body each affects. For example, stimulating a point on the leg may help with headaches or stomachaches. When providing treatment, the acupuncturist will only stimulate the points he or she believes will benefit that specific patient.

Training to Be An Acupuncturist

To become an acupuncturist, a person usually attends a three-year program in acupuncture and Asian medicine, which includes practical (hands-on) experience in a clinical setting. There are both accredited and non-accredited schools (accredited schools must adhere to certain standards that qualify its students for professional practice). Shorter programs do exist that only require 50 to 200 hours of study in acupuncture. These programs, which are not accredited, are usually taken by medical professionals who want to incorporate acupuncture into their practices.

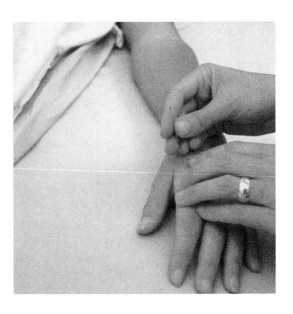

In more than half of U.S. states, an acupuncturist must be licensed to practice. To become licensed, certain requirements, which can vary among states, must be met by a candidate.

These requirements may include providing proof of the satisfactory completion of a formal study program, having practical experience, and passing a licensing examination given by the state.

If a state does not require licensing, an acupuncturist usually takes the certification examination offered by the National Commission for the Certification of Acupuncture & Oriental

Acupuncturist inserting a needle into a point on the large intestine meridian on a patient's left hand. (Science Photo Library/Custom Medical Stock Photo. Reproduced by permission.)

Medicine (NCCAOM). A person who completes one of the shorter programs in acupuncture cannot qualify for taking the NCCAOM examination or state licensing examinations.

ART THERAPIST

Using different art forms and a variety of craft activities, art therapists treat emotional, mental, and physical disabilities in patients. An art therapist will engage a patient in the artistic process through drawing, painting, creating collages, taking photos, sculpting, or other art forms to help patients express their feelings and to promote self-awareness. This form of therapy is especially useful when dealing with people who are unable to talk directly about their problems.

Often times, an art therapist is able to make a breakthrough with a patient's therapy when efforts by other therapists have failed to help the patient move forward.

A typical session with an art therapist may involve the therapist directing a patient to work on a drawing or painting of a scene that mirrors something that is happening in that patient's life. In a group setting, the therapist may have patients work together on a mural; an exercise of this nature can help patients learn to interact with others in a productive manner.

A profession that began in the twentieth century, art therapy became popular in the 1930s as art instructors recognized the value of children's artwork as a representation of their emotional and mental states. At the same time, psychiatrists (doctors who specializes in mental illness) began to look at artwork done by their patients in order to determine whether or not a link existed between the art and a patient's illness.

Art therapy is used to treat people of all ages, races, and ethnic backgrounds. It can help people with problems of a developmental, educational, medical, social, or psychological nature. Oftentimes, art therapy will be employed in a number of settings, ranging from a private therapist's office to a school to a hospital. Art therapy can be used with individuals, couples, families and groups of people with similar issues.

An art therapist works with a young female patient. (Photograph © 1993 Peter Berndt M.D., P.A. Custom Medical Stock Photo. Reproduced by permission.)

Whether art therapists work in hospitals, shelters, or schools, they will usually work with teams of physicians, psychologists, registered nurses, social workers, and teachers in order to best serve a patient. With the combined knowledge of all of these individuals, art therapists are able to come up with effective mental health programs. Art therapists working in a private office may consult with these other professionals even though they may be their patient's primary therapist.

Training to Be an Art Therapist

Formal training for art therapists involves a four-year college degree in either art therapy or psychology with a concentration in art therapy, as well as a master's degree in art therapy. One needs a master's degree to be a registered art therapist. One can get a job in art therapy without a master's degree, but not be an actual therapist. To become a registered art therapist (A.T.R.), one thousand hours of direct client contact hours must be completed in a supervised setting. On a personal level, art therapists are, ideally, sensitive to people's needs and expressions. Patience, attentiveness, and good people skills are all characteristics of an effective art therapist. Furthermore, a solid understanding of psychology (the study of the mind and behavior) and of different art forms is necessary.

CHIROPRACTOR

Chiropractors are well known for treating patients who are experiencing back and neck problems. In general, they address ailments of the muscular, skeletal, and nervous systems. They handle problems with these bodily systems through the manipulation and adjustment of certain areas of the body, particularly the spinal column. While chiropractic (derived from the Greek word "cheir" meaning "hand," and "prakticos" meaning "skillful use of") is considered an alternative medicine, it is the fourth largest health profession in the United States.

Daniel David Palmer (1845-1913) founded the practice of chiropractic in the 1890s. He believed that disease is the result of interference with the normal function of the nervous system.

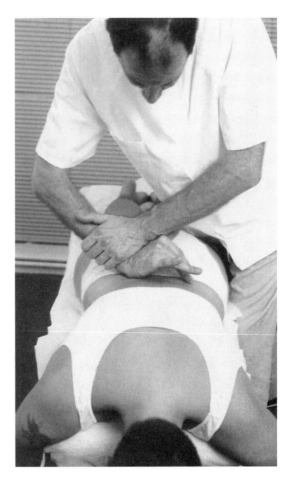

A woman has her back adjusted by a chiropractor. (Custom Medical Stock Photo. Reproduced by permission.)

He determined the interference is caused by subluxation, or the slight dislocation of two vertebrae in the spinal column. The subluxation impairs nerve function that in turn upsets the functions of other parts of the body influenced by those nerves. According to chiropractors, this leaves the body more open to disease. Chiropractic addresses subluxation by manually realigning the spinal column. Once the vertebrae are realigned, nerve function should improve and allow the body's natural healing process to work better.

When treating a patient, a chiropractor takes into account the patient's history, current lifestyle, and response to treatment. Therefore, communication between chiropractor and patient is an important factor. A chiropractor will ask patients about their exercise, dietary, and sleep habits, their genetics, and their living and work conditions. Chiropractic treatment works to improve the patient's overall well-being.

As well as manipulating and adjusting the spinal column with their hands, chiropractors may use other forms of treatment such as massage, ultrasound, and water, heat, light or electric therapies. They may also counsel their patients in proper nutrition and healthy living. They do not perform surgery or prescribe drugs for their patients. An interesting fact is that chiropractors are trained in obstetrics (the branch of medicine relating to the care of women during pregnancy and childbirth) and gynecology (the branch of medicine relating to treatment of the female reproductive system) and have the ability to deliver babies, however, most chiropractors never use this training. Also, some chiropractics can lawfully perform minor surgery in certain states.

Training to Be a Chiropractor

To study chiropractic care, a person may attend a chiropractic college. Palmer founded the first school of chiropractic in Davenport, Iowa, in 1897. To qualify for admittance to a chiropractic college, a person must have a minimum of two years of college course work that includes classes in biology and chemistry. Some states do require chiropractors to have a bachelor's degree (a four-year college degree), and in the future, chiropractic colleges will probably require bachelor degrees to qualify for admittance. The chiropractic programs are full-time for four years. Upon satisfactory completion of a chiropractic program, students earn the doctor of chiropractic degree and the initials D.C. may follow their names.

In order to practice after graduation, a chiropractor must pass a state board examination to become licensed. Continuing education is required for chiropractors to maintain their li-

"STRAIGHTS" AND "MIXERS"

There are two major categories of chiropractors: the "straights" and the "mixers." The straights generally perform chiropractic in the traditional manner, focusing on the manipulation and adjustment of the spinal column. The mixers, on the other hand, employ a variety of therapies in their chiropractic work, including acupressure, massage, nutritional counseling, or physical therapy. Thus they "mix" straight chiropractic with other therapies. Only about 15% of practicing chiropractors graduating today are considered "straights."

censes. Areas of specialty do exist for chiropractors. These include neurology, orthopedics, nutrition, sports injuries, or internal disorders. Chiropractors typically work in solo or group practices or for other chiropractors. Some work in hospitals or clinics; others teach or conduct research.

DENTIST

Seeing a dentist on a regular basis is an important part of preventive dental care. Dentists today are focusing more and more on preventive care (that is, taking care of teeth *before* there is a problem) in order to help people avoid having to undergo complicated dental procedures for painful conditions, such as gum disease. In addition to providing people with advice on preventive dental care and good oral hygiene, dentists diagnose and treat problems of the teeth and gums. This ranges from cleaning teeth to filling cavities, taking X rays, and repairing damaged teeth.

A typical visit to a dentist will entail the dentist using a variety of tools, such as X-ray machines and instruments (mouth mirrors and probes), to examine the teeth. After evaluating a patient's X rays, a dentist will treat problems, for example tooth decay, and clean the teeth. The dentist may then advise a patient as to how to improve the home dental care routine, offering advice on brushing or flossing techniques as well as recommending new products, such as a new oral rinse.

Other services, like sealing children's teeth to prevent cavities, pulling teeth, and making dentures (false teeth), are familiar tasks to dentists. Dentists also provide cosmetic services, including whitening the teeth.

Most dentists work in either private practice or in group practices with other dentists who provide similar or different dental services. These dentists are often supported by dental hygienists (who clean teeth and provide instruction on good oral care) and dental assistants (who assist the dentist and the hygienist in procedures). Other dentists may work in large clinics. Still other dentists may become instructors or researchers.

Dentists, like medical doctors, often specialize in treating different populations of people, like pediatric dentists who treat children, or provide particular dental services, such as orthodontics, periodontics, or oral surgery. Orthodontists, the largest group of specialists, concentrate on straightening the teeth. Periodontists treat the gums and the bone supporting the teeth. Oral surgeons operate on the mouth and the jaws.

Training to Be a Dentist

Training for dentists begins with a bachelor's degree (four-year college degree), which usually includes a course of study that focuses on the sciences, such as biology and chemistry. Applicants to dental schools then take

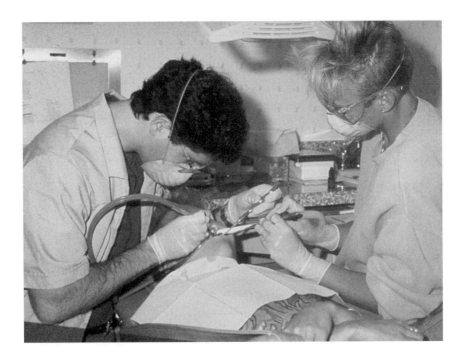

A dentist and dental hygienist perform a procedure on a patient. (Custom Medical Stock Photo. Reproduced by permission.)

the Dental Admissions Test (DAT). Once students have entered four-year dental schools, they study in the classroom and laboratory. From there, dental students treat patients in dental clinics under the supervision of licensed dentists. After students graduate from dental school with degrees of doctor of dental surgery (D.D.S.) or doctor of dental medicine (D.M.D.), they must pass written and practical licensing exams in order to practice dentistry.

Specialists, such as oral surgeons and pediatric dentists, usually must go through an additional two to four years of postgraduate education. Many states then require that a specialty license be obtained before a dentist may practice as a specialist.

In addition to educational requirements, the best dentists are those with good diagnostic ability and manual (hand) skills. A good visual memory, excellent judgment of space and shape, and strong communication skills are also essential.

DIETITIAN

Preventing disease and illness before it begins has a lot to do with what people eat. With more and more people now watching what they eat, the need for dietitians has increased greatly.

Dietitians provide nutritional counseling to their clients. (Custom Medical Stock Photo. Reproduced by permission.)

Dietitians can help prevent and treat illnesses by promoting healthy eating habits, planning nutrition programs for schools and hospitals, and advising patients as to how they can improve their diets.

Dietitians work in a variety of settings, depending upon the type of work they do. Most hospitals, schools, and nursing homes work with dietitians to help map out healthy meal plans, educate people about the importance of good nutrition, and create special diets for people with special needs (such as diabetics who must carefully control the amount of sugar they eat).

Dietitians work closely with dietetic technicians (who assist dietitians), nutritional counselors (who typically counsel individuals on eating habits and nutritional problems), and food-service personnel (who help prepare and serve meals). There are four main types of dietitians:

CLINICAL DIETITIANS. Clinical dietitians can be found working in institutions such as hospitals and nursing homes. These professionals will look closely at the needs of the patients or residents and develop a nutritional program (including planning meals) that will meet the different needs of all the patients. Clinical dietitians monitor the effectiveness of their programs and are constantly seeking ways to make sure that people's nutritional needs are being met. Often, these dietitians consult with doctors and other health care professionals to ensure that a patient's medical care and nutritional plan complement one another. It is not uncommon for clinical dietitians to specialize in treating specific patient populations, such as pediatric, diabetic, or geriatric (elderly).

COMMUNITY DIETITIANS. Community dietitians offer nutritional counseling to people in a certain community or to members of a certain organization in order to help these people prevent disease and maintain their health. These dietitians can be found working in community health care clinics, health maintenance organizations (HMOs), and home health agencies. Like clinical dietitians, community dietitians evaluate dietary needs by listening and talking to individual patients about their lifestyles. The dietitian then develops nutritional care plans for the patients and advises their families. The advice a community dietitian provides can range from tips on grocery shopping to instruction on food preparation.

CONSULTANT DIETITIANS. Many consultant dietitians see patients in their own private practices or work for an established health care facility. In either case, these dietitians most often provide nutritional screening for patients. Nutritional screening is a process in which dietitians evaluate the eating habits of their patients. Based on the results of screenings and patients' concerns, consultant dietitians can counsel patients how to lose weight, reduce their cholesterol, or adopt a high-fiber and low-fat diet. Consultant dietitians may also work with supermarkets, sport teams, and food manufacturers.

MANAGEMENT DIETITIANS. Management dietitians are experts at planning meals for large numbers of people, such as those found in major health care facilities, corporate cafeterias, prisons, and schools. Hiring, training, and supervising other dietitians and food-service workers are just part of the management dietitian's job. They also have to handle the budgeting for and purchasing of food and supplies and make certain that safety and sanitary regulations are followed.

Training to Be a Dietitian

Dietitians must have a bachelor's degree (four-year college degree) with a major in dietetics, foods and nutrition, food-service systems management, or a related area. Most bachelor's programs require students in dietetics to serve internships or have supervised work experience. Some dietitians also hold a master's degree in nutrition science. Dietitians can become registered dietitians (R.D.) by passing a certification exam that may be taken only after completing their education and supervised work experience or internship.

EMERGENCY MEDICAL TECHNICIAN (EMT)

When a medical emergency occurs, such as a car accident or a heart attack, emergency medical technicians (EMTs) are most often the first to arrive at the scene. Working in teams of two, EMTs drive ambulances with special

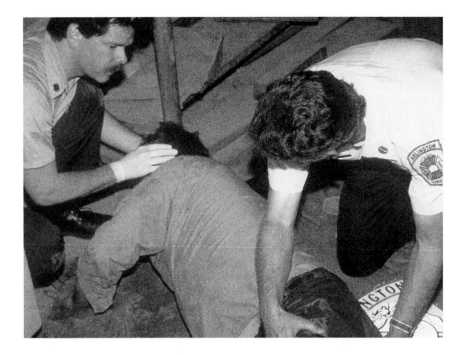

EMTs must work quickly at the scene of an accident. (Custom Medical Stock Photo. Reproduced by permission.)

equipment that allows them to examine patients and treat injuries and illness. After EMTs determine the seriousness of an emergency, they give people immediate medical care. They must follow strict guidelines when treating their patients. Once treatment has been given, one EMT continues to monitor and treat the patient in the ambulance while the other EMT drives to the nearest hospital.

There are three skill levels for an EMT: EMT-Basic; EMT-Intermediate; and EMT-Paramedic. The differences among them revolve around what type of emergency care they are trained for and allowed to give. All EMTs can do the following:

- help with childbirth
- control bleeding and bandage wounds
- restore breathing and administer oxygen
- treat victims for shock and heart attack
- treat poison and burn victims
- use an automated defibrillator (equipment that uses an electric shock to restore a regular heartbeat)

EMT-Intermediates have more training than an EMT-Basic so they can use more sophisticated equipment and procedures to treat medical emergencies. EMT-Paramedics have the most training and are able to give a victim the most extensive care. This includes administering drugs, reading electrocardiograms (EKGs, or machines that monitor heart problems), and performing endotracheal intubations (insertion of a breathing tube down the throat).

When EMTs arrive at a hospital, they give the emergency room doctors information regarding the patient, including the patient's medical status and any procedures that have been performed on the patient. Once the patient is at the hospital, the EMTs' job is done, until they are called to help in another emergency.

EMTs' work can be very challenging because the workday usually involves life-and-death situations. Along with the challenges and the excitement, however, comes stress and sometimes danger. EMTs must remain calm in emergency situations, as well as calm others at the scene. If EMTs are called to handle a victim who's had a drug overdose or a patient suffering from a mental illness, the EMTs may have to deal with angry and/or violent reactions from their patients.

Training to Be an EMT

In order to become an EMT, one must be at least eighteen years old and have a high school diploma and a valid driver's license. The training an EMT must undergo is different for each skill level. Moving from one level to the next involves a certain amount of classroom work and field work, as well as written and practical examinations. In order to become registered, or certified, one must pass an examination that is given by the National Registry of Emergency Medical Technicians. Many communities colleges offer courses in EMT Training.

EMT-Basic requires 110 to 120 hours of work in the classroom as well as ten hours interning in the emergency room of a hospital. Upon completion of the EMT training program, graduates must pass the National Registry's written and practical exam.

Moving from EMT-Basic to EMT-Intermediate requires more classroom work, usually between 35 and 55 hours. It also requires another examination, as well as a certain amount of practical experience in the field.

Most EMT-Intermediates go on to become EMT-Paramedics. This requires still more education and training. Training can last from 750 to 2,000 hours. Once training is completed, a person must take yet another written and practical exam, as well as gain more experience in the field.

All EMTs must reregister every two years to continue working in the field. To do so they must continue to take classes and learn about advances in the equipment they use and the medicines they give their patients.

HEALTH SERVICES ADMINISTRATOR

Hospitals and other health care facilities, such as nursing homes, health clinics, HMOs (health maintenance organizations), and group practices are places where people expect to receive good medical care. At these facilities, there is usually one person who makes sure everything is running smoothly. That person is the health services administrator. The job of a health services administrator (also referred to as health services director) involves the many responsibilities that are part of running a health care facility.

Health services administrators oversee the day-to-day operations of the facility, which requires a tremendous amount of planning, and organization, as well as financial management. They ensure that all patients are receiving the best possible health care at all times.

Health services administrators must also supervise a staff of assistant administrators, who are in charge of different areas, from food service and housekeeping to marketing and public relations. Public relations and marketing are important to a health care facility. These departments reach out to the community to learn how to improve the facility for the people who need and use it.

A large part of a health services administrator's job is planning for the future. Health care is always changing as new technologies are constantly being developed. Health services administrators need to stay aware of these changes in order to make improvements in the facility.

They need to decide how to best spend the facility's money, either by hiring more staff, buying new equipment, or expanding the facility. Once a decision is made as to how to spend the money, health services administrators also must be sure that the improvements don't cost more than the facility has to spend.

All health care facilities must follow government regulations. These regulations are enforced to make sure that people are receiving quality health care. Health services administrators must be sure their facilities meet the standards set by government agencies, as well as insurance companies, who routinely check up on facilities and evaluate their performance.

There are many opportunities for health services administrators since there are many different types of health care facilities throughout the United States. Work settings range from small clinics to large hospitals. The amount of responsibility for health services administrators depends on the size of the facility in which they work.

Training to Be a Health Services Administrator

In order to pursue a career as a health services administrator, one should have a bachelor's degree (four-year college degree) with a major in social sciences, health administration, or business administration. A bachelor's degree enables one to apply to a master's program in hospital administration, public health, or health administration. Licensing is not required for all health services administrators. Some states require that those working in nursing homes or long-term care facilities become licensed by passing a written exam.

Health services administrators must be able to deal with people effectively, communicate well, and handle many tasks at once. While there are assistants to take some of the responsibility, health services administrators are usually the only ones able to make important decisions. At a hospital or other health care facility, this can happen at any time, seven days a week, twenty-four hours a day.

MENTAL HEALTH COUNSELOR

Mental health counselors help people work through problems in their lives and improve their overall mental health. They counsel patients with problems associated with most areas of life, including family, career, or school, as well as poor self-esteem, abuse, suicidal tendencies, drug and alcohol addiction, or stress. Patients may vary in age from small children to the elderly.

PATIENT ADVOCATE

Patient advocacy is a relatively new field in health care. Patient advocates are people who help patients and their families when patients believe there are problems with the quality of health care they are receiving. When patients feel they have been treated poorly, patient advocates will meet with them and listen to their concerns. Patient advocates may then speak with the health services administrators to discuss a solution to the problem.

The job of a patient advocate is not to determine whether an actual problem exists. Rather, patient advocates provide a forum for patients to express their concerns. Sometimes, patient advocates solve problems just by listening to the patients. Other times, patient advocates work with health services administrators to develop a resolution to the problem.

Patient advocates are also responsible for collecting information regarding patient problems and writing reports that can be used to make improvements to the health care facility. By work-

ing with patients and health services administrators, patient advocates help both sides understand each other better. By helping patients with their problems, patient advocates can prevent possible lawsuits against their health care facility. Sometimes, a change in policy will result from the work of patient advocates.

Since it is a new field, there are no educational requirements for patient advocates. It is possible to work in the field with a high school diploma or an associate's degree (degree granted from two-year college institutions). Some patient advocates enter the field with on-the-job training or by volunteering. However, it is recommended to earn a bachelor's degree. The most important thing for those who wish to pursue a career as a patient advocate is to have experience working in a hospital or another type of health care facility.

Patient advocates must be compassionate and sympathetic to patients who are often angry or frustrated with the way they've been treated. This requires that patient advocates have good communication skills and like working with people.

A mental health counselor, center, conducts a group therapy session. (Photograph ©
1993 Mike Moreland. Custom Medical Stock Photo. Reproduced by permission.)

Most mental health counselors specialize in certain age groups, such as
adolescents or adults, or they may specialize in areas, such as abuse or marriage. Mental health counselors can provide individual, group, or family counseling. They may work in private practice or at community or social services
agencies, drug rehabilitation centers, group homes, health maintenance organizations, mental health clinics, prisons, or schools.

During a session, a mental health counselor talks with a patient about
any concerns that the patient may have. This may sound easy, but it can be
hard since many people find it hard to talk about their feelings. It is the responsibility of the counselor to make the patient feel comfortable and to
keep a dialogue going between them. A counselor must also be very patient
for it may take a long time for a person to open up or to want to make life-
changes.

Based on the patient's problems or concerns, a mental health counselor
will develop a treatment plan for the patient. During treatment the counselor
will keep records of the patient's progress. The goal in mental health counseling is to have a patient work through problems and regain control of his
or her life. Mental health counseling also places emphasis on preventive care;
therefore, counselors try to develop ways to teach people about maintaining
good mental health.

Training to Be a Mental Health Counselor

health care
careers

To work as a mental health counselor, a person is required to obtain a master's degree (a college degree that ranks above a four-year bachelor's degree) in counselor education. Mental health counseling programs are accredited by the Council for Accreditation of Counseling and Related Educational Programs (CACREP). To graduate from an accredited program, a person must successfully complete 48 to 60 semester hours of course work as well as gain a certain amount of practical experience. Doctoral programs (programs that grant degrees beyond the master's degree level) are also available, which is a good foundation for those interested in conducting research.

The National Board for Certified Counselors (NBCC) offers certification to all counselors, whether their particular state requires certification or not. To be certified by the NBCC, a person must have graduated from an accredited master's program, practice as a counselor in a supervised, professional setting for two years, and pass the certification exam given by the NBCC called the National Counselor Examination for Licensure and Certification.

OCCUPATIONAL THERAPIST

Having a disabling condition, such as arthritis, paralysis, cerebral palsy, muscular dystrophy, or mental illness, can mean having to learn or relearn how to perform routine activities for daily living and working. Occupational therapists, or registered occupational therapists (O.T.R.), help patients suf-

SUBSTANCE ABUSE COUNSELORS

Substance abuse counselors focus on counseling people with alcohol and drug addictions. These counselors evaluate their patients' conditions, devise treatment programs with the help of other medical professionals, and counsel their patients in individual or group therapy sessions. Recovery from drug or alcohol addiction is a lifelong struggle that may have periods of relapse; therefore, substance abuse counselors must have compassion and patience. They may work in private practice or at drug rehabilitation centers, hospitals, or government agencies.

These counselors have strong knowledge of drugs and their effects on the human body, both mentally and physically. They are trained in the characteristics of drug and alcohol addiction. In fact, some substance abuse counselors have firsthand knowledge of the destructive effects of the drugs and the difficulties of recovery because they are former addicts themselves.

Training to Be a Substance Abuse Counselor

A master's degree is not required to become a substance abuse counselor, but it is preferred. Certification is available, which is recommended since most employers will only hire certified substance abuse counselors. Standards for certification usually include supervised practical experience as a substance abuse counselor for two years, two- to three-hundred training hours, a case presentation, and an examination. A Master Addictions Counselor (MAC), which is the highest level of certification in this field, must have a master's degree, three years' practical experience, five hundred training hours, and an examination.

fering from these conditions set and reach goals for accomplishing activities such as eating, dressing, and writing. Occupational therapists also design and make special devices that help patients adapt to their home and work space and communicate with others more effectively. A major goal of occupational therapy is to have the patient become more independent. Occupational therapists also strive to improve the patient's quality of life.

Some techniques employed by occupational therapists include physical or mental exercises and the use of computer programs that help improve a patient's problem-solving, decision-making, and memory skills. For example, if a patient suffers from memory loss, an occupational therapist will instruct the patient in exercises that work to improve memory and prevent forgetfulness. An important part of treatment is patient participation. Patients are expected to use what they learn in therapy in real life. Many activities, then, are planned that require the active participation of the patient. In creating and using various techniques, occupational therapists must be imaginative and have a great deal of patience.

Occupational therapists work with other health care professionals on the rehabilitation of a patient. Rehabilitation is the general name given to training and therapy techniques designed to help a person return to normal daily activities. A physician heads the rehabilitation process of the patient and refers the patient to an occupational therapist. The occupational therapist evaluates patients, plans treatment programs with reachable goals for them, and monitors their progress.

Work settings for occupational therapists can vary from hospitals to schools or rehabilitation centers to the homes of their patients. Some may choose to work specifically with children or with the elderly. Others may work primarily with mentally ill patients or with patients with specific physical disabilities, such as cerebral palsy. Occupational therapists who specifically help patients with workplace needs are called industrial therapists. Occupational therapists may also teach or conduct research.

Occupational therapists work with occupational therapy assistants, or certified occupational therapy assistants (C.O.T.A.), who aid in the treatment of the patients. Occupational therapy assistants do not evaluate patients, but they

An occupational therapist works on eye-to-hand coordination with a patient. (Photograph © 1994 K. Glaser & Associates.Custom Medical Stock Photo. Reproduced by permission.)

do administer the treatments devised by occupational therapists and document the patients' progress.

Training to Be an Occupational Therapist

To become an occupational therapist, a person may acquire a bachelor's or master's degree in occupational therapy or, a person with a bachelor's degree in another field may also enter a post-bachelor's certificate program in occupational therapy. During a program, a student studies behavioral, biological, and physical sciences as well as completing practical experience in the field. Occupational therapy programs receive accreditation from the Accreditation Council for Occupational Therapy Education of the American Occupational Therapy Association.

In order to practice, an occupational therapist must be licensed. Candidates who successfully complete an accredited occupational therapy program may take a national certification examination given by the American Occupational Therapy Certification Board. After passing the exam, they become registered occupational therapists. Continuing education is necessary for all occupational therapists to keep on top of the latest advancements in the field.

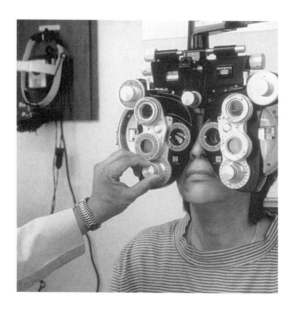

An optometrist uses this piece of equipment to measure a patient's vision. (Custom Medical Stock Photo. Reproduced by permission.)

OPTOMETRIST

When people have problems with their vision, they may go to see an optometrist. Optometrists, also referred to as doctors of optometry, examine patients' vision and treat any eye infections or diseases. During an eye examination, optometrists give patients different tests using instruments or merely observing a patient's eyes. They test for sharpness of vision, depth perception, color perception, and ability to focus. Once the tests are complete, optometrists review the test results and prescribe treatment. Most times, optometrists prescribe corrective lenses, such as glasses or contact lenses, for vision problems. Sometimes, they use vision therapy to treat a problem. If an infection or disease is present, optometrists prescribe medication. Optometrists do not, however, perform eye surgery on patients. This job is performed by ophthalmologists, physicians who specialize in eye health and can perform surgery on the eyes.

According to the American Optometric Association, two-thirds of all optometrists have their own private practice. This means they are not only treating patients, but they are also running a business. Running a business usually involves hiring people, taking care of the finances, finding new patients, updating equipment, and investing in new technology. There is a growing trend among optometrists to work together, sharing a practice with one or more optometrists. This allows the optometrists to share the responsibilities of running a business or to have the flexibility to work in other environments, such as clinics or vision care centers.

There are other career options for optometrists who do not open a private practice. Some optometrists choose to specialize in other areas of the field. They may work specifically with children or the elderly, or they may focus on improving the vision of people working in certain environments who are vulnerable to eye problems on the job. Some optometrists even specialize in sports vision, helping athletes with any vision problems. In addition, optometrists may also work in hospitals, at HMOs, or for ophthalmologists. A smaller number of optometrists choose to work as consultants for insurance companies or other companies, conduct research, or teach.

Training to Be an Optometrist

In order to become an optometrist, one must receive a doctor of optometry from an optometry school that is accredited by the Council on Optometric Education of the American Optometric Association. A person must have a bachelor's degree (four-year college degree) from a college or university in order to apply to an optometry program. Optometry schools accept students who have studied math and science in college and who have passed the Optometry Admission Test.

A student in an optometry program, which lasts four years, will do classroom and laboratory work as well as have practical training. After completing optometry school, it's necessary to take another examination given by the state in which the school is located in order to receive a license to practice optometry. Optometrists must continue their education so that they can renew their license every one to three years. If optometrists wish to specialize in other areas, teach, or conduct research, postgraduate work is necessary.

PHARMACIST

Prescription drugs, which are prescribed by physicians or other health care practitioners, are not available over the counter. Pharmacists, usually in drugstores, dispense them. This is to ensure proper dosages are given to patients with accurate instructions on how to administer the drug. Pharmacists also inform patients of side effects or possible interactions, either with food or other drugs, that can cause problems. If pharmacists work in hospital settings, they fulfill requests from physicians for drugs for their patients. They are also available to advise physicians and other staff on the characteristics of a particular medicine.

Pharmacists may have to mix preparations to form certain prescriptions, which is called compounding, but most drugs sold today by pharmacists are made by drug companies.

Pharmacists are required to know how a drug should be used, what it is made of, and what effect it gives when taken. They keep records of the prescriptions they fill, usually in a computer database. As well as keeping their business organized, these records allow pharmacists to warn patients if their records show that a patient has filled a prescription that is going to interact negatively with another drug he or she is already taking.

Even though they are primarily responsible for dispensing prescription drugs, pharmacists do have knowledge of over-the-counter drugs (drugs that

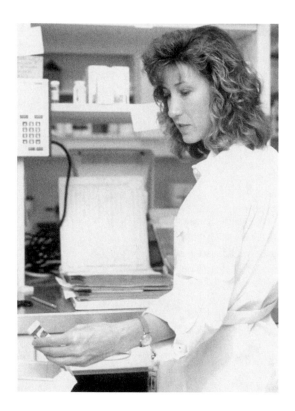

are available to the public without a prescription, such as aspirin or certain cold medications) and can advise drugstore customers on their proper usage. They also have knowledge of any medical equipment being sold in the drugstore. In some drugstores, pharmacists may have the responsibility of stocking other nondrug-related merchandise, such as cosmetics, and hiring and managing personnel.

In addition to dispensing drugs and fielding drug questions from hospital staff, pharmacists working in hospitals usually monitor patients' drug treatments during their stay and order medical supplies. If patients have questions about the drugs they are taking, hospital pharmacists are available to answer their questions, too. Other areas in which a pharmacist may be employed include the pharmaceutical industry, home health care, or research facilities.

Training to Be a Pharmacist

To become a pharmacist, a person must graduate with either a bachelor's degree in pharmacy or a doctor of pharmacy (Pharm.D.) degree. The bachelor's degree in pharmacy is a five-year program and the doctor of pharmacy degree is a six-year program. However, by the year 2004,

A pharmacist is a familiar sight at the neighborhood drug store. (Photograph © 1991 L. Steinmark. Custom Medical Stock Photo. Reproduced by permission.)

it is planned that all accredited programs will only offer the doctor of pharmacy. Some pharmacy programs accept students directly out of high school. For others, there is a prerequisite of one or two years of undergraduate college classes. Master's and Ph.D. (doctoral) degree programs in pharmacy are also offered by some schools.

Before pharmacists can begin to work, they must become licensed by the state in which they will be working. There are certain requirements a person must meet for licensure. Those include successfully completing a program in pharmacy from an accredited college, taking and passing a licensing examination given by the state, and completing an internship supervised by a licensed pharmacist. Like most health care fields, continuing education is very important. In fact, in order to maintain a license in some states, continuing education is required.

PHYSICAL THERAPIST

Physical therapy is a very popular, competitive career with many job opportunities. Physical therapists evaluate and treat patients who suffer from the effects of injuries or diseases. They have important roles in the rehabilitation of their patients. They work to relieve symptoms, correct existing problems, and prevent further physical disabilities associated with a patient's condition. Their patients may suffer from diverse conditions such arthritis, cerebral palsy, back pain, head injuries, or fractures.

Physical therapists design specific treatment programs for their patients, depending on the patient's injury or disease. For example, if a patient has lower back pain, the physical therapist may design a program that includes hot packs and traction. They are responsible for outlining the program and its desired outcome in a treatment plan. It is required in most states for a patient to be referred to a physical therapist by a physician. The referral may give the physical therapist the freedom to devise the patient's treatment program or the physician may give specific treatment instructions.

Some treatments physical therapists use to address their patients' conditions include exercise, massage, ultrasound, hydrotherapy (water therapy such as whirlpools), electrical stimulation (when electricity is used to massage deep tissue or to relieve swelling), hot packs, ice, paraffin (hot wax), and traction (when a person's body is gently pulled by a machine to stretch muscles and increase circulation). During the first visit, a patient is evaluated and a treatment program is developed. On following visits, the patient receives treatment by the physical therapist, a physical therapy assistant, or aide.

During the evaluation of the patient, the physical therapist performs diagnostic tests. These tests provide the therapist with information on muscle function, strength, and range of motion, balance, coordination, and areas of weakness, and whether the patient has suffered any brain damage. This information, along with the patient's medical history and diagnosis from the patient's physician, helps the therapist devise an effective treatment program and monitor the patient's progress.

Physical therapists work in a variety of settings, including private practice, hospitals, clinics, and rehabilitation centers, or they provide home health care for their patients. They may specialize in pediatrics (children), geriatrics (elderly), sports injuries, cerebral palsy, or mental illnesses. They may also teach or conduct research.

Physical therapy assistants help physical therapists in administering treatment to patients and maintaining documentation of a patient's progress. They usually interact more with the patients than the physical therapists, who are often overloaded with administrative duties and supervisory responsibilities.

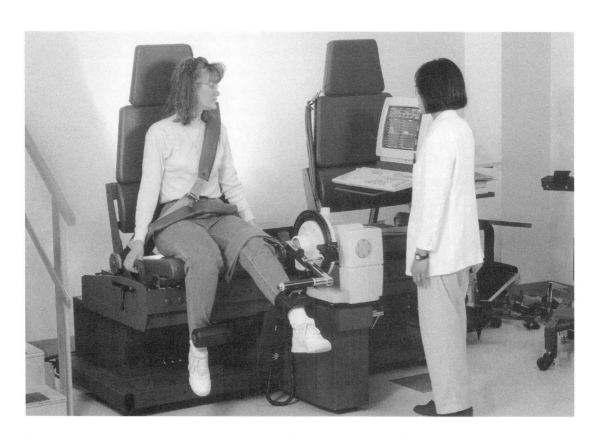

A physical therapist works with this patient to strengthen her left knee. (Custom Medical Stock Photo. Reproduced by permission.)

Training to Be a Physical Therapist

A physical therapy program is typically a three-year, full-time program. It requires two to three years of prerequisite (required) undergraduate college courses that include biology, chemistry, and physics, before a student may apply for the program. Practical experience in the field as a physical therapy aide is also a requirement. Most programs offer a master's degree but some still only offer the bachelor's degree. In 2001, however, all programs will offer the master's degree.

In order to practice, a physical therapy graduate must pass a state licensing examination. Some states require continuing education to maintain a license. To keep up on the latest advances in the field, physical therapists should seek continuing education whether the state in which they are practicing requires it or not.

PHYSICIAN

Physicians are the foundation of all health care systems. Physicians diagnose and treat illnesses. Aside from helping patients overcome illness, physicians help people maintain good health with preventive care. Regular checkups from a family physician or pediatrician help people stay healthy. However, physicians do much more than simply provide physical examinations. They take medical histories and order, perform, and evaluate diagnostic (used in diagnosis) tests. If the tests show irregular results or indicate the presence of a disease, the physician will decide upon a course of treatment that may include medication, a surgical procedure, or therapy of some sort.

There are two different kinds of physicians and that difference lies in their training. The most common type of physician is a doctor of medicine (M.D.). M.D.s are also known as allopathic physicians. There is also the doctor of osteopathic medicine (D.O.). Both types of physicians use all accepted methods of treatment to treat patients; however, because of their training in osteopathy, D.O.s tend to pay closer attention to a patient's musculoskeletal (mus-

A SAMPLING OF SPECIALTIES

Here are just a few areas of medical specialty and what parts of the body they involve:

Anesthesiology: anesthesia or drugs used to make an individual lose consciousness/feeling (as when undergoing surgery)

Cardiology: the heart

Dermatology: the skin

Gastroenterology: the stomach and the intestines

Gynecology: the reproductive systems of women

Neurology: the brain and nervous system

Obstetrics: pregnancy and childbirth

Oncology: cancerous growths and tumors

Ophthalmology: the eyes

Orthopedics: the bones

Otolaryngology: ears, nose, and throat

Pathology: disease

Pediatrics: care of children

Psychiatry: the human mind and behavior

Pulmonary: lungs

Radiology: the use of radiation to treat disease

Thoracic: the midsection of the body

Urology: urinary tract

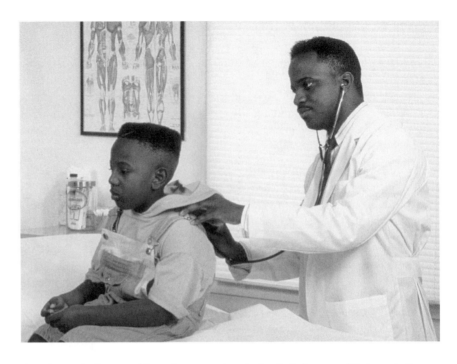

Listening to the heart and lungs is a normal part of a doctor's exam. (Photograph ©
1994 T. McCarthy. Custom Medical Stock Photo. Reproduced by permission.)

cles and bones) system and employ holistic (treating both the body and the
mind) care.

Both M.D.s and D.O.s can specialize in a variety of areas. There are
primary (initial) care specialties that include general internal medicine and
general pediatrics. There are also what are categorized as medical specialties, such as cardiology, dermatology, obstetrics/gynecology, and pediatric
cardiology. Surgery in and of itself is a specialty; there are general surgeons
as well as surgeons who specialize in neurological surgery, plastic surgery,
or thoracic surgery. Beyond these, there exist numerous other areas of specialty that include anesthesiology, emergency medicine, psychiatry, and
radiology.

Approximately seven out of ten physicians work out of an office-based
private or group practice. This can include health care clinics and HMOs
(health maintenance organizations). When physicians work in a private or
group practice, they will also have privileges to admit and supervise the care
of their patients who require hospitalization and/or surgery. There are physicians who do not have outside practices and work on staff at a hospital. They
are often known as attending physicians. Physicians can also be found working for the federal government, in government-funded hospitals and clinics,
or for the Department of Health and Human Services. Most physicians who

are on staff at hospitals that are associated with medical colleges also function as instructors at those colleges.

Physicians are often supported by physician assistants. Physician assistants are trained and certified to perform many duties that normally would be carried out by a physician, such as treating cuts and burns or setting broken bones. Physician assistants are also able to interpret lab tests, and they may even make preliminary diagnoses. Like physicians, physician assistants often specialize in a certain type of medicine, such as pediatrics or surgery. Physicians also work directly with nurses (see entry) and medical assistants, who perform clerical and organizational duties as well as assist doctors with procedures.

Pediatric cardiologist Dr. Sean Levchuck. (Photograph by Richard Levchuck. Reproduced by permission.)

SPOTLIGHT ON PEDIATRIC CARDIOLOGY

Dr. Sean G. Levchuck is a pediatric cardiologist. He diagnoses and treats heart ailments in children from infancy through twenty-one years of age. Many of the heart problems that children suffer from are known as congenital (existing at birth) heart disease. In fact, eight out of every 1,000 children are born with a heart ailment. One of the most common ailments that pediatric cardiologists such as Dr. Levchuck treat are holes between the heart chambers.

Congenital heart disease can be treated with surgery, but often, a pediatric cardiologist can close the hole using a catheter (plastic tubing). Medication can also be used to treat congenital heart disease or to prevent arrhythmias (irregular heartbeats) from occurring. But, if the hole is too large to be treated with either of these techniques, a pediatric cardiologist will make sure the child is healthy enough to undergo surgery. A surgeon will then operate under the direction of the pediatric cardiologist to mend the hole in a child's heart.

In addition to seeing patients in a private office and making rounds in hospitals to check on the status of any patients he has admitted, Dr. Levchuck spends time in the cath lab, doing catheterizations on his patients. Catheterizing a patient enables Dr. Levchuck to open a closed valve in a child's heart or to simply get a better idea of what is happening in and around the heart.

Dr. Levchuck became a pediatric cardiologist because he found cardiology very interesting, especially congenital heart disease. And he loves helping children. To become a pediatric cardiologist, Dr. Levchuck went to medical school and then served a three-year residency in pediatrics. To specialize even further, he did a three-year fellowship in pediatric cardiology at a different hospital. He says that the hardest thing about his job is "the fact that some kids die; that's always the worst part." But, Dr. Levchuck says, "we can help everybody in some way, which is not how it has always been. Dramatic advances [in pediatric cardiology] have been made, especially in the last ten years."

There are only about 1,700 pediatric cardiologists in the world.

Training to Be a Physician

There is a great deal of education and training involved in becoming a physician of any type. First, an individual must earn a bachelor's degree with a focus on pre-medical studies. Toward the end of undergraduate studies, people wishing to enter medical school must take the Medical College Admission Test (MCAT). After gaining admission to a medical school, medical students then spend two years on classroom studies, taking courses such as anatomy and histology. The following two years are spent working in clinics and hospitals learning acute, chronic, preventive, and rehabilitative care under the supervision of physicians. Students rotate through different areas of care, such as internal medicine, psychiatry, and surgery in order to have a well-rounded knowledge of medical care.

After graduating from medical school, both M.D.s and D.O.s do internships (supervised practical experience) for one year. (Often, a M.D.'s internship will be considered the first year of residency.) The internship is followed by a residency (advanced training in a medical specialty) in a particular area, such as internal medicine or pediatrics, that can last two years or more. Physicians who wish to specialize even further, such as going into pediatric neurology, must do a fellowship (advanced study and research) that can be an additional three or more years. After this training is completed, physicians must pass a licensing exam. Beyond that, to become a certified specialist by the American Board of Medical Specialists (ABMS), an additional exam must be passed.

Because of the demanding nature of both the training and daily activities of physicians, individuals entering this field need to be very motivated and determined. In order to deliver quality care and truly help patients, physicians should have a good bedside manner (the ability to put a patient at ease and communicate effectively) and strong decision-making abilities.

PSYCHOLOGIST

Psychology is the study of behavior and the mind. There are many different types of psychology and many different kinds of psychologists. All psychologists are concerned, though, with some aspect of the behavior of an individual or an organization, or with the human or animal mind. When most people think of a psychologist, they think of a professional who diagnoses and treats mentally ill people. However, there are many psychologists who focus on research rather than actually treating individuals as practitioners do.

Working in laboratories or out of research centers, psychologists who conduct research can study anything from functions of the brain to the way large organizations, such as corporations, function. Some psychologists focus exclusively on the work habits and work environments of different people and are employed by privately owned businesses or the government. Other psychologists work in private practice, clinics, or hospitals with patients and clients to help those individuals overcome mental illness, such as attention deficit disorder or post-traumatic stress disorder. Psychologists are also instructors at universities, training others to become psychologists. And, a psychologist's role in education doesn't end there. Many psychologists work with students to help them with learning disabilities and violence prevention in schools. Finally, psychologists can be found working in and around a community, assisting in planning programs at community centers or providing counseling services within jails or juvenile-detention centers.

There is a wide range of specialties within psychology that individuals training to be psychologists can focus upon as they complete their training and prepare to enter the workforce:

CLINICAL PSYCHOLGIST. The most popular specialty in psychology, clinical psychologists interview, diagnose, and treat patients in a variety of settings, including counseling centers, private practices, hospitals, or universities. They are trained to provide individual, couples, family, and group therapy, all of which can help people overcome mental and emotional problems. Clinical psychologists are often instructors at colleges and medical schools.

DEVELOPMENTAL PSYCHOLGIST. Just as the name suggests, developmental psychologists are most concerned with the development of the human mind and behavior throughout a person's life. Developmental psychologists may focus their interests on research or treat persons who develop mental disorders during a particular time of development, such as infancy or adolescence. Specific developmental disabilities, such as mental retardation and autism, can also be a developmental psychologist's area of specialty.

INDUSTRIAL/ORGANIZATIONAL (I/O) PSYCHOLOGIST. Trying to improve productivity in the workplace, I/O psychologists use psychological principles and research to determine what motivates individuals and groups of people at work. I/O psychologists also work to improve the quality of work life so that both employee and employer are satisfied. Human resource specialists and trainers in the workplace are often trained I/O psychologists.

NEUROPSYCHOLOGIST. To be a neuropsychologist, one must first be a clinical psychologist. Because neuropsychologists concentrate on the relationship between the activities of the brain and a person's behavior, they often work with people who have suffered strokes or head injuries. Neuropsychologists also study the functions of memory as well as how certain diseases can affect people's emotions and behavior along with the rest of their mental functioning.

RESEARCH PSYCHOLOGIST. Human beings and animals, such as rats, monkeys, and pigeons, are often studied by research psychologists. Research psychologists usually work in university and private research centers as well as laboratories and for governmental organizations. They research and study things such as motivation, learning and memory, and the effects of substance abuse on the mind.

SOCIAL PSYCHOLOGIST. Working in settings as diverse as conducting research in a university or studying consumer likes and dislikes at an advertising agency, social pychologists study how people interact with others and the social environment. Social psychology research provides a greater understanding of how and why people form different opinions about certain people or things. This is especially helpful in overcoming problems like discrimination and prejudice.

SPORTS PSYCHOLOGIST. Athletes, both professional and amateur, must prepare both their bodies and their minds for a competition. Often, individual athletes or entire teams need help to become more mentally focused on goals or to become more motivated. Sports psychologists work with this population, helping athletes to achieve their goals. Along the way, the sports psychologist might also help an individual overcome anxiety and a fear of failure before an event or competition.

Training to Be a Psychologist

Individuals working in the field of psychology usually hold bachelor's degrees (four-year college degree) in psychology. From there, an individual may choose to earn a master's degree in psychology and work as an I/O or a school psychologist. Clinical psychologists and other psychologists specializing in other areas usually hold doctorates of philosophy (Ph.D.) degrees in psychology. A doctor of psychology (Psy.D.) degree is also awarded at some universities.

PSYCHIATRISTS VS. PSYCHOLOGISTS

Psychiatrists and psychologists are similar in that both are mental health care providers. The difference between the two lies in the training for each profession as well as their approaches to treating mental or behavior problems.

Psychiatrists are medical doctors. They attend college and go on to medical school just as all physicians do. After completing their schooling, psychiatrists do their residency in psychiatry, just as a pediatrician would do a residency in pediatrics. Psychologists go to college as well, but they go on to a graduate program where they earn a Ph.D. or a Psy.D. While psychologists do learn about the human body to a certain degree, they focus mainly on applying psychological principles when assessing and treating mental and developmental disorders. In contrast, psychiatrists, because they are physicians, focus on the biological and chemical causes behind mental illness as well as using psychological principles to diagnose and treat an individual.

Both of these types of mental health professionals can help people with mental illness or emotional and behavioral problems. Psychiatrists, however, are allowed to prescribe medications that are often used to treat anxiety, depression, or schizophrenia (see Chapter 12 Mental Illness). A psychologist treating an individual with any of these disorders would need to work closely with a psychiatrist in order to provide a patient with proper physical and psychological therapy.

A Ph.D. can take anywhere from five to seven years to complete. Near the end of the program, Ph.D. candidates must write a dissertation (an in-depth research paper) based on original research that the student has conducted. A Psy.D. program is different in that it can often be based more on hands-on work and traditional exams rather than on a research-based dissertation. Most Ph.D. and Psy.D. students are also required to perform an internship.

Psychologists must be certified and licensed to practice psychology professionally. This certification and licensing usually involves passing written and oral exams.

RADIOLOGICAL TECHNOLOGIST

Radiological technologists are trained to take images of the inside of the human body. Some radiological technologists work with radiation to take these images. When most people hear the term radiation, they think of a harmful substance. While exposure to radiation can cause illness, small doses of radiation given in controlled settings can be helpful to doctors and patients. Radiation is used to create images, called X rays, of the inside of the body. Radiation, however, does more than produce images; it is also used to treat cancer.

The different types of radiological technologists include radiographers, radiation therapy technologists, and sonographers. Sonographers are unique in that they don't work with radiation. Rather, they use sound waves to take pictures of the human body. All radiological technologists work closely with radiologists, doctors specializing in radiology, who give them strict instructions for each patient. It's also important for radiological technologists to protect themselves and their patients from overexposure to radiation. Lead gloves, aprons, and equipment that monitors levels of exposure help to protect against overexposure to radiation.

RADIOGRAPHER. When doctors need to see the inside of the body to diagnose a medical problem, they order X rays, or radiographs, of a specific body part. Radiographers are responsible for producing these X rays.

First, radiographers explain to the patient how the procedure will work. Patients must remove any jewelry from their bodies, as X rays cannot pass through jewelry. Radiographers then position patients so that the X rays can reach the right part of the body and only that part. Finally, a lead shield is placed over the exposed body part to protect patients from radiation.

Once patients are positioned and protected, radiographers then measure the thickness of the body part being X-rayed. This allows radiographers to

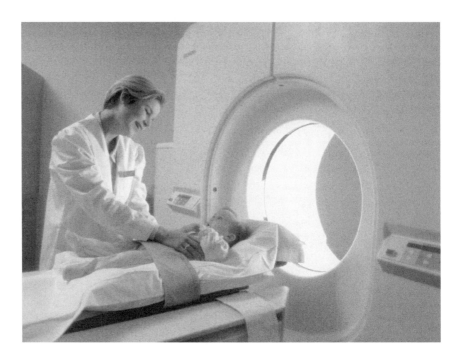

A radiological technician comforts a young patient. (Photograph © 1995 Sean O'Brien. Custom Medical Stock Photo. Reproduced by permission.)

set the X-ray machine at the right levels to release the right amount of radiation. Once the machine takes the picture, radiographers then develop the film for the doctor.

RADIATION THERAPY TECHNOLOGIST. Patients who are diagnosed with cancer sometimes receive radiation therapy to treat the disease. This involves getting certain doses of radiation from a radiation therapy technologist, or radiation therapist. Radiation therapists are trained to use equipment that releases radiation. Their jobs require extreme accuracy when giving treatments to patients. Once they have positioned patients properly, radiation therapists give specific doses of radiation to the affected body part, while also protecting the rest of the body from exposure.

Radiation therapy can cause patients to lose hair, feel nauseated, or experience skin problems. Radiation therapists are trained to help patients deal with these difficult side effects. Radiation therapy can also be emotionally difficult as many patients are struggling with cancer, which can be a life-threatening diseases. Radiation therapists and their patients usually develop a strong bond due to the intense nature of the treatment, which can last from a few weeks to many months.

SONOGRAPHER. Sonographers also take pictures of the inside of the body, but they use a different method that involves high-frequency sound waves. The sound waves are directed into the body and create echoes. Special equipment turns these echoes into images. Sonographers and patients can watch the images on a screen while the process takes place. Then a doctor views the images directly from the screen or from photographs that are taken by the sonographer. A diagnosis can be made from seeing the sonograph. Sonographers must also be extremely accurate when taking images of patients so that the doctor can make a diagnosis from examining the image.

Many sonographers specialize in certain parts of the body. For example, a sonographer who specializes in the female reproductive system will take sonographs of a baby in the womb as it grows to make sure it is healthy. Other specialties include the brain, the heart, the liver and kidneys, and the eyes.

Training to Be a Radiological Technologist

People interested in work as a radiological technologist can get training in a few different ways. These include programs in hospitals, vocational schools, colleges and universities, and the Armed Forces.

Programs offer either a certificate (one-year program), an associate's degree (two-year program), or a bachelor's degree (four-year program). Most people work toward an associate's degree. Certificate programs are for people who already have a medical background but wish to change careers. All programs, which require a high school diploma to enter, involve both classroom work and clinical instruction. While becoming registered with the American Registry of Radiologic Technologists (ARRT) is not required by law, most people like to hire those who are registered. Once a student has graduated from a radiological technologist program, it's necessary to pass an examination to become registered.

REGISTERED NURSE (R.N.)

There are many opportunities for those interested in a career as a registered nurse (R.N.). The many jobs available in the field continue to grow every year; in fact, nursing is one of the fastest growing occupations today. R.N.s not only treat patients who are sick, but they work to help people maintain good health as well as prevent and cope with illness and disease. While most R.N.s work directly with individual patients in different settings, they can also help entire communities improve health by acting as health care advocates for groups of people and families who are not receiving necessary medical care.

The basic duties of a R.N. are to:

- examine and record a patient's symptoms
- observe a patient's progress or a patient's reaction to treatment

Nurses are a great source of comfort and assistance to hospitalized patients. (Custom Medical Stock Photo. Reproduced by permission.)

- give medication to a patient
- assist doctors in the examination and treatment of a patient
- help with the patient's recovery

R.N.s usually work in hospitals. Most often, they are assigned to a specific area of the hospital, such as the pediatrics (children's) ward or the emergency room. However, R.N.s have many workplace options; they can work in a private doctor's office, as a home health nurse (caring for people in their homes), in a nursing home, with the government, in schools, in offices, or with health maintenance organizations (HMOs).

Working as a nurse can be very rewarding; however, like most jobs, there is stress involved. Many R.N.s spend most of the day on their feet. They also must deal with people's suffering on a daily basis. The amount of stress an R.N. experiences can depend on the setting in which the R.N. works. For example, an R.N. in the emergency room of a hospital may have more stress than an R.N. in a private doctor's office, as emergency room patients need immediate care. In addition, any R.N. in a hospital may have to work odd hours, as patients need to be cared for twenty-four hours a day. Most R.N.s at one point or another will work night shifts, as well as weekends and holidays.

CERTIFIED NURSE-MIDWIFE (C.N.M.)

Midwives have existed for thousands of years giving women support and care through the birthing process. Even though midwives, or wisewomen as they were often called, have practiced for centuries, their profession was not officially recognized until recently. Midwifery as a formal profession began in 1921 when nurses who worked with the Frontier Nursing Service and Maternity Center Association saw that poor communities in New York City and Appalachia greatly needed their services because they couldn't afford to give birth in hospitals. Certified nurse-midwives (C.N.M.s) were officially recognized by the American College of Obstetricians and Gynecologists in

1971. Now, many hospitals employ C.N.M.s, who have been educated through graduate programs specializing in the birthing process, prenatal care, and aftercare for new mothers.

C.N.M.s offer women a safe, and often less costly, alternative to giving birth in a traditional hospital setting. They are committed to meeting the individual needs of their patients and giving women freedom to make choices during the birth, such as who will be present during the delivery and in what position the women want to give birth. While they are licensed to give drugs to their patients and provide patients with any technological assistance, C.N.M.s use technology only when it's absolutely necessary. Their mission is to give women a natural and normal birthing experience in a calm,

Training to Be a Registered Nurse

In order to become an R.N., a person has three choices. These include earning an associate's degree (A.D.N.) through a junior or community college, which takes approximately two years; getting a diploma through programs offered in hospitals, which usually takes two to three years; and, finally, getting a bachelor of science degree in nursing (B.S.N.) at a university, which takes four to five years to complete.

While these three options are still acceptable, many state governments are now considering changing the requirements for an R.N.'s education. The new standards would require all R.N.s to have a B.S.N. It's beneficial now for all R.N.s to have a B.S.N. because it gives them greater opportunities in the field. Many R.N.s with a diploma or an associate's degree enroll in a bachelor's program, often having their employers pay for their schooling. All nursing education involves classroom work as well as practical experience in a hospital or other health care facility. After the schooling is completed, a person must take an examination to become a registered nurse.

Some R.N.s go on to do graduate work, which enables them to enter into specialized nursing fields, such as nurse practitioner (a nurse who is trained and licensed to act in place of a physician), certified nurse-midwife, or certified registered nurse anesthetist (who is responsible for anesthetizing a patient during an operation).

SOCIAL WORKER

The job of a social worker is a challenging one. They help people cope with many types of problems, including personal, family, and work-related

caring atmosphere and to prevent any complications before, during, and after the birth.

The American College of Nurse-Midwives (ACNM) regulates the standards for C.N.M.s. All the schools that offer programs in nurse midwifery must be accredited by ACNM. All C.N.M.s must pass a national examination given by ACNM Certification Council.

C.N.M.s can work in many different settings. Some have their own practices, and some work with private doctors, hospitals, and birth centers. No matter where they work, C.N.M.s always work with a doctor, who remains available in case of a problem or emergency with the birth.

Some physicians are happy to cooperate with C.N.M.s and offer their assistance to them. However, other physicians may refuse to work with them because they don't agree with C.N.M.s' mission or are afraid of losing business to C.N.M.s. While C.N.M.s are licensed health care practitioners and covered by most insurance policies, they are relatively new as a formal profession compared with other health-related careers. At times, certain standards that the medical system has incorporated, such as a requirement to use certain technology during labor, make it difficult for C.N.M.s to do their jobs. Despite these obstacles, C.N.M.s are in high demand, and most women who use them choose to work with them again.

issues. When people face financial problems, unemployment, serious physical or mental illness, disabilities, conflicts at school or on the job, social workers are there to guide them toward helpful resources and give them support through their difficult times. Social workers act as counselors and give special attention to the poor, who are unable to afford other types of counseling. Because they deal with so many problems, social workers often practice in several different environments. They can be found working in schools, hospitals, mental health clinics, welfare offices, and employment offices.

When people first meet with social workers for help, they talk one-on-one with the social worker about their problems. Social workers help their patients uncover their specific concerns and then review the possible solutions available to them. Because of their education and training, social workers may be able to offer solutions that their patients have never considered or weren't aware of. Finally, once a solution is agreed upon, social workers help their patients take action. This may involve helping patients fill out job applications or other types of forms and arranging for counseling services. By investigating the many resources that can help their patients, social workers can be instrumental in changing the course of their patients' lives.

The job of social workers can be very intense and emotional, as they often become intimately involved with their patients' lives. Social workers offer their services even after their patients are getting help from other sources for their problems. Through the follow-up care, social workers can ensure that the help their patients are receiving is the type of care they need. If something isn't working for their patients, social workers can direct them to a different service or program that may be more effective.

Almost all social workers specialize in a certain area:

- Family services social workers work with children and youths who are having trouble adjusting with an issue at home or at school.
- Child or adult protective services social workers investigate reports of abuse in the home. They take action to ease the problem or possibly take children or adults out of abusive homes and place them in safe homes or other facilities.
- Mental health social workers help people with mental or emotional problems cope with their daily lives.
- Health care social workers help people who are dealing with a serious or chronic illness, such as AIDS or Alzheimer's disease.
- School services social workers handle students' problems, such as pregnancy, bad behavior, or poor performance in school.
- Criminal justice social workers help convicted criminals and their families with court procedures and issues that arise after a person is released from prison.

- Occupational services social workers help people who have problems with their jobs, such as stress, or who have personal problems that are affecting their work.
- Gerontological services social workers deal with the concerns of elderly people and their families.

Training to Be a Social Worker

People who want to become social workers must have a bachelor's degree in social work (B.S.W.), which allows them to get an entry-level position in the field. This involves studying four years at a college or university whose program has been accredited by the Council on Social Work Education. In addition to classroom work, a student must have 400 hours of supervised training in the field.

For those who wish to work in the health or mental health area, it's necessary to have a master's degree in social work, which usually takes an additional two years of study, 900 hours of supervised training or an internship. A master's degree will also broaden the opportunities for social workers, allowing them to work in positions that supervise or train other people. All social workers must be licensed by the state in which they work; each state has its own requirements for licensing.

JANE ADDAMS: PIONEER SOCIAL WORKER

Jane Addams (1860-1935) is considered a trailblazer of social reform. She dedicated her life to helping the poor and was responsible for starting one of the first settlement houses (a place that provides free services to communities) in the United States. Addams and her friend Ellen Starr established Hull House in Chicago, Illinois, in 1889 as a way to help poor and troubled families, as well as immigrants, who were living in the slums of the city. Addams worked and lived there until her death in 1935.

The seeds for planning Hull House were planted in Addams's head after a trip to Europe when she was a young woman. In London, she visited another settlement house called Toynbee Hall, where young women were helping poor people.

One year after her return to America, she rented a house (the Hull mansion) and offered a variety of services, such as day-care centers for working mothers and recreational activities for children and teens. Through Addams's dedication and hard work, Hull House expanded with money from private citizens and grants from social agencies. Soon after its opening, Hull House became famous throughout the United States. It grew from one building to thirteen and offered medical care, legal aid, and English classes, as well as art, music, and drama instruction. By 1893, Hull House was helping more than 2,000 people each week.

The success of Hull House continued after Addams's death. Today, the original Hull House stands as a museum, but the Jane Addams Hull House Association continues to help many poor communities of Chicago.

SPEECH-LANGUAGE PATHOLOGIST

Speech-language pathologists help people of all ages who have difficulty communicating. They treat people who stutter, have lost the ability to speak due to brain injury or brain disorder, have trouble speaking clearly, or have problems with the quality of their voice, meaning their voice is either too loud or too high. People who have hearing loss and speech problems because of emotional issues, or the inability to understand or produce language will also seek treatment from a speech-language pathologist.

With therapy and special equipment, speech-language pathologists evaluate patients, diagnose problems, and provide the appropriate treatment. Over the course of several weeks or even months, speech-language pathologists meet with patients and help them improve their voices, teach them to make certain sounds, and increase their language abilities. Sometimes, speech-language pathologists use a videostroboscopy, an instrument that allows them to view and monitor a patient's vocal chords for any abnormalities.

For both patients and speech-language pathologists, the therapy process requires patience, as it takes time to make significant progress. Sometimes, therapy is unsuccessful. With severe cases, speech-language pathologists may recommend an alternative to therapy. This includes sign language and devices, such as computers, that enable patients to communicate.

During treatment, speech-language pathologists may also work closely with parents or other family members to teach them how to cope with a loved one who has communication problems. They will also work with social workers or teachers, who can also help with a patient's progress and make sure the patient receives the best possible treatment.

Speech-language pathologists have many different job settings available to them. They may have their own private practice, while others may specialize in certain areas, working in schools with children, in hospitals with stroke victims, or in nursing homes or rehabilitation centers. Some speech-language pathologists are more interested in doing research than working directly with patients. They are usually employed at universities and study the origins of speech problems, as well as the impact of communication disorders on patients. They may also develop new techniques, equipment, or drugs to treat patients.

Training to Be a Speech-Language Pathologist

Becoming a speech-language pathologist requires a master's degree in speech-language pathology from a university that is accredited by Educational Standards Board of the American Speech-Language-Hearing Association. A master's degree involves classroom work, as well as 350 hours of practical experience. And, most states require speech-language pathologists to become licensed. To get a license to practice speech-language pathology, a graduate must pass a written exam, complete 375 hours of practical experience supervised by another licensed

The speech-language pathologist works to help a patient correct her speech disorder. (Photo Researchers, Inc. Reproduced by permission.)

speech-language pathologist, and complete at least thirty-six weeks of professional experience in the field. Some states require that speech-language pathologists continue their education every few years in order to renew their license.

FOR MORE INFORMATION

Books

Baxter, Neale and Philip A. Perry. *Opportunities in Counseling and Development Careers.* Lincolnwood, Ill.: VGM Career Horizons/NTC Publishing Group, 1997.

Camenson, Blythe. *Real People Working in Health Care.* Lincolnwood, Ill.: VGM Career Horizons/NTC Publishing Group, 1997.

Field, Shelly. *Career Opportunities in Health Career: A Comprehensive Guide to Exciting Careers Open to You in Health Care.* New York: Facts on File, Inc., 1997.

Krumhansl, Bernice. *Opportunities in Physical Therapy Careers.* Lincolnwood, Ill.: VGM Career Horizons/NTC Publishing Group, 1993.

Lund, Bill. *Getting Ready for a Career in Health Care.* New York: Capstone, 1998.

The Occupational Outlook Handbook 1998-99. Compiled by the United States Department of Labor, 1998.

Reeves, Diane Lindsey. *Career Ideas for Kids Who Like Science.* New York: Facts on File, Inc., 1998.

Shafer, R.C. and Louis Sportelli. *Opportunities in Chiropractic Health Care Careers.* Lincolnwood, Ill.: VGM Career Horizons/NTC Publishing Group, 1994.

Weeks, Zona R. *Opportunities in Occupational Therapy Careers.* Lincolnwood, Ill.: VGM Career Horizons/NTC Publishing Group, 1996.

Web sites

American Art Therapy Association. [Online] www.arttherapy.org (Accessed August 21, 1999).

American Association of Colleges of Pharmacy. [Online] http://www.aacp.org (Accessed August 21, 1999).

American Association of Oriental Medicine. [Online] http://www.aaom.org (Accessed August 21, 1999).

American Chiropractic Association. [Online] http:// www.amerchiro.org (Accessed August 21, 1999).

American Counseling Association. [Online] http://www.counseling.org (Accessed August 21, 1999).

American Dental Association. [Online] http:// www.ada.org (Accessed August 21, 1999).

American Medical Association. [Online] http://www.ama-assn.org (Accessed August 21, 1999).

American Nurses Organization. [Online] http://www.nursingworld.org (Accessed August 21, 1999).

American Occupational Therapy Association. [Online] http://www.aota.org (Accessed August 21, 1999).

American Optometric Association. [Online] http://www.aoanet.org (Accessed August 21, 1999).

American Physical Therapy Association. [Online] http://www.apta.org (Accessed August 21, 1999).

American Psychiatric Association. [Online] http://www.psych.org (Accessed August 21, 1999).

American Psychology Association. [Online] http://www.apa.org (Accessed August 21, 1999).

American Society of Radiologic Technologists. [Online] http://www.asrt.org (Accessed August 21, 1999).

American Speech-Language-Hearing Association. [Online] http://www.asha.org (Accessed August 21, 1999).

Association for University Programs in Health Administration. [Online] http://www.aupha.com (Accessed August 21, 1999).

National Association of Emergency Medical Technicians. [Online] http://www.naemt.org (Accessed August 21, 1999).

National Association of Social Workers. [Online] http://www.socialworkers.org (Accessed August 21, 1999).

8

Preventive Care

Illnesses and injuries affect everyone at some point in life. That is why it is important to think about how to prevent getting sick or injured. There is a saying: "An ounce of prevention is worth a pound of cure." This means that even a small amount of prevention will save a lot of time lost from getting sick or injured. Amazingly, there is a wide variety of ways that each individual can try to protect her or his own health and well-being. Starting in childhood, a person can establish a healthy diet and physical fitness program and begin other healthy habits that will greatly reduce the likelihood of future illnesses and injuries.

This chapter will examine three aspects of preventive care: illness prevention, injury prevention, and preventive medicine. The discussion on illness prevention will detail the many ways that an individual can avoid contracting diseases or developing painful or life-threatening conditions. Injury prevention will examine safety precautions, good habits, and equipment that protect people from getting hurt at home and at play. Information on preventive medicine such as vitamins, minerals, and herbal medicines that help the body fight off disease and infection will also be discussed.

Illness Prevention

Injury Prevention

Preventive Medicine

ILLNESS PREVENTION

Experts agree there are many things a person can do to keep from getting ill. Illnesses are usually caused by living organisms—bacteria, parasites, fungi, or viruses—that are transmitted from one person to another. A healthy person's immune system usually can attack and destroy these organisms before the person becomes ill, but when this system is weakened by factors such as poor nutrition or stress, sickness or disease may be the result.

People can take many actions that can help guard their bodies against these infections and build up their immune systems to make them strong and resistant to illness. These actions include good habits like eating well, getting plenty of exercise and sleep, managing stress, practicing good hygiene, and getting frequent physical checkups and complete immunizations.

Eating Well

A healthy diet—making sure to get enough of certain kinds of foods, such as fruit and vegetables, and not too much of other kinds, such as hamburgers and French fries—can prevent a host of health problems. These problems can include allergies, Alzheimer's disease, cancer, cataracts, diabetes, digestive problems such as bloating and diarrhea, headaches, heart disease, high blood pressure, Parkinson's disease, and premature aging. The best way to maintain a healthy diet is to eat a variety of foods, paying special attention to eating the right proportions as suggested by the U.S. government's Food Guide Pyramid, which is a guide to good nutrition. [*See also* Chapter 1: Nutrition.]

FIBER. In general, a person should concentrate on eating a diet high in fiber. Sufficient dietary fiber intake helps prevent colon cancer and irritable bowel syndrome, as well as constipation, hemorrhoids, and diarrhea. Fiber also promotes bowel regularity. It is possible that eating enough fiber may lower cholesterol and, in diabetics, slow the absorption of sugar, which may decrease the need for insulin. Foods high in fiber include whole

INCREASE FIBER INTAKE BY EATING HIGH-FIBER SNACKS LIKE NUTS, POPCORN, FRESH OR DRIED FRUITS, AND WHOLE GRAIN CRACKERS.

WORDS TO KNOW

Adrenaline: A chemical that blocks the histamine response in an allergic reaction.

Alzheimer's disease: A severe condition usually found in the elderly that affects the parts of the brain that control thought, memory, and language.

Anemia: The condition of low iron in the blood.

Antibodies: A substance made in the body that protects the body against germs or viruses.

Antioxidants: Powerful molecules found in certain foods and vitamins that help neutralize free radicals, which are damaging molecules.

Bacteria: Single-celled micro-organisms, which can be either beneficial or harmful.

Carbon monoxide: A highly toxic, colorless, odorless gas that is produced whenever something is burned incompletely, or in a closed environment.

Collagen: Fibrous protein found in connective tissues such as the skin and ligaments.

Cruciform: The term for certain vegetables with long stems and branching tops, such as broccoli and cauliflower.

Emphysema: A lung disease usually caused by smoking that produces shortness of breath and relentless coughing.

Enzyme: A complex protein found in the cells that acts as a catalyst for chemical reactions in the body.

Esophagus: The muscular tube that connects the throat with the stomach.

Free radicals: Harmful molecules in the body that damage normal cells and can cause cancer and other disorders.

Fungus: An organism of plant origin that lacks chlorophyll; some fungi cause irritation or disease.

grains, fruits, vegetables, and legumes (peas, beans), but some people prefer to take fiber supplements available at grocery and drug stores.

FRUITS AND VEGGIES. Everyone has heard: "an apple a day will keep the doctor away," or "eat your vegetables, they're good for you!" Fruits and vegetables are good for everyone, but many people find it hard to eat enough of them, and some don't like them at all. They may not taste as good as ice cream or chocolate to most people, but it is important to try to eat them anyway. They benefit a person's health in many ways.

One group of vegetables, called cruciform, includes broccoli, cauliflower, brussels sprouts, kale, kohlrabi and Swiss chard. Eating vegetables from this group helps prevent the development of stomach, colorectal (large intestine and rectum), and lung cancers. Dark green and deep yellow vegetables like spinach, carrots, sweet potatoes, cantaloupes, and apricots are good sources of vitamin A. Oranges, grapefruit, strawberries, and green and red peppers contain vitamin C. Vitamins A and C are antioxidants, which are important vitamins that help neutralize harmful molecules called free radicals in the body. Free radicals damage normal cells and can cause cancer, as well as cataracts, diabetes, heart disease, high blood pressure, and both Alzheimer's and Parkinson's disease.

MORE ABOUT ANTIOXIDANTS. In addition to vitamins A and C, the antioxidant vitamin group includes beta-carotene, selenium, and vitamin E.

Hemoglobin: A protein found in red blood cells, needed to carry oxygen to the body's many tissues.

Hemorrhoids: Enlarged and swollen veins in the anus that may bleed.

Hepatitis: One of several severe liver-damaging diseases specified by the letters A, B, C and D.

Histamines: Chemicals released in an allergic reaction that cause swelling of body tissues.

Immune system: The body's own natural defenses against germs and other infectious agents.

Immunization: The introduction of disease-causing compounds into the body in very small amounts in order to allow the body to form antigens against the disease.

Insomnia: Chronic sleeplessness or sleep disturbances.

Insulin: The substance in the body that regulates blood sugar levels.

Larynx: The voice box.

Monosodium glutamate (MSG): A substance that enhances flavor but causes food intolerance in some people.

Mucous membranes: The lining of the nose and sinus passages that helps shield the body from allergens and germs.

Osteoporosis: A degenerative bone disease.

Parasite: An organism that lives on or inside another organism at the expense of its host.

Parkinson's disease: A progressive disease that causes slowing and stiffening of muscular activity, trembling hands, and a difficulty in speaking and walking.

Virus: A tiny organism that causes disease.

Many people take supplements of these vitamins, but a person with a healthy, varied diet should take in enough to help prevent certain diseases. Increasing the body's level of antioxidants also has been shown to help prevent premature aging and skin damage, minimize stress, and prevent acne. Antioxidants can also prevent or lessen the severity of allergies like hay fever.

REDUCE THE FAT AND PROCESSED FOODS. A diet low in fatty foods, which are foods that contain unsaturated or saturated fats, is helpful in the prevention of certain diseases. Research has shown a relationship between high dietary fat intake and the occurrence of prostate, colorectal, and other cancers. Dietary fat is one of the main generators of damaging free radicals. Because of this connection, eating less fat, both saturated and unsaturated, lessens a person's risk of cancer, cataracts, diabetes, heart disease, high blood pressure, and both Alzheimer's and Parkinson's disease. Lowering fat intake also helps prevent or reduce acne. The same benefits can be realized by avoiding foods rich in white, processed flour and sugar.

AVOID FRIED AND SMOKED OR BARBECUED FOODS. Fried foods are high in fat, and many smoked and barbecued foods contain nitrates and other chemicals that are known to cause cancer. A person should reduce the amount of these foods in the diet, which may help to prevent cancer, as well as headaches, allergies, and acne problems.

Garlic is a healthy addition to a diet. (Photograph by Robert J. Huffman. Field Mark Publications. Reproduced by permission.)

OTHER BENEFICIAL FOODS, VITAMINS, AND MINERALS

There are other foods and supplements that have been found to be beneficial and to help prevent various disorders:

- Garlic fights heart disease and cancer and prolongs the life span of skin cells.

- Vitamins A and E, zinc, and chromium can reduce acne, and along with selenium, can protect the mucous membranes, which shield the body from allergens and germs.

- Magnesium helps relieve constriction in the lungs due to allergies and asthma, and can help prevent migraine headaches.

- Vitamin C blocks histamines, which are present in allergic reactions, and reduces inflammation.

- Bioflavonoids may help reduce asthma-related inflammation.

- Riboflavin, magnesium and calcium taken regularly help prevent migraine headaches.

Drink Alcohol in Moderation

Adults of legal drinking age who do choose to drink alcohol should do so in moderation. High alcohol consumption increases the risk of liver cancer and cirrhosis of the liver (a condition in which liver tissue is destroyed). If alcohol is combined with smoking or chewing tobacco, a person will have greater risk of cancers of the mouth, larynx, throat, and esophagus. In addition, alcohol is high in sugar content and calories that can contribute to weight gain and the creation of harmful free radicals in the body.

No Smoking, Please

Almost everyone knows that smoking is hazardous to one's health. But why? It is now known that smoking produces free radicals, which can cause premature aging and wrinkles, cancer, and heart disease; raise blood pressure; damage the skin and connective tissues; and lead to other diseases in the body. Smoking also aggravates sun damage and reduces the body's ability to fight off infection. It can also cause emphysema (a lung disease) and chronic bronchitis, which can eventually be fatal. Smoking cigars or chewing tobacco may not be as intense in their effect as cigarettes, but lead to the same problems, and more: increased risk of oral cancer, such as in the cheek or gum, tongue, lips, esophagus, larynx, and pancreas. Chewing tobacco can also lead to gum disease.

It is important to try to avoid secondhand smoke—cigarette, cigar, or pipe smoke that is exhaled by smokers—because it can lead to cancer, even in nonsmokers. Inhaling secondhand smoke causes the heart to beat faster, blood pressure to rise, and the level of carbon monoxide in the blood to increase, which can, over time, result in heart disease, high blood pressure, and reduced lung capacity.

Drink Plenty of Water

Drinking an adequate amount of water every day (between 4 and 8 eight-ounce glasses) prevents dehydration and helps flush out the body, removing harmful substances, toxins, and free radicals. Most public water systems in the United States also provide supplemental fluoride that strengthens children's teeth.

However, one should not drink any water of unknown safety. Tap water in most American cities and small towns is likely to be safe, as is most bottled water. But, water in streams and

BUTTER VS. MARGARINE

For many years, nutritionists and diet experts have been advising people to avoid butter, which is high in fat, in favor of margarine. It turns out that many margarines have as much fat and calories per serving as butter. The important difference is that margarine has less saturated fat than butter and more unsaturated fat, which is better for you. Saturated fat is known to increase blood cholesterol levels, which can lead to heart disease.

Among the different kinds of margarine, soft margarine has less saturated fat than stick margarine. This is because the process to harden margarine increases saturated fat and forms what are called trans-fatty acids, which have been linked to heart disease. Thus softer margarine is preferred. Diet or low-fat margarines tend to have less fat and fewer calories than regular margarine or butter, but a better solution is to try to use less of any of these spreads.

rivers may be contaminated with either cancer-causing chemicals or with parasites that could make a person sick. When camping or traveling, if in doubt, drink bottled water.

Avoiding Certain Foods

Just as one should pay special attention to eating the right foods, one should also consider avoiding certain others. Some foods have been shown to increase the risk of certain specific disorders. One example is chocolate, which may cause or aggravate acne and also trigger migraine headaches. Other foods to avoid for people who suffer from headaches, especially migraines, include:

- cheddar cheese and bacon, which cause blood vessels to constrict and then dilate, triggering a pounding pain;
- chocolate ice cream, as the chocolate and the cold temperature both can trigger headache pain;
- coffee, which causes headaches if not drunk in moderation;
- dark wines and alcohol, which contain the headache-triggering chemical tyramine;
- foods containing MSG (monosodium glutamate), nitrites, or aspartame (artificial sweetener); and
- pickled herrings, chicken livers, lentils, snow peas, navy beans, peanuts, and sunflower seeds, all of which contain tyramine.

Food Allergies and Intolerance

Food allergies and intolerance can cause, among other things, abdominal pain; diarrhea; nausea or vomiting; fainting; hives; swelling of the lips, eyes, face, tongue or throat; nasal congestion; or asthma. The difference is that in a true allergic reaction, the body produces histamine and other sub-

FOOD SAFETY

The following simple principles will help a person avoid getting sick from food poisoning, which can make one extremely uncomfortable at the least, and can be fatal at worst. Symptoms of food poisoning include loss of appetite, nausea, vomiting, diarrhea, and stomachache.

- Keep hot food hot and cold food cold, whether in the home or on a picnic. Use an insulated cooler when transporting food, and don't put cold groceries in a hot car trunk or let them sit out at room temperature too long before putting them in a refrigerator.

- Wash hands thoroughly before handling food and in between handling raw meat or eggs and other foods.

- Don't let food sit out for more than an hour under any circumstances. Food that sits at room temperature is at high risk for developing harmful bacteria.

- Avoid eating raw eggs, which are likely to contain illness-causing salmonella bacteria (this includes eating uncooked batter or dough when baking).

- Avoid raw shellfish, such as oysters and mussels, which may contain bacteria for hepatitis A.

stances that cause this reaction. In food intolerance, the chemistry is different; the culprit is likely the absence of an enzyme needed to digest food fully.

Common foods that can cause allergic reactions include:

- cow's milk
- whole eggs or egg whites
- peanuts and peanut butter
- wheat
- soybeans
- berries
- shellfish
- corn

Kitchens can be breeding grounds for bacteria. To decrease the spread of bacteria, always wash hands before and after handling raw meat and clean the work space with soap and warm water or an antibacterial cleaning product when finished. (Photograph by Robert J. Huffman. Field Mark Publications. Reproduced by permission.)

- beans
- gum Arabic (a thickener found in processed foods)
- certain food dyes

Food allergies are usually diagnosed through an elimination diet in which the patient removes suspected foods from the diet for a week or two, then slowly adds them back, one at a time, until the reaction occurs again. This food can then be avoided in the future. In addition, people with severe, life-threatening allergies may carry an injection kit containing adrenaline, a chemical that blocks the histamine response.

Food intolerance is in some ways more difficult to spot than true allergies because people may be sensitive to various "hidden" chemicals used to process foods. These chemicals include monosodium glutamate (MSG), a flavor enhancer commonly used in Chinese restaurants and other cuisine; food dyes; sulfites, which are found in wines, seafoods, potatoes, and some soft drinks; and salicylates, which appear in fruits, vinegar, cider, and wine made from fruits.

Probably the most common type of food intolerance is called lactose intolerance, a hypersensitivity to a sugar called lactose found in milk. About 70 percent of the world's population is unable to fully digest lactose. Symptoms of lactose intolerance include bloating, pain, gas and diarrhea. Lactose intolerant people can prevent the symptoms by avoiding milk and eating other dairy products, such as yogurt, hard cheeses and sour cream, in which most of the lactose is already broken down. Some also choose to use special lactose-free milk or take over-the-counter pills that help the body digest lactose.

Another common food intolerance involves gluten, found primarily in wheat products. Severe intolerance to gluten can lead to celiac disease, a painful condition of the small intestine.

Exercise and Health

Exercise has many benefits, both physical and mental. It helps to minimize the risk of cancer, stroke, heart disease, diabetes, and premature aging. It also reduces anxiety, fatigue, and tension. Regular exercise has been shown to effectively manage stress, which helps prevent acne and the occurrence of tension headaches. Exercise helps people sleep better, which, in turn, contributes to a stronger immune system and

MINI-MEALS MAKE THE DIFFERENCE

Research has shown that the traditional three meals a day may not be the best way to eat for optimum health. More and more, it appears that eating five to seven "mini-meals," snack-sized meals of about 250-500 calories each, throughout the day promotes better nutrition and health.

Spreading out these small meals throughout the day helps maintain a normal blood sugar level (rather than high spikes and low dips caused by waiting a longer time between meals). Studies show this normalized blood sugar level reduces damage to collagen and DNA, which can cause wrinkles, age spots, and cataracts (an eye disorder). Mini-meals also normalize insulin levels; high levels of insulin, which regulates blood sugar, are a known risk factor for heart disease.

greater ability to fight illness and infection. In general, people who exercise enjoy a higher energy level than others, and are better able to concentrate at school or at work.

A physically fit person is more likely to recover quickly from illness and injury and from surgery. If exercising regularly, a person will strengthen his or her heart and muscles and improve the flexibility of the joints. Aerobic exercise, which raises the heartbeat, improves the condition of other organs as well as the heart, and increases one's overall conditioning and endurance. Women who exercise are at a decreased risk of developing osteoporosis (a degenerative bone disease).

People who participate in muscle-toning exercises can experience special benefits. Strong stomach muscles help protect the back and lessen the risk of back injury. In addition, a stronger, more physically fit person can lift heavy things more easily, again lessening the strain on the back. A toned individual takes surer steps, is less likely to fall down, and generally experiences less risk of injury from falls because the muscles are pliable and strong. [See also Chapter 2: Physical Fitness.]

Manage Stress

One of the most important aspects of a personal health regimen is to manage stress. Stress is the body's normal response to dangerous or high-pressure situations, anything from an upcoming test at school, to a big game, to facing surgery, or being lost in an unfamiliar place. No matter the source of the stress, the body's response is the same: the body produces adrenaline (a hormone) and chemicals that cause the pulse to quicken, the muscles to tense, and the blood pressure to increase. This is known as the "fight or flight" response, which might have been more useful to ancient peoples facing predators than to today's average person.

EXERCISING SAFELY

A good rule of thumb is to try to exercise for about thirty minutes three times a week. Exercise should include a variety of activities, including aerobic activities that raise the heartbeat, stretching and flexibility exercises, and muscle-strengthening activities. Usually, participation in sports, either at school or with friends, provides enough physical activity for a healthy young person.

School-age young people should be warned not to overdo exercise. It is wise to check with a doctor before beginning an exercise program. Start slow, with short exercise sessions, and build up to the thirty-minute goal. Each time a person exercises, he should start by stretching and warming up to prepare the joints, muscles, and tendons for the activity, and cool down afterward with a period of slower and gentler exercise. The warm-up and cool-down periods prevent soreness and stiffness later.

Anyone who experiences faintness, chest pain or pressure, or excessive tiredness or pain during exercise should stop working out or playing the sport and check with a doctor.

A little stress can be beneficial in certain situations. The increased adrenaline and stimulation of the body can help an athlete perform to his or her best in a big game, or allow a student to focus better on an important exam. However, too much stress, or ongoing stress that is not addressed, eventually takes a physical toll on the body. Over an extended period of time, uncontrolled stress produces the free radical molecules that can cause premature aging, cancer, heart disease, strokes, diabetes, acne, and increased risk of infections.

There are a number of well-documented ways to manage and reduce stress. One of the best of these is exercise. A regular exercise program, whether it consists of structured aerobics classes or a few casual games of tennis or racquetball a week, reduces stress and also promotes healthy sleep, which in itself helps reduce stress.

Ensuring that one gets a healthy night's sleep every night is a second way to manage and reduce stress. A person can improve sleep patterns in the following ways:

- Avoid sleeping on the stomach.
- If sleeping on the back, put a pillow under the knees to flex the spine.
- If snoring is a problem, sleep on the side.
- Use a low pillow to support the head without flexing the neck.
- Be sure to dress warmly for bed and/or use enough blankets.
- Have plenty of room to move around in bed.

Eating a healthy diet is a third way to reduce stress in life. One should especially concentrate on ingesting enough antioxidants, which can be found in green leafy vegetables, yellow and deep orange veggies, and many fruits. If getting a variety of fruits and vegetables is a problem, a person can take an antioxidant supplement, which can be found in almost any drugstore or the pharmacy section of the local supermarket.

Another good way to manage stress is to find ways to relax. Again, there are a number of different methods; each individual can choose a method that works best.

- Some people use deep breathing to relax. Breathe in, hold it for five seconds, then exhale.
- Another relaxation technique is to lie down, close the eyes, and concentrate on slowly relaxing each part of the body. Start with the feet and relax each muscle group until a feeling of deep relaxation and peace surrounds the body.
- Some individuals find a particular kind of music soothing.
- Humor or laughter is a great way to relax both body and mind.
- Another method that some people enjoy is aromatherapy, in which scented oils, candles, lotions, or bath beads are used to calm the senses. Lavender is one recommended soothing scent.

- Milder forms of exercise, such as yoga or tai chi (a gentle martial art), are also popular.

The power of positive thinking should not be underestimated in reducing the effects of stress. This can include talking positively to oneself and refocusing negative thoughts and situations into positive ones. Concentrating on some of the activities mentioned above is one way to make an effort to stop negative thoughts.

Another very important, way to manage stress is to seek support from peers. Getting together with peers for social or sports activities, studying, games, and fun helps one focus on the positive. Socializing helps relax the body and mind and greatly reduces the effects of everyday stress.

Hanging out with friends is a great stress reducer. (Photograph by Robert J. Huffman. Field Mark Publications. Reproduced by permission.)

Get Enough Sleep

Getting plenty of sleep is essential to maintaining good health. The body uses the time spent sleeping to repair and rejuvenate itself while storing energy for the next day. For many reasons, however, sleep is often elusive for busy Americans, even the very young. Yet numerous studies have shown that chronic sleeplessness leads to many serious disorders. Most authorities claim that the average person needs eight hours of sleep a night to function adequately; some individuals believe they need only six or seven, whereas others think they need nine or ten.

Sleep deprivation (not getting enough sleep) is a major cause of accidents. It raises blood pressure, a risk factor for heart disease and stroke, and is a known cause of psychological disturbances. And lack of sleep seriously compromises the immune system's ability to fight disease. Getting enough sleep is one sure way to help fight off common colds, the flu, and mild infections.

There are several ways to prevent insomnia, or chronic sleeplessness. Set a regular sleep schedule and try to stick to it. Try not to take naps during the day, as this prevents deep, refreshing sleep at night. Get regular exercise, reduce caffeine intake, avoid smoking, and, for those of legal drinking age, drink alcohol only in moderation. Alcohol may make a person sleepy, but the type of sleep it causes is shallow and not beneficial to the body's self-healing processes.

Try to reserve the bedroom for sleep only. Take steps to make the bedroom as appealing, quiet and relaxing as possible, while avoiding such activities as watching TV or doing homework in bed.

Observe Good Hygiene Practices

Illnesses are usually spread from person to person through the spread of germs, viruses, and other organisms. One of the best ways to be protected against these illnesses is to follow basic good hygiene techniques. [*See also* Chapter 3: Personal Care and Hygiene.]

Good hand-washing habits are one of the most important ways to prevent the spread of illnesses such as colds, the flu, and viruses, as well as those caused by parasites. One should always wash his or her hands with warm water and plenty of soap after using the bathroom (especially public rest-rooms, which may not be cleaned as frequently as personal bathrooms) and before preparing or eating food. Washing hands is also important after coming in contact with someone who is ill or after handling trash or playing with pets.

Good dental hygiene—brushing and flossing every day and seeing a dentist at least once a year—will help prevent bad breath, tooth decay, cavities, and gum disease later in life. Gum disease puts adults at risk for strokes because it can lead to blockages of the carotid arteries, which supply blood to the head.

No matter your age, getting the proper amount of sleep is important to maintaining good health. (Photograph by Robert J. Huffman. Field Mark Publications. Reproduced by permission.)

Keeping the hair clean will help minimize the risk of developing head lice, while bathing or showering frequently and keeping the body clean helps to prevent skin problems and rashes, jock itch, and athlete's foot.

Physical Examinations

Eating well, practicing good hygiene, managing stress, and exercising are all proven ways to prevent illness and disease. However, even a person who follows all of these techniques should still visit a medical professional regularly for a physical examination or checkup. Some authorities recommend checkup visits for children at the following ages: two to four weeks, two, four, six, nine, twelve, fifteen, and eighteen years.

Checkups are important because they allow the health care provider to review the patient's growth and development, perform tests, and give shots (vaccines), if necessary. Anyone who has a health concern or question should be sure to ask the doctor or other health professional at this visit. Often, catching a problem early can prevent it from becoming much more severe. For example, doctors will usually examine patients for scoliosis (curvature of the spine) starting at around fifth or sixth grade. Catching a mild curvature at this age allows it to be treated with a brace and can reduce the likelihood of severe problems that might require surgery later in life.

Some diagnostic tests that may be performed during an examination include:

- Anemia: Young people should be tested for anemia (a blood disorder) early in life as a preventive measure. Anemia can be treated better if caught early.
- Auscultation: This is a medical term for listening, the process by which a doctor or other professional determines whether the sounds coming from the lungs, heart, and abdomen are normal. Abnormal sounds can signal such problems as a heart murmur or irregularity, an aortic aneurysm, fluid in the lungs, or serious intestinal problems. One example that a doctor might listen for would be an absence of bowel sounds, which could indicate a rupture of the intestines. This condition could rapidly become fatal if not treated immediately.
- Blood pressure check: High blood pressure in young people can lead to serious problems, such as heart disease and strokes.
- Cholesterol level: High levels of cholesterol have been linked with heart disease and heart attacks. Testing is especially important if there is a family history of these problems.
- Inspection: This process of "looking" at and observing the patient's external appearance is usually the first step in a checkup. A doctor might spot, for example, a mole on a patient's arm that has grown or changed in appearance, signaling the possibility of skin cancer. Skin cancer is a condition that can be very successfully treated or even prevented if caught early.
- Palpation: This term means "feeling" and refers to the doctor's methods of touching affected body parts to determine their size, consistency, texture, location, and tenderness. Palpation might allow the provider to spot a tumor or cyst while it is still small enough to be removed successfully.

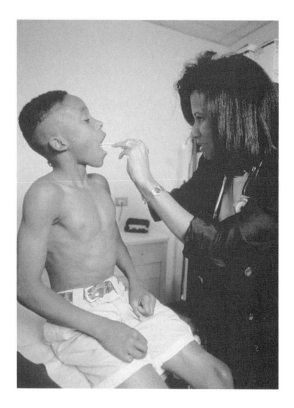

Regular physical exams can help keep people healthy by catching any sicknesses or disorders before they become serious. (Custom Medical Stock Photo. Reproduced by permission.)

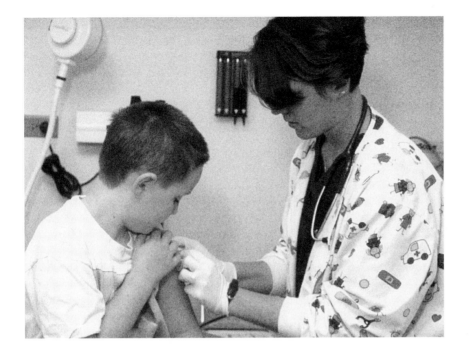

While receiving vaccines may not be fun, the protection they provide against disease is invaluable. (Custom Medical Stock Photo. Reproduced by permission.)

- Percussion: A method of "tapping" of body parts during a physical examination with fingers, hands, or small instruments to evaluate the size, consistency, borders, and presence or absence of fluid in body organs.
- Tuberculosis (TB): This test is generally only necessary if one has been in close contact with a person who has TB (a disease of the lungs).

RECOMMENDED VACCINES

The federal government recommends that all Americans receive the following course of vaccinations:

- Polio (OPV or IPV): At 2 months, 4 months, 6 to 18 months, and 4 to 6 years.
- Diphtheria-Tetanus-Pertussis (DTaP, DTP): At 2 months, 4 months, 6 months, 15 to 18 months, and 4 to 6 years. Tetanus-Diphtheria (Td) at 11 to 16 years.
- Measles-Mumps-Rubella (MMR): At 12 to 15 months and either 4 to 6 years or 11 to 12 years.

- Haemophilus influenzae type b (Hib): At 2 months, 4 months, 6 months, and 12 to 15 months; or 2 months, 4 months and 12 to 15 months depending on the vaccine type.

- Hepatitis B (HBV): At birth to 2 months, 1 to 4 months, and 6 to 18 months.

- Chickenpox (VZV): At 1 to 12 years.

The schedule of immunizations does change with new research, so individuals should check with their doctors to see if there are any new vaccines available.

• Vision and hearing tests: The health care provider has tests to determine if there are any potential problems with vision or hearing. Problems like glaucoma (an eye disease) or hearing loss can be treated successfully or at least minimized if caught early.

Complete Immunizations

Many infectious illnesses (ones that may be passed from person to person) caused by viruses or bacteria are now preventable through immunization. Immunization means being injected with a vaccine (a tiny amount of the disease that is not infectious), which allows the body to create defense mechanisms against the disease. These defense mechanisms, which include antibodies or white blood cells, protect the body if the person is later exposed to the infectious disease.

INJURY PREVENTION

At home, at school, and at play, hazards exist that can lead to injuries. Just as a person can take steps to prevent illness and disease, one can take steps to prevent getting hurt as well. Following good household safety precautions, using the right equipment for sports and play, and remembering to warm up before and cool down after any physical activity are just three of the ways people can prevent minor injuries. The following section will explore many more.

SHOULD YOU GET A FLU SHOT?

Not on the list of standard childhood vaccinations, but something to consider, is an annual "flu shot." Each year, doctors receive a supply of vaccine for the type of influenza or "flu" virus that is expected to strike. Many people go to their doctors for this annual vaccine to prevent a bad case of the flu. However, some people avoid the shot for fear that the vaccine itself will give them the flu—and some cases like this have been reported. Also, a small percentage of people do experience a slight fever and muscle ache from the immunization. Because of this risk, the vaccination is more likely to be recommended for adults over sixty-five or those with weak immune systems. Check with your doctor for advice on whether to be vaccinated for influenza.

Household Injuries

Accidents can happen anywhere, even in one's own home. Taking precautions around the house can increase the safety level and prevent falls, cuts and burns, accidental poisoning, medicine overdoses, and electrocution—some of the potential hazards in a typical household environment.

PREVENTING FALLS. Preventing falls generally means removing obstacles around the house and yard that can cause someone to fall. This is a cooperative effort on the part of everyone who lives there. However, one of the best ways to prevent falls is by exercising regularly. Exercising improves muscle strength, flexibility, and coordination, all of which help keep a person from accidentally falling down, as well as reducing the likelihood of serious injury if one does fall. Here are some more tips for preventing falls:

• Clean up any spills around the home immediately.

Never horse around on ladders or step stools. Always climb carefully and maintain proper balance. (Photograph by Robert J. Huffman. Field Mark Publications. Reproduced by permission.)

- Keep stairways clear and well lit, and hold on to handrails while going up and down stairs.
- Put nonslip pads under rugs to hold them down and prevent tripping.
- Use nonskid wax on kitchen and bathroom floors.
- Place nonskid strips on the bottoms of showers and bathtubs. Install grab bars or handrails in the bathtub and shower.
- Keep small objects and cords off the floor or at least out of the pathways of travel throughout the home.
- Store items that are frequently used in places where they are easily reached without climbing.

The liquid from an aloe vera plant can soothe minor burns. Many people keep an aloe plant in their home for this reason. (Photograph by Robert J. Huffman. Field Mark Publications. Reproduced by permission.)

- Improve the lighting throughout the house.
- Wear sturdy shoes.
- Avoid walking on icy sidewalks and pavement.

CUT AND BURN PREVENTION. Using a little common sense with sharp objects is the best way to prevent accidental injuries involving cuts. Knives, forks, scissors, and other sharp tools should be kept in a drawer with a safety latch if there are young children in the home. Also, they should not just be thrown in a drawer. This could lead to cuts when reaching in to grab something. There are different kinds of products available to help organize sharp objects in drawers and other spaces.

When using a sharp object, like a knife or scissors, one should always hold it by the handle and not walk around with it. It is also important to use caution with appliances that have sharp blades, such as blenders or food processors. One should be very careful when cleaning these appliances and should always unplug the appliances if it is necessary to have a hand near the blades. One should also never reach into a garbage disposal with his or her hand.

Other kitchen safety tips include keeping glass objects within easy reach to prevent breakage from dropping or falling. When loading and unloading the dishwasher, one should take special care handling knives, or other sharp tools. Taking out the garbage can also result in injuries if one is not careful. If someone threw away broken glass or a metal can with a sharp edge, the person handling the garbage could cut himself.

As well as the kitchen, the garage may hold some things that could cause injuries. All tools, including those used for gardening, automotive, and lawn care, should be put away in a safe manner. When mowing the lawn, one should always wear shoes.

The following precautions should be taken to avoid the possibility of an accidental burn:

- Never smoke in bed.
- Do not leave burning candles unattended, even for a short while.
- If using a space heater be sure it is not placed near curtains or a bedspread that could start a fire, or where a small child could reach the heating elements.
- Avoid overloading electrical sockets with too many appliances.
- Do not leave hot appliances like hair curlers or coffeepots plugged in.
- Avoid reaching over stove burners with long hair or loose sleeves hanging down.
- When cooking, always use the back burners on the stove, and be sure to turn the pot handles away from the front where they could be knocked easily or grabbed by a small child.
- Always test bath water with the tips of the fingers before stepping in to make sure it is not too hot.
- Never go to sleep with a heating pad on. Even on low settings, a heating pad can cause serious burns.

PREVENTING ACCIDENTAL POISONING. One of the biggest hazards in any household is the presence of numerous substances that can be poisonous if ingested or, in some cases, handled at all. The best method of prevention for accidental poisoning is to be aware of these substances, which ones are dangerous, how they should be handled, and how to avoid them.

A poison warning label on a paint solvent can explains how to treat accidental ingestion of the product. (Photograph by Robert J. Huffman. Field Mark Publications. Reproduced by permission.)

Household cleaning products and aerosol sprays are one source of potential poisoning. They should be stored in clearly marked containers out of reach of small children, and never in old soda bottles or containers that were once used for food.

One should avoid handling roach powders or rat poison, and never leave such items where small children or pets can reach them. If using pesticides is unavoidable, read the product label before use and follow all recommended safety precautions during and after use. Some safety tips for using pesticides include wearing gloves and protective clothing, avoiding breathing the fumes or vapors, and washing hands or showering right after applying pesticides.

When using mouthwash, one should be careful not to swallow much of it as many mouthwashes contain substantial amounts of alcohol. Remember that alcohol poisoning can be severe and often fatal. Sometimes paint in older homes or on old furniture contains lead, which can cause lead poisoning in

A fireman at a poison prevention display explains to his audience the dangers of some common household poisons. (Photograph by Robert J. Huffman. Field Mark Publications. Reproduced by permission.)

THE DANGERS OF CARBON MONOXIDE

One type of household poisoning is caused by carbon monoxide. Carbon monoxide, or CO, is a colorless, odorless gas that is produced whenever something is burned incompletely or in a closed environment. It is toxic to all animals and to humans, and it is especially dangerous because it is so difficult to detect.

The best way to prevent carbon monoxide poisoning is to have a CO detector installed in the house. Check with friends and family to see if their homes also are protected. Avoid staying in homes or buildings where old gas furnaces, water heaters, or space heaters are in use, and be sure that when a fireplace or charcoal grill is lit, it is properly ventilated.

Never use lawnmowers, leaf blowers, and other small gasoline-powered equipment inside, even when performing repairs. Do not start any automobile in an enclosed garage, even just to warm it up in the wintertime. Also, if a household pet, which may show the effects of CO poisoning earlier than a human, suddenly becomes ill or dies, think of the possibility of a toxic exposure and have the house checked.

[For more information on carbon monoxide, see Chapter 5: Environmental Health.]

---

humans. Other things that may contain lead and should be avoided are dust and debris from older building renovations, some cosmetics and ceramics, leaded gasoline fumes, and auto battery storage casings.

Other poisons can actually be found in plants. Take time to learn all the names of the plants in the house, and remove any that could be toxic. Many household plants can be poisonous if accidentally ingested by either humans or pets. Do not play with or try to break open batteries, either the regular type used in radios and headsets or automotive batteries; both contain acid that is poisonous and can cause painful burns.

MEDICINE CABINET SAFETY. Medicines are a leading cause of serious and sometimes fatal accidental poisonings, even among adults who simply mistake one medicine for another or take the wrong dose. For this reason, special precautions should be taken to store medicines properly and to take them only as directed.

All family members should take care not to leave vitamin bottles, aspirin bottles, or other medications on the kitchen table, countertops, bedside tables, or dresser tops. When guests are in the house, be sure they do not have access to the family medicine cabinet, and that the guests' medications are safely stored away.

One should always keep medications in their original containers with the labels intact. Pills left in purses or liquids stored in unmarked bottles are too easily mistaken for something else. In addition, always check the label before taking medication and only give medication to the person for whom it was prescribed. Another precaution is to not take medicine or even vitamins in the dark, in case of an accidental switch or overdose. After taking or administering medication, be sure to reattach the safety cap and store the med-

The average medicine cabinet is filled with dozens of products to keep people well, but many products can be fatal if taken accidentally or not taken as directed. (Photograph by Robert J. Huffman. Field Mark Publications. Reproduced by permission.)

ication away safely. Also, dispose of any out-of-date or expired medication safely, preferably by taking it to a pharmacy where it can be disposed of as hazardous waste.

SAFETY WITH ELECTRICITY. Another major safety hazard in any home is the electrical system and all electrical appliances. The following are steps that a person can take to avoid being burned or even electrocuted (a potentially fatal accident) by a mishap with electricity.

- Do not touch the electrical system panel.
- Tell a parent or other adult if lights dim or the size of the television picture shrinks often; if there are sparks or bright light flashes or unusual sounds from the system; or if parts of the system, such as outlet covers or plugs, feel warm.
- Try to avoid the use of extension cords, and never use frayed or damaged ones.
- Replace damaged or frayed cords, which can cause shock or fire.
- Do not secure cords with nails or staples, which can present fire and shock hazards. If nails or staples need to be removed, disconnect the power first.
- Do not try to plug a three-prong plug into a two-hole outlet. Use an adapter, which grounds the current and helps prevent shocks. Never stick a finger into an outlet.
- Use caution in bathrooms, kitchens, basements and garages where people can touch heating radiators, water pipes, electric heaters, electric stoves

Examples of safety trigger locks for handguns. (Photograph by Robert J. Huffman. Field Mark Publications. Reproduced by permission.)

FIREARM SAFETY

Guns take the lives of sixteen children in the United States each day, through homicide (one person killing another), suicide (the taking of one's own life), or accidental shootings. Many young people have easy access to these deadly weapons, which is resulting in major tragedies across the nation. The best advice is to avoid handling firearms altogether, and if at all possible, to avoid being in a house where there are guns. However, in any household where guns are kept, safety precautions can be taken to prevent a tragic accident.

- Never play with or joke around with a gun, even if you are "sure" that the gun is not loaded. Never point a gun at yourself or anyone else.

- All guns should be stored in a locked cabinet, unloaded, with the safety mechanism on.

- Ammunition should be stored separately in a securely locked container.

- If possible, all guns should be secured with childproof devices such as trigger locks or padlocks that prevent them from being fired.

- Take a firearm safety course to learn the safe and correct way to handle any gun.

and water in sinks and bathtubs. If a person touches one of these and a faulty electrical appliance at the same time, he or she can receive a shock and may be electrocuted.

- Unplug all small appliances when not in use.
- Do not ever use a hair dryer or other electric appliance in or near a sink or bathtub. If it is plugged in, even if the power is off, it can deliver a powerful shock if it comes into contact with water.
- Never reach into water to get an appliance that has fallen in without being sure the appliance is unplugged.
- Use electric blankets according to the manufacturer's instructions.
- Never go to sleep with a heating pad that is turned on.

Recreation and Sports

Just as there are dangers inside the home, hazards exist in the outside world as well. Even when participating in fun activities such as games and sports, people must take precautions to prevent injuries.

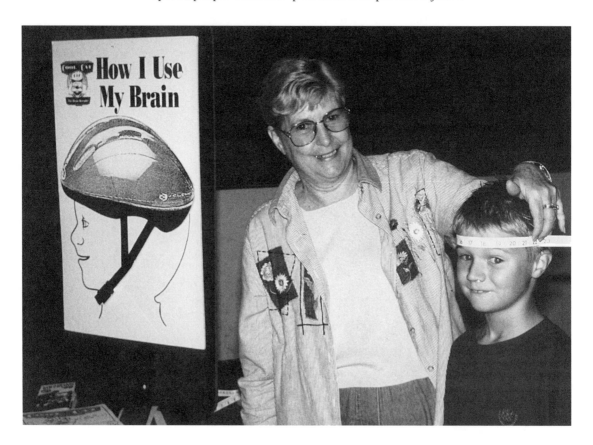

Proper fit is essential to the effectiveness of a bicycle safety helmet. (Photograph by Robert J. Huffman. Field Mark Publications. Reproduced by permission.)

PROTECTIVE EQUIPMENT. One of the most important ways to prevent injury during sports and recreation is to be sure to wear the right clothing and protective gear.

FOOT PROTECTION. Good footwear is essential to prevent foot injuries, such as Achilles tendon strains and bruising. Never wear worn-out shoes; try to choose footwear that is sturdy enough and appropriate for the activity being conducted.

HEAD GEAR. Proper helmets are essential gear for almost any sport, including bicycling, in-line skating, skateboarding, playing roller hockey, baseball or softball, and of course football. It is estimated that two-thirds of the bicycle related deaths each year are caused by head injuries, and the universal use of helmets could save one life per year. In addition to helmets, find out what other protective gear is right for the particular sport being played. Face masks, mouth guards, shin guards, and other protective items greatly reduce the likelihood and severity of injuries.

SHIELD THE EYES. Eye injuries are the leading cause of blindness in children, and sports are the major cause of eye injuries in school-age children. Always wear some kind of face mask, face guard, or goggles, whatever is appropriate for the sport. People who already wear eyeglasses should consider investing in a special pair for sports use.

SPORTS AND SPECIAL EQUIPMENT. There are many sports that require their own special equipment. Before starting a new sport, learn what kinds of equipment are necessary and how to use them.

Baseball and softball are examples of sports that require their own special gear, both for players and for the playing field. Each player should have his own glove, bat, and cleated shoes. Make sure the equipment meets league requirements. Most leagues supply batting helmets, which are extremely important; if the league doesn't supply one with a face guard, buy one. Check out the baseball field and be sure it has breakaway bases that help prevent ankle fractures and sprains. The field should be well maintained and free of

ACCORDING TO THE NATIONAL YOUTH SPORTS SAFETY FOUNDATION, AS MANY AS ONE-THIRD OF IN-LINE SKATING EMERGENCY-ROOM-TREATED INJURIES COULD BE PREVENTED OR LESSENED IN SEVERITY BY THE USE OF PROTECTIVE EQUIPMENT.

BICYCLE SAFETY

- Make sure the bicycle is adjusted properly; the rider should be able to stand over the top tube.

- Check to make sure all parts are secure and working well. The handlebars should be firmly in place and turn easily. The wheels must be straight and secure.

- Always check brakes before riding.

- Ride slowly in wet weather and apply brakes earlier; it takes more distance to stop.

- Wear fluorescent or other bright-colored clothes.

- Avoid biking at night.

- Always keep a lookout for obstacles.

- Stay alert at all times.

- Use special care on bridges.

- Ride on the right side in a straight predictable path.

- Always be aware of the traffic in the area.

- Learn the rules of the road and obey traffic laws.

- Never wear headphones while riding as they impair your ability to hear traffic.

A runner demonstrates good warm-up technique. (Photograph by Robert J. Huffman. Field Mark Publications. Reproduced by permission.)

SAFE IN-LINE SKATING

All in-line skaters should wear a proper helmet, wrist guards, and knee pads. To avoid injuries, practice and prepare before striking out on the street. Always be aware of a safe place to "bail out" if that becomes necessary. Learn to "crash" in grass or other soft surfaces while skating. Avoid skates with toe stops, which should never be used on in-line skates, and use heel brakes instead. Be sure the liner is well cushioned and supports the foot, and that the laces or buckles on the skate give as close as possible to a customized fit.

ruts and debris. In fact, in any sport, the facility should be clean and well maintained, the equipment should be frequently inspected, metal equipment should not be rusty, and floors should be safely maintained to prevent slips and falls. To learn about other sports and the equipment necessary to use when playing, one may consult coaches, sport stores, books, magazines, or the Internet.

DON'T OVERDO IT. Overuse injuries such as teenager's knee, Little League elbow, swimmer's shoulder, and gymnast's back are becoming much more common than in the past. These injuries produce symptoms of redness, swelling, stiffness, soreness, and pain in the affected areas and are simply caused by "overdoing it"—failing to recognize when enough is enough.

Warming up and cooling down appropriately will help minimize overuse injuries, as will stretching before playing or engaging in a sport. Learn the proper technique for the particular activity, and do a variety of practice drills so that the technique is perfected and the skills are done properly and not dangerously.

Don't exceed restrictions, such as the limit on the number of innings Little Leaguers can pitch in one week. Consider playing more than one sport. Specializing all year in one sport can put too much stress on particular parts of the body, such as the back and wrists in gymnastics.

WARM UP AND COOL DOWN. When engaging in any sort of physical activity, make it a rule to warm up before starting and to cool down afterward. Before starting, take three to five minutes to stretch and loosen the muscles and joints that will be used in the activity. This simple precaution significantly decreases the risk of muscle sprains, pulls, and strains.

Similarly, at the end of the activity, cool down by walking slowly, doing another gentle activity, and finally stretching once again. This

Helmets, knee pads, and elbow pads can lessen the severity of an in-line skating spill. (Photograph by Robert J. Huffman. Field Mark Publications. Reproduced by permission.)

is essential to help prevent and reduce the severity of any strains, injuries, or soreness from the activity.

TAKE IT SLOW. It takes time to learn a new sport and be good at it. When starting a new sport, a person should first learn the rules of the game and what equipment is required. After that, learn and practice a few skills until one feels more comfortable. In the beginning, one should focus on relaxing and having fun with the sport, and as skills improve, then try more advanced techniques. Many injuries occur when people try to perform at a level that is too advanced for their skills.

There are a few precautions that can be taken by anyone playing a sport or game to reduce the risk of injury:

- A person should not lift any weight that he or she has to strain to lift even once.
- People's motor skills develop at different rates, so they should not try to force themselves to play a sport for which they are not suited. Individuals should try different things until they find the right one.
- Do not return to sports after an injury if there is any limited motion in a joint compared to its uninjured opposite joint (such as in the right elbow compared to the left), joint swelling, or a limp.
- Be especially careful when playing sports during growth spurts. During growth spurts, the muscles, tendons, and ligaments get tighter, increasing the risk of injury.
- Prepare for weather conditions. When the temperature is higher than 85 degrees and humidity is greater than 70 percent, there is a danger of heat exhaustion or heat stroke. Be sure to drink plenty of fluids on such days. Always apply sunscreen with a sun protection factor (SPF) level of 15 or higher before going outside. In cold weather, make sure to be properly dressed in warm, insulating layers, with the head well covered, if permitted.

Always lift heavy objects by bending at the knees and using the leg muscles, not the back muscles. Never lift anything that causes the body too much strain. (Photograph by Robert J. Huffman. Field Mark Publications. Reproduced by permission.)

PREVENTIVE MEDICINE

People usually think of medicine as something to be taken to make a person well after he or she has gotten sick. Preventive medicines are things a person can take when well to help prevent becoming sick.

Vitamins, minerals, and even herbal supplements, when taken regularly in the right amounts, can help prevent many different illnesses, conditions, and even minor symptoms. However, a well-balanced diet should contain most, if not all, of the vitamins and minerals necessary to maintain health. The key to taking vitamins, minerals, or herbal supplements is knowing which ones to take. Before taking any kind of supplement, one should always consult a medical professional to know if it is safe to be taking the supplements, and the right doses, because some vitamins or herbs can be harmful in high doses. Lists of basic, well-documented helpful supplements can be found below.

Vitamins

Vitamins are organic (natural) compounds that are usually not made by the body, but must be acquired from food. They are necessary for the proper growth and development of the body and its continued well-being. Deficiencies of certain vitamins can lead to various bodily disorders.

VITAMIN A (BETA CAROTENE). One of the antioxidant group, this vitamin helps neutralize free radicals, which in turn can reduce the signs of premature aging, heart disease, strokes, cancer, and diabetes. It also can protect the mucous membranes, which shield the body from allergens and germs.

VITAMIN C. Vitamin C is known to help reduce the risk of certain kinds of cancers, such as colon and cervical. It also blocks histamines, which are present in allergic reactions, and reduces inflammation.

VITAMIN D. Vitamin D helps maintain desired blood levels of calcium and enhances calcium absorption. Proper calcium levels can help prevent migraine headaches and, later in life, can help prevent osteoporosis.

VITAMIN E. Another antioxidant, this vitamin is sometimes difficult to get in large amounts from food. It is well known to help reduce the risk of heart disease, and, like vitamin A, it can help prevent or lessen the effect of allergies.

Minerals

Unlike vitamins, which are organic compounds, minerals are inorganic. Like vitamins, however, they are also needed for the growth, maintenance, and repair of body tissues and bones. There are two kinds of minerals: macrominerals, which are needed in large amounts, and trace minerals, which are only needed in small amounts.

CALCIUM. Proper levels of calcium in the body are needed to maintain healthy blood and cardiac function, as well as a healthy nervous system. In addition, maintaining a balance of calcium in the

Vitamins come in many different formulas, even children's chewable vitamins. (Photograph by Robert J. Huffman. Field Mark Publications. Reproduced by permission.)

Healthy Living **233**

blood helps prevent migraines. And it is essential for girls and young women to absorb adequate calcium now to prevent osteoporosis later in life.

COPPER. Copper helps prevent anemia by enhancing hemoglobin (red blood cells that transport oxygen throughout the body) formulation and stimulating the absorption of iron.

IRON. Iron is important in the production of red blood cells. Correct iron levels are essential for preventing anemia.

MAGNESIUM. This mineral works together with calcium to help prevent migraine headaches. It also helps relieve constriction in the lungs due to allergies and asthma.

POTASSIUM. This important mineral is essential to proper heart function. In extreme cases, a severe deficiency of potassium can lead to a heart attack.

SELENIUM. Along with vitamin A, selenium helps protect the mucous membranes, which are the body's first defense against germs, pollen, and other irritants.

ZINC. Zinc, like selenium and vitamin A, can help protect the body from allergens and germs. Recent studies have shown that zinc lozenges coat the throat and can help prevent people from contracting the common cold.

Herbal Medicine

Herbs have been used since the time of the earliest civilizations for their healing properties. Today, some traditional medicines are still made from herbs, while many medical practitioners both in the United States and worldwide use herbs in their practices. Furthermore, many Americans are choosing to make their own health choices by using herbal supplements to prevent and treat various ailments. As with any treatment, a person should check with a medical professional before using herbal medications to find out exactly how they should be taken.

Indigestion Medicine

Indigestion is not a disease in and of itself but a "catch-all" term used to describe various abdominal symptoms, such as heartburn, general discomfort, nausea, a feeling of fullness, and/or a bloated sensation.

Sometimes indigestion has an obvious and specific cause, such as the ingestion of a certain food or the consumption of alcohol. In that case, the best prevention is to avoid consuming that food or beverage. If indigestion does not seem to have an identifiable cause, however, one should check with a doctor; the symptoms could be the sign of a more serious underlying condition, such as an ulcer, gastritis, or gallbladder disease.

For those who are lactose intolerant there are many lactose-free foods that allow one to reap the nutritional benefits of dairy foods without the painful side effects. (Photograph by Robert J. Huffman. Field Mark Publications. Reproduced by permission.)

Herbal formulas that can prevent indigestion include peppermint and ginger, both of which can be drunk in the form of an herbal tea. These teas are commonly available in grocery stores, drugstores, and health food stores.

Traditional over-the-counter medications that combat indigestion include antacids and acid-reducing medicines such as cimetidine, ranitidine, nizatidine, or famotidine, and stomach-coating medications like sucralfate or the brand name product Pepto-Bismol. Recent studies have shown that travelers who plan to be in countries where the water supply might contain parasites or organisms that cause intestinal distress can minimize and even prevent these problems by taking Pepto-Bismol regularly starting a few days before the trip.

Lactose Intolerance Medicine

Lactose is a sugar found in cow's milk that, in humans, requires an enzyme called lactase to digest. Some people do not produce enough lactase to break down milk and other dairy products and, as a result, they experience symptoms such as abdominal pain, cramps, bloating, diarrhea, and excessive gas from eating these foods. Some studies show that as much as 70 percent of the world's population is somewhat lactose intolerant. (About 30 million Americans, mostly those of Mediterranean, African American, or Asian heritage, are believed to have some degree of lactose intolerance.)

One way to prevent the symptoms of lactose intolerance is to cut down on the amount of milk consumed, to drink it only with food, or to consume other dairy products such as cottage cheese and yogurt that are already partly broken down (cultured). Alternatively, one can buy lactose-free milk and ice cream in health food stores and some grocery stores. Finally, several over-the-counter medications exist that contain lactase and help to break down the lactose in milk. Lactaid and Dairy Ease are two brand names of lactase preparations that can be mixed into milk to prevent the painful symptoms.

A SAMPLING OF HERBS

There are a number of ways to ingest herbs, from pills to teas to rubbing them on the skin. Many herbs are available in health food stores and without a prescription. It is important not to self-medicate oneself with herbal supplements, however, before checking with a doctor. The herbs listed below have been shown to have useful properties when used with care and according to direction:

- Aloe Vera: Helps prevent constipation by maintaining regular bowel function.

- Angelica (also known as dang qui): Prevents arthritis and combats certain cancers.

- Astragalus: Boosts the immune system.

- Bilberry Fruit Extract: Bilberry contains compounds that help strengthen the capillaries and protect them from damaging free radicals.

- Black Walnut: Fights athlete's foot and jock itch; helps prevent certain cancers.

- Burdock: Helps prevent diabetes.

- Cayenne (Red Pepper): Lowers cholesterol, which has been linked to a higher risk of heart disease.

- Celery Seed: May help prevent certain cancers; regulates blood pressure; reduces cholesterol.

- Cilantro (Coriander): Prevents infection in minor wounds.

- Cinnamon: Controls blood sugar in diabetics, prevents stomach ulcers, wards off urinary tract infections, fights tooth decay and gum disease, and prevents vaginal yeast infections.

- Coffee: Combats drowsiness, which can lead to accidents; prevents asthma attacks.

- Cranberry: Cranberry juice helps prevent urinary tract and bladder infections by making the urine more acidic.

- Dill: Fights flatulence; prevents infectious diarrhea in children by inhibiting the growth of certain bacteria.

- Echinacea: Fights infections and stimulates the immune system.

- Fenugreek: Controls diabetes, reduces levels of cholesterol.

- Feverfew: Helps prevent migraine headaches.

- Garlic: Research indicates that garlic helps reduce cholesterol levels, as well as maintain normal blood pressure levels, both essential elements for reducing the risk of heart disease and stroke. Garlic also helps prevent cancer and contributes to the longer life span of healthy skin cells.

- Ginger: Prevents motion sickness. Also helps kill the influenza virus and helps the immune system wage war on infection.

Books

Duff, John F., M.D. *Youth Sports Injuries.* New York: Macmillan, 1992.

Flegel, Melinda. *Sports First Aid.* Rev. ed. Human Kinetics, 1997.

Garvy, Helen. *The Immune System: Your Magic Doctor.* Los Gatos, Calif.: Shire Press, 1992.

Hyde, Margaret O., and Elizabeth H. Forsyth, M.D. *The Disease Book: A Kid's Guide.* New York: Walker and Company, 1997.

Micheli, Lyle J., M.D. *Sportswise: An Essential Guide for Young Athletes, Parents, and Coaches.* New York: Houghton Mifflin, 1990.

- Ginseng: Relieves stress, which is a factor in premature aging, heart disease, cancer, acne, allergies and other infections. Also regulates blood pressure and enhances immunity.

- Goldenseal: This herb contains a compound called berberine that kills many of the bacteria that cause diarrhea. Berberine also helps the immune system neutralize the bacteria that cause colds and sinus infections.

- Grape Seed Extract: This plant extract contains antioxidant compounds that can be beneficial in the same way as other antioxidants like vitamins C and E.

- Green Tea: Green tea extract is a popular beverage that also happens to contain large amounts of antioxidants.

- Guarana: This herb can prevent drowsiness and reduce the risk of heart attacks.

- Hawthorn: Regulates blood pressure, which is helpful for preventing heart disease.

- Licorice Root: Another plant extract with antioxidant properties.

- Milk Thistle: Protects against liver damage from alcohol, hepatitis and chemical toxins. It is also a powerful antioxidant, which, like vitamins A and C, helps neutralize cell-damaging free radicals.

- Oregano: Enhances digestion.

- Peppermint: Aids digestion; soothes stomachs; freshens breath.

- Pycnogenol: This plant extract is an antioxidant that helps maintain healthy cells, prevent collagen damage that can lead to premature aging, and neutralize the production of free radicals.

- Rosemary: May prevent certain cancers; like peppermint, rosemary aids digestion.

- Sage: Thought to fight diabetes by boosting the action of insulin, which helps to regulate blood sugar levels.

- Tarragon: Helps prevent certain cancers and helps against the flu.

- Tea: Prevents certain cancers; wards off heart disease by helping to lower blood cholesterol and regulate blood pressure. Tea also helps to rid the body of excess fluids.

- Thyme: A natural antiseptic, thyme kills bacteria and fungi.

- Turmeric: Turmeric is thought to protect the liver, fight heart disease, prevent ulcers, and help reduce the risk of certain cancers.

- White Willow: "The Herbal Aspirin," helps prevent heart attacks and strokes, combat certain cancers, and prevent migraine headaches.

Web sites

Dr. C. Everett Koop. [Online] http://www.drkoop.com (Accessed October 26, 1999).

Health Central. [Online] http://www.healthcentral.com (Accessed October 26, 1999).

Kids' Health for Parents. [Online] http://www.kidshealth.org (Accessed October 26, 1999).

On Health. [Online] http://www.onhealth.com (Accessed October 26, 1999).

Prevention Magazine. [Online] http://www.healthyideas.com (Accessed October 26, 1999).

Sports Illustrated for Kids. [Online] http://www.sportsparents.com (Accessed October 26, 1999).

9

Over-the-Counter Drugs

When people are ill, often times they are able to seek relief from medications available at their local pharmacy without having to visit a physician for prescription medicine. Typically, the conditions are minor and not life threatening. People use nonprescription, or over-the-counter (OTC), drugs to treat less serious conditions that are either transient (will pass relatively quickly), such as the common cold, or chronic (lasting for a long time or recurring frequently), such as allergies.

There are over 100 thousand different OTC drugs. The Food and Drug Administration (FDA) classifies these drugs in over eighty categories such as allergy and cough/cold medications, pain relievers, aids for digestive problems, stimulants, sleep aids, and antibacterial drugs. There are also herbal remedies, which are not regulated by the FDA and which may or may not be effective at treating ailments.

Even though a drug is OTC rather than prescription, it can still have side effects. In fact, many OTC drugs have drug interactions with prescriptions and other OTC drugs. Interactions usually cause one of the drugs to work less effectively, but they can also have dangerous, even deadly, results. In fact, there are many OTC drugs that can aggravate certain medical conditions. In this and similar cases, that particular OTC drug should be avoided altogether. Furthermore, due to certain ingredients or for other reasons, many OTC drugs should be used only by adults and older children (generally over the age of twelve), unless it is a formula made especially for younger children. This is why the use of OTC drugs requires a careful reading of a drug's label and instructions so that a consumer will have a full understanding of the drug and its proper uses. If a person doesn't understand something on the package label, a pharmacist can usually help.

This chapter presents the most common OTC drugs, from pain relievers such as acetaminophen and aspirin, to cold and flu remedies, to more controversial remedies such as sleep aids and weight loss aids.

Acne Medicine

Analgesics (Pain Relievers)

Antacids

Antibacterial Drugs

Antidiarrhea Medicine

Antihistamines and Allergy Drugs

Cold and Cough/Flu Medicines

Hemorrhoid Medicine

Laxatives

PMS Medicine

Yeast Infection Medicine

Other Common OTC Drugs

Herbal Medicine

ACNE MEDICINE

over-the-counter
drugs

Acne is an inflammatory disease of the oil glands of the skin. Both superficial (surface) acne and deep acne are caused by a combination of bacteria, hormones, and inherited tendencies.

During puberty, an increase in hormones causes oil glands on the face, neck, back, and chest to become stimulated. The glands produce large amounts of sebum, a fatty substance. Sebum normally flows out of the skin

WORDS TO KNOW

Acetaminophen: A generic name for a compound that affects the brain and spinal cord, altering the perception of pain and lessening it.

Allergy: A chronic condition in which an allergic reaction occurs when the immune system responds aggressively to a certain foreign substance.

Analgesic: A drug that alleviates pain without affecting consciousness.

Antacids: A medication used to neutralize up to 99 percent of stomach acid.

Antibiotics: Drugs used to treat bacterial infections.

Antihistamine: The drugs most commonly used to treat allergies.

Anti-inflammatory: Chemical that counteracts inflammation.

Antiseptic: A substance that prevents the growth of germs and bacteria.

Antitussive: A type of cough medication that calms the part of the brain that controls the coughing reflex.

Aromatherapy: A branch of herbal medicine that uses medicinal properties found in the essential oils of certain plants.

Arthritis: Inflammation of the joints. The condition causes pain and swelling.

Astringent: Something that tightens the skin.

Caffeine: An organic compound that has a stimulating effect on the central nervous system, heart, blood vessels, and kidneys.

Carcinogens: Substance that produces cancer.

Clinical trial: A study that evaluates how well a new drug works, positive effects, negative side effects, and how it is best used.

Cortisone: A hormone from the steroid family that originates in the adrenal cortex and is known for its anti-inflammatory properties.

Decongestant: A compound that relieves a stuffy nose by limiting the production of mucus and reducing the swelling in the mucous membrane by constricting the blood vessels in the nose, opening the airways and promoting drainage.

Diarrhea: An increase in the frequency, volume, or wateriness of bowel movements.

Echinacea: A plant (also known as purple coneflower) that herbalists believe bolsters the immune system and treats certain ailments.

Endorphins: Hormones that the brain produces that stop the sensation of pain from being transmitted from cell to cell.

Ephedra: A type of plant (also known as Ma Huang) used to treat ailments, including bronchial problems, and as a decongestant.

Expectorant: A type of cough medication that helps clear the lungs and chest of phlegm.

Feverfew: An herb used to treat migraines.

Ginkgo biloba: A tree (the oldest living kind of tree, in fact) whose leaves are believed to have medicinal value, particularly in aiding memory and treating dizziness, headaches, and even anxiety.

Ginseng: An herb used as a kind of cure-all, with benefits to the immune system and aiding the body in coping with stress. Some also believe it aids concentration.

along the hair follicles. However, too much sebum, combined with skin debris, can form a plug in the hair follicle called a blackhead. Once the hair follicle becomes plugged, bacteria grow in it. This bacterial infection is called acne. In severe cases of deep acne, inflamed cysts may form; sometimes these cysts can cause permanent scars.

Acne can also occur in people who aren't experiencing puberty. Certain drugs, industrial chemicals, oily cosmetics, or hot, humid conditions can also cause it. Some people believe that stress can cause or worsen adult acne.

Hallucination: A vision of something that is not actually there; can occur because of nervous system disorders or in response to drugs.

Hemorrhoids: A form of varicose veins that occurs when the veins around the anus become swollen or irritated.

Ibuprofen: The generic name for a type of analgesic that works in the same manner as aspirin but can be used in instances when aspirin cannot.

Indigenous: Occurring naturally in an environment.

Insomnia: Abnormal inability to get adequate sleep.

Insulin: Hormone used to metabolize carbohydrates.

Interaction: When two drugs influence the effects of each other.

Laxatives: Drugs that alleviate constipation, the inability to have a bowel movement.

Metabolism: Process by which substances are handled by the body.

Neurotransmitters: A substance that transmits nerve impulses.

Nicotine: An organic compound in tobacco leaves that has addictive properties.

Nonproductive cough: A dry and hacking cough.

Organic: Occurring naturally.

Osteoporosis: A disease whereby, over time, bones mass (and therefore bone strength) is decreased.

Palpitation: Rapid, irregular heartbeat.

Panacea: A cure-all.

Phenylpropanolamine (PPA): A chemical that disrupts the hunger signals being sent by the brain; it is often used in weight loss aids.

Phlegm: Sticky mucus present in the nose, throat, and lungs.

Productive cough: A cough that brings up phlegm.

Prostaglandin: A hormone-like substance that affects blood vessels and the functions of blood platelets, and sensitizes nerve endings to pain.

Rapid-Eye movement (REM) sleep: A deep stage of sleep during which time people dream.

St. John's Wort: An herb used as an anti-inflammatory drug, to treat depression, and as an analgesic.

Side effect: A secondary (and usually negative) reaction to a drug.

Stimulant: Substance that produces temporary increase in ability.

Topical: Designed for application on the body.

Toxins: Poisonous substances.

Transient: Passes quickly into and out of existence.

Vasoconstrictor: A drug that constricts the blood vessels to affect the blood pressure.

Yeast infection: A common infection of a woman's vagina caused by overgrowth of the yeast Candida Albicans.

Acne is usually treated with OTC topical (applied on the body) drugs such as sulfur or benzoyl peroxide, which can be found in products such as Clearasil and Stridex medicated pads. Unfortunately, these ingredients can dry the skin too much. In particular, the FDA is currently studying the effects of benzoyl peroxide on skin that is exposed to the sun. Because the effects are unknown at this time, it is advisable to avoid unnecessary sun exposure and use sunscreen if treating acne with benzoyl peroxide.

Another type of topical drug commonly used is keratolytic skin ointment. The ingredients in these ointments peel off the dead and hardened skin cells that form the skin surface and contribute to the sebum plug. This can cause soreness or redness, especially during the first few uses. Some OTC topical acne drugs also contain antibiotics to prevent or treat infection. Antibacterial soaps can be somewhat helpful, although they may cause irritation.

Mild cases of acne do not necessarily need to be treated with drugs. Regular washing and moderate exposure to sunlight will usually control the acne.

ANALGESICS (PAIN RELIEVERS)

Pain relievers, or analgesics, are familiar products found in most medicine cabinets. These products help consumers relieve headaches, muscle aches, fever, and other pain-related symptoms. With so many brand name products and different strengths and formulas, today's consumer has a variety of pain relieving products from which to choose. What follows are descriptions of the various pain-relieving agents available as OTC drugs.

Aspirin

Acetylsalicylic acid is known by a much more familiar name—aspirin. It is a common analgesic, or drug that alleviates pain without affecting consciousness. In the fifth century B.C., Greek physician Hippocrates, considered "the father of medicine," used powder extracted from willow tree bark to treat pain and reduce fever. The active ingredient, sodium salicylate, was discovered centuries later. This ingredient was the predecessor to aspirin.

IN 1897, GERMAN CHEMIST FELIX HOFFMAN DEVELOPED ASPIRIN WHILE TRYING TO FIND A WAY TO RELIEVE THE PAIN OF HIS FATHER'S ARTHRITIS. HE WORKED FOR A COMPANY CALLED BAYER.

Aspirin works by inhibiting the release of a hormone-like substance called prostaglandin. This chemical affects blood vessels and the functions of blood platelets and sensitizes nerve endings to pain. By limiting the prostaglandin, aspirin affects blood clotting, eases inflammation, and prevents the nerve ending at the site of the pain from becoming stimulated. It is used for headaches, muscle pain, arthritis, and to reduce fevers.

While it seems like a wonder drug, aspirin does have certain drawbacks. It can irritate the stomach lining, causing heartburn, pain, or nausea. Coating aspirin capsules helps reduce this irritation by preventing the release of the aspirin until it has passed through the stomach and into the small intestine; however, coating also slows the absorption of aspirin and increases the amount of time before it starts to work. Buffered aspirin reduces the acidity of the stomach's contents to lessen irritation. Taking aspirin with an antacid or after a meal will also reduce the stomach irritation. Because of these possible adverse effects, people should not take aspirin if they have a bleeding

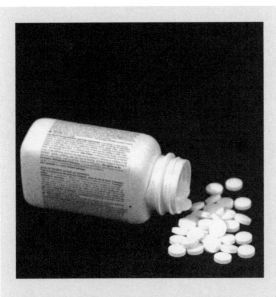

Aspirin can be used to reduce the risk of heart disease. (Photograph by Robert J. Huffman. Field Mark Publications. Reproduced by permission.)

ASPIRIN FOR THE HEART?

The Bayer Company ran an advertisement for its aspirin in the 1920s that read, "DOES NOT AFFECT THE HEART." But Bayer was wrong; aspirin does affect the heart. Fortunately, aspirin has been found to be beneficial to the heart, and some of today's aspirin advertisements feature the American Heart Association's seal of approval.

It is estimated that Americans use 80 million aspirin tablets a day, and most are not taken for aches and pains. They are used to reduce the

risk of heart disease. The FDA has approved the use of aspirin to treat serious cardiovascular conditions such as heart attack and stroke. It has been proven to reduce the risk of:

• Strokes and heart attacks in those who have already had one.

• Death or complications from a heart attack if taken at the first signs of one.

• Recurring blockage in those who have had heart bypass surgery to clear blocked arteries.

The secret to aspirin's protective properties in relation to the cardiovascular system lies in aspirin's ability to reduce the body's production of prostaglandin, which causes blood platelets to stick together. This phenomenon can eventually lead to blocked blood vessels and clots. A blood clot in the brain causes stroke, while a blood clot in the heart causes heart attacks. By reducing the prostaglandin, the risk of heart attacks and strokes is reduced.

The American Heart Association believes that out of the nine hundred thousand lives lost each year to cardiovascular disease, five to ten thousand could be saved if more people used aspirin at the first signs of a heart attack (intermittent chest pain, shortness of breath, and fatigue). In the important first moments of a heart attack, aspirin provides "head start" therapy and a better chance for survival.

Because of its possible serious side effects, aspirin is not approved for daily use by healthy people who are not at risk for heart disease. For those who do need it, the recommended dose varies from 50 to 325 milligrams daily. Above all, aspirin should never replace a healthy lifestyle.

disorder, stomach ulcer, or gout (a painful disease of the joints, especially legs, hands, and feet).

Other side effects include the fact that high doses of aspirin may cause ringing in the ears. Furthermore, if children or adolescents infected with chicken pox or influenza (flu) are given aspirin, they could develop Reye's Syndrome, a sudden loss of consciousness that may cause death. Allergy sufferers should also watch their aspirin intake. If people are allergic to aspirin, they may have difficulty breathing or develop hives, itching, or swelling. Also, aspirin should not be given to someone directly before or after surgery because it decreases the blood's ability to clot, which could cause excessive bleeding.

People who consume a lot of alcohol need to be careful, too—liver damage and stomach bleeding can result when heavy drinkers use aspirin. Finally, aspirin should not be given to children under the age of twelve or to pregnant women, especially during the last three months of pregnancy since it could cause complications during delivery.

Acetaminophen

Acetaminophen is the generic (non-trademarked) name for the pain reliever found in brand name products such as Tylenol and Excedrin. It is also used to treat fever, headaches, and minor aches and pains. Acetaminophen works by affecting the brain and spinal cord, altering the perception of pain. Acetaminophen is similar to hormones that the brain produces called endorphins. These hormones stop the pain sensation from being transmitted from cell to cell. It reduces fevers by affecting the area of the brain that regulates temperature. Like aspirin, acetaminophen limits the production of prostaglandin in the brain. Aspirin affects prostaglandin production in the rest of the body as well, but acetaminophen only affects the brain. For this reason, acetaminophen does not reduce inflammation. It cannot affect swelling from arthritis, sprains, or muscle pain. It does have fewer side effects than either aspirin or ibuprofen (see below). Therefore, people with blood clots, ulcers, chicken pox, influenza, or gout can safely take acetaminophen instead of aspirin.

Individuals with liver disease should not take acetaminophen; in fact, an overdose of this drug can cause serious liver and kidney damage. Like other pain relievers, this drug should not be taken with alcoholic beverages. A risk of liver damage exists from combining large amounts of alcohol and acetaminophen. It should not be taken for more than ten days or by children under the age of twelve.

Ibuprofen

Originally available only by prescription, this drug has been available in lower strength as an OTC pain reliever since 1984. Ibuprofen can be used to treat headaches, muscle aches, arthritis, swelling, menstrual pain, and to reduce fevers. Like aspirin, it works by inhibiting production of prostaglandin, which aids blood clotting and makes nerve endings sensitive.

The possible side effects of using ibuprofen include drowsiness, heartburn, upset stomach, nausea, vomiting, or dizziness. Taking the drug with food or milk often helps to avoid these problems. Pregnant women and people with diabetes or congestive heart failure should not take ibuprofen.

Ibuprofen is a stronger analgesic than either aspirin or acetaminophen and a better anti-inflammatory than aspirin. It can be found in brand name products such as Advil, Motrin IB, and Nuprin.

Ketoprofen and naproxen are pain relievers similar to ibuprofen. Ketoprofen has had OTC status since 1994; naproxen has been available over the counter since 1995. Ketoprofen and naproxen share side effects similar to those of ibuprofen, including heartburn and upset stomach.

ANTACIDS

The stomach is a very busy organ. It stores food, mixes food with gastric secretions, and empties food into the small intestine for digestion and absorption. Gastric acid helps with digestion and absorption of food, and it also kills bacteria found in the stomach. Acidity is measured using a pH value. The pH of gastric acid is extremely high, approximately 3 million times more acidic than the pH of blood. The stomach has a lining to protect it from this acid. The lining secretes mucus and bicarbonate, which form a barrier against the acid.

There are substances that interfere with this lining and cause the stomach to become irritated by the acid. These substances include medications, alcohol, and caffeine. Smoking and certain diseases affect the lining as well. When acid irritates the stomach, the result is heartburn, gas, indigestion, and sometimes ulcers. There are two main types of antacids to treat these problems: H2-antagonists and non-H2-antagonists. (H2 is a type of acid. The antacid types are called such because some people have an overproduction of acid.)

NON-H2-ANTAGONISTS. Non-H2-antagonists were the first antacids to be available without a prescription. They work by neutralizing the gastric acid in the stomach. This makes it easier for the lining to protect the stomach. These antacids

FROM BEHIND THE COUNTER TO OVER THE COUNTER

Many former prescription medicines can now be bought over the counter, such as Advil (pain reliever), Aleve (pain reliever), Monistat (treats yeast infections), and Tagamet HB (antacid). The FDA switches a prescription to OTC status if it determines that people can safely and effectively use the medicine after reading the medicine's package label and without physician instruction. The FDA also looks at how the medicine interacts with other drugs, how safe it is in high doses, and the risk of abusing this medicine before it approves a medication's OTC status. OTC drugs that used to be prescription medicines are usually sold in lower doses than could be prescribed by a physician.

contain calcium carbonate, sodium bicarbonate, aluminum salts, or magnesium salts as their main ingredients.

Calcium carbonate takes longer to dissolve than the other ingredients but is more effective in neutralizing the acid. Calcium carbonate antacids are intended for short-term use only. Some people believe that the calcium in antacids can be used as a dietary supplement, but the amount of calcium that is absorbed by the body is actually very small.

Antacids that use sodium bicarbonate offer almost instant relief, but should not be taken by people who are on a low-sodium diet, have congestive heart failure, high blood pressure, cirrhosis, swelling, or kidney failure because of the sodium (salt) that the body absorbs from these antacids.

Aluminum salts dissolve very slowly and take longer to work. These antacids can cause constipation. They are often combined with magnesium salts, which cause diarrhea. Magnesium salts neutralize acid better than aluminum salts, but not as well as calcium carbonate or sodium bicarbonate, and they don't provide long-term relief. People with kidney failure should not use aluminum salt or magnesium salt antacids.

Some antacids have other ingredients such as aspirin or a chemical called simethicone, which relieves gas. Sometimes sodium bicarbonate antacids also contain alginic acid. This acid reacts to the sodium bicarbonate and makes a foam that treats heartburn.

H2-ANTAGONISTS. H2-antagonist antacids are now available without prescription. Originally designed to treat ulcers, they also work well for heartburn, acid relief, and sour stomachs. These antacids work by blocking the formation of excess acid in the stomach. They do not neutralize the acid that is already there. These antacids should not be taken for more than two weeks.

Antacids in liquid form absorb faster than the other varieties, so they provide faster relief. Chewable tablets should be chewed thoroughly and work best if taken with water. Some interactions with other drugs may occur because the other drugs can bind to the antacids and will not get fully absorbed. Pregnant women should not use antacids unless recommended by their doctor.

ANTIBACTERIAL DRUGS

Antibacterial drugs work by attacking the bacteria that are causing the infection. Antibacterial medicine was first used in 1935. These early drugs were called sulfa drugs. They were so effective against a wide range of bacterial infections that they were included in the first aid pouches the U.S. Army supplied to soldiers in World War II (1939–45). The descendants of these early antibacterial drugs are called sulfonamides.

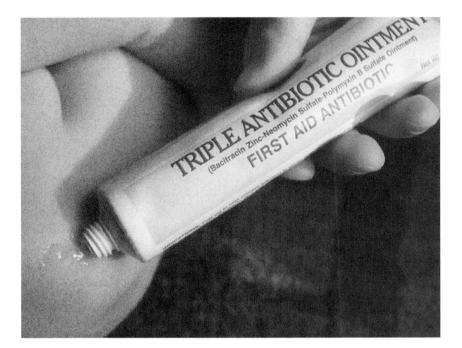

Applying antibacterial ointment to a skinned knee is a good way to help the wound heal. (Photograph by Robert J. Huffman. Field Mark Publications. Reproduced by permission.)

OTC antibacterial drugs such as Neosporin are intended to treat minor cuts and scrapes, and they contain one or more of three different antibiotics designed to treat specific types of microorganisms. Combinations of antibiotics give a broader range of treatment. Some antibacterial drugs also contain local anesthetics to alleviate the pain that can accompany infections. Other antibacterial drugs include antiseptics to prevent or slow down bacteria growth in the infected area. Mineral oil or lanolin may also be found in these drugs to speed the medication's absorption.

To further promote the effectiveness of antibacterial drugs, a person should keep the infected area clean, cool, and dry, and drink plenty of water (topical medicines are poorly absorbed by the skin if it is dehydrated). Antibacterial drugs can cause allergic reactions such as rashes and fever. These problems can often be resolved by changing to a different drug. Like many OTC drugs, antibacterial medications should not be used for more than seven days.

Cortisone

Cortisone is an organic (naturally occurring) compound from the steroid family (a group of fat-soluble organic compounds). It is a hormone that originates in the adrenal cortex (part of the adrenal glands, which are located one above each kidney), and is known for its anti-inflammatory properties. It was first introduced in 1948 as a treatment for rheumatoid arthritis. It provides relief from rheumatic fever, some kidney diseases, certain skin conditions, and allergies.

Available in many OTC creams and ointments, such as Cortaid, cortisone can cause problems with sodium, potassium, and nitrogen imbalances within the body and can sometimes cause swelling.

ANTIDIARRHEA MEDICINE

When the digestive tract is functioning normally, food and fluid pass from the stomach into the small intestine and colon. Cells that line the small intestine and colon absorb nutrients and water, then pass the waste along. If these cells become irritated, they cannot absorb the nutrients and water, as they should. The food and fluids then move through the colon too fast, which results in a watery stool called diarrhea.

There are a number of things that can irritate the cells lining the small intestine and colon. The most common culprits are allergies to certain foods and parasites or bacteria found in the food and water of some foreign countries. Stressful situations, poisons, blood pressure drugs, and drinking too much alcohol may also lead to diarrhea.

OTC antidiarrhea drugs, such as Imodium and Kaopectate, cannot cure diarrhea; rather they only control its symptoms. People who are experiencing diarrhea should try to rest, eat small amounts of food at a time, and avoid dehydration by drinking plenty of fluids. Antidiarrhea drugs should not be used for more than two days.

READ THE LABEL

The FDA has labeling guidelines for OTC drugs that make the packages easier to read and understand for consumers. The label must detail:

- Active ingredients, or the primary ingredients.
- The use, or the types of symptoms that the drug treats.
- Directions, or the amount a person should take, how often it should be taken, and for how long.
- Warnings, or possible interactions with other drugs or side effects the medicine may cause and what should be done if these things occur.

ANTIHISTAMINES AND ALLERGY DRUGS

The body's immune system protects the body from sickness and infection. To do so it must recognize and respond to any foreign substance it encounters. Histamine is an organic substance that plays an important role in the human body's response to injury or invasion. When an injury or allergic reaction occurs, the body releases histamine in response. An allergic reaction occurs when the immune system responds aggressively to a foreign substance. There are two main types of allergies; each is triggered by different substances. Perennial (year-round) allergies are usually a reaction to things such as animal dander, paint fumes, certain foods, drugs, dyes, or chemicals. Seasonal (occurring at certain times of the year) allergies are generally environmental. They are a reaction to pollens, trees, grass, ragweed, and mold spores.

Antihistamine drugs used to treat allergies are called H1 blockers because they only block histamine on H1 receptors. H1 receptors are found mostly in the small blood vessels in the skin, nose and eyes. High levels of histamine in these receptors cause an allergic reaction, usually in the way of a stuffy nose or sneezing. Allergic reactions may include itching or swelling skin such as hives, eczema, itching from insect bites, or irritation of the eyes. Antihistamines are synthetic (human-made) drugs that block the action of histamine by replacing it at one of two sites where it binds to the receptor, which prevents reactions from occurring. This reduces the irritation in the eyes and nose, congestion and breathlessness in the lungs, and redness, itching, or swelling of the skin.

Antihistamines also pass from the blood to the brain where they cause general sedation (drowsiness) and depression of certain brain functions, such as the vomiting and coughing mechanisms. Since most antihistamines have this sedative effect on the brain, they are often used in sleep aid drugs (see section on sleep aids). They are also used to control nausea and motion sickness.

Some experts believe that antihistamines should not be available over the counter because of the drowsiness and sluggishness that is associated with their consumption. Other side effects include blurred vision, dry mouth, constipation, and light-headedness (all of which are particularly prominent in elderly users). Pregnant women and sufferers of chronic bronchitis, emphysema, and glaucoma should avoid antihistamines. Like many

GRAPEFRUIT JUICE

Some people may know that drinking grapefruit juice when taking medication can help with the body's absorption of certain drugs. But a recent study at the University of California at San Francisco has shown that in some cases, grapefruit juice may actually decrease the absorption of drugs.

Grapefruit juice increases absorption of drugs by reducing the level of an intestinal enzyme known as CYP3A4. This enzyme breaks down drug molecules before they reach the bloodstream. A University of California study, however, found that an unknown substance in grapefruit juice activates a mechanism in the intestinal tract increasing the likelihood that certain drugs will not enter the bloodstream. Some of the drugs affected by this mechanism are those used to combat cancer, treat congestive heart failure, suppress organ rejection after a transplant, control high blood pressure, and treat allergy symptoms.

Depending on the drug, grapefruit juice may either increase or decrease levels of the drug in the bloodstream; thus, people may get too much or too little medication, both of which could be dangerous situations. In most cases, doctors recommend that people avoid taking drugs with grapefruit juice until more is known about how it affects drug absorption.

drugs, most antihistamines should not be taken with alcohol, antidepressants, or sedatives.

Antihistamines are not usually helpful in treating the common cold. They are sometimes used to treat fever, rash, and breathing problems that result from reactions to blood transfusions, and allergic reactions to drugs. Antihistamines containing diphenhydramine are sometimes used in the early stages of Parkinson's disease.

These drugs should not be used for longer than seven days or by children under the age of six. Avoiding the substances that cause allergic reactions is usually the best treatment for allergies, when possible. If OTC allergy drugs do not help alleviate symptoms, allergy shots administered by a physician may be a viable alternative.

Decongestants

The lining of the nasal (nose) passages is called the mucous membrane. When infection, such as a cold or an allergic reaction, occurs, the blood vessels that supply the mucous membrane become enlarged and the mucous membrane swells. Fluid accumulates in nearby body tissue and mucus (the sticky substance secreted by the mucous membrane) is produced in larger amounts than usual. The result is a stuffy nose. Decongestants relieve a stuffy nose by limiting the production of mucus and reducing the swelling in the mucous membrane by constricting the blood vessels in the nose. This opens the airways and promotes drainage of nasal passages.

There are two types of decongestants: topical (applied to the body) and oral (taken by mouth). Topical decongestants are sprays or drops that are used directly in the nose, such as Neosenephrine. There are short- and long-acting topical decongestants that can provide relief from four to twelve hours; they usually start to work within a few minutes. Topical decongestants should not be used for more than three days because there is a risk of developing a problem called rebound congestion. When a person stops using a topical decongestant after using it for longer than recommended, the blood vessels in the mucous membrane will suddenly widen because they are no longer constricted by the drug. This causes congestion to occur all over again.

Oral decongestants, such as Drixoral, are taken through the mouth. Their effects are usually longer lasting than those of topical decongestants but they also take longer to yield noticeable relief. They are also more likely to cause side effects, such as increased heart rate and trembling, than topical decongestants. Both topical and oral decongestants should be used only by adults or children over the age of twelve unless advised by a doctor.

People with high blood pressure, diabetes, heart disease or an overactive thyroid should only use decongestants with their physician's approval. If a

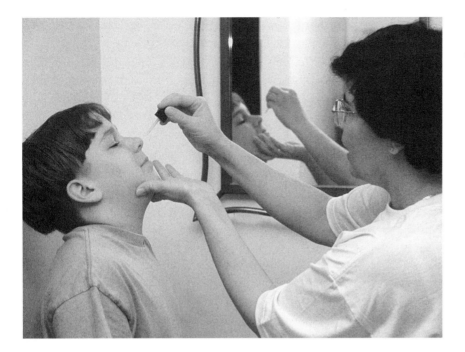

Decongestant nose drops help clear stuffed nasal passages on contact. (Photograph by Robert J. Huffman. Field Mark Publications. Reproduced by permission.)

person uses decongestants too frequently, she or he may develop problems, such as nervousness, insomnia, dizziness, headaches, or palpitations.

COLD AND COUGH/FLU MEDICINES

Contrary to popular belief, going outside on a cold day with wet hair does not cause a person to catch the common cold. Viruses, tiny disease-producing particles, are the culprits. Viruses can easily be transferred from person to person via the air (when a person sneezes, for example) or via objects such as door knobs and telephones. (That is why washing one's hands often helps cut down on the transmission of viruses.) The symptoms of a cold are a runny or stuffy nose, coughing, sneezing, and a sore throat. These symptoms usually last five to seven days. If the symptoms persist for seven to ten days and include fever, tiredness, and headache, it could be influenza (flu).

There is no cure for a cold or flu; the only medical option available is the treatment of the symptoms to provide a person with some relief. OTC cold and flu medicines, such as Nyquil, usually contain antihistamines, decongestants, and analgesics, such as aspirin or ibuprofen.

COUGH MEDICATIONS. There are two types of cough—productive and nonproductive. Productive coughs bring up phlegm (mucus produced by the mucous membranes in chest and lungs) and can often be treated by inhaling steam, which makes it easier to cough up the phlegm. If steam doesn't work, expectorants like Robitussin are used to help clear the phlegm from the chest and lungs. Nonproductive coughs are dry and hacking. This kind of coughing is treated with antitussives, which calm the part of the brain that controls the coughing reflex. Antitussives have a sedating effect on the brain and nervous system, so drowsiness and other side effects are common.

Most cough medicines are made up of active ingredients and flavorings added to a syrupy base. Some cough medicines contain active ingredients that work against each other, such as expectorants that produce phlegm and antitussives to suppress the body's ability to cough it up. A person must carefully read the label and choose a cough medicine that treats the kind of cough one has. Using the wrong type of cough medicine could cause the condition to worsen. If a cough lasts longer than two days or symptoms such as fever or blood in the phlegm are present, a physician should be consulted immediately.

It is a good practice to cover the nose and mouth when sneezing to minimize the spread of germs. (Photograph © 1990 Linda Steinmark. Custom Medical Stock Photo. Reproduced by permission.)

Because many cough and cold remedies contain antihistamines, users should be certain that they are not taking another product containing antihistamines at the same time. Furthermore, cough and cold medicines should not be taken with tranquilizers or sedatives or for more than seven days. Sufferers of asthma, emphysema, glaucoma, heart disease, high blood pressure, or thyroid disease should avoid using these drugs. People with diabetes need to choose a sugar-free product. Most cold and cough remedies offer specific formulas for both adults and children.

HEMORRHOID MEDICINE

Hemorrhoids are a form of varicose (swollen or knotted) veins that occur when the veins around the anus become swollen or irritated. This is usually the result of prolonged back pressure from pregnancy or frequently sitting for long hours at a time. Hemorrhoids will cause itching, burning, pain, swelling, irritation, or bleeding around the anus. Constipation can make hemorrhoids worse.

There are two ways to treat hemorrhoids using OTC drugs. There are creams and suppositories that relieve most of the symptoms. These drugs usually consist of a soothing agent that contains an antiseptic, an astringent (such as bismuth, witch hazel, and zinc oxide), or a vasoconstrictor (shrinks blood vessels). These ingredients reduce swelling, burning, and itching, and restrict blood supply to the area. Some also contain a local anesthetic (pain blocker) to ease the pain. These drugs may cause irritation or a rash. The second method of treatment is to relieve constipation, which makes hemorrhoids more uncomfortable, with laxatives. Laxatives soften waste to ease its passage through the intestines.

Neither treatment actually shrinks the hemorrhoids. They simply provide relief while the problem corrects itself naturally. OTC hemorrhoid drugs are available in ointments, suppositories, and medicated pads with witch hazel, such as Tucks. Severe or persistent hemorrhoids may need to be removed surgically. If a person has hemorrhoids, it is a good idea to see a doctor as the hemorrhoids could be a sign of a more serious bowel disorder.

LAXATIVES

When people's bowels do not move as often as usual and the waste becomes hard and difficult to pass, they have constipation. Other symptoms may include lower back pain, a distended stomach, or a headache. Constipation is usually the result of limited water intake or a diet that is lacking in fiber. Fiber naturally provides bulk, which makes the waste soft and easy to pass. A diet that includes more fruits, vegetables and whole grain breads will provide more fiber. Also, certain diseases and drugs such as narcotic analgesics, antidepressants and antacids that contain aluminum may cause constipation. Lack of exercise may be a contributing factor as well.

Constipation is commonly treated with OTC drugs called laxatives, which stimulate bowel muscles or affect waste consistency. Laxatives are also used to prevent pain for people suffering with hemorrhoids or after childbirth or abdominal surgery. Laxatives should only be used for short-term therapy (no longer than a week) and should not be used to achieve weight loss. Overuse of laxatives is dangerous and can lead to severe deficiencies in vitamins and minerals. People can also develop a dependency on laxatives if they are used for too long; this can lead to chronic constipation.

There are two main types of OTC laxatives, and both affect the large intestine. Bulk-forming laxatives, such as Metamucil, absorb water, increasing the volume of waste in the bowel and making it softer and easier to pass. These laxatives produce results within twelve to seventy-two hours. Stimulant laxatives, such as Ex-Lax and Senokot, use senna to make the bowel muscle contract, which speeds the passage of waste through the intestine. Overuse of stimulant laxatives can cause dehydration, severe cramping, and loss of protein and potassium. Products such as Doxidan contain both a stimulant laxative and stool softener.

Laxative users should visit their doctors if they experience nausea, vomiting, bleeding, dizziness, or weakness while using OTC laxatives. Children under six should not use laxatives unless they have been so advised by their doctor.

FDA APPROVAL

By law, all new drugs have to be proven effective and safe before the Food and Drug Administration (FDA) will approve them. Even with FDA approval, however, no drug is completely safe; there is always a risk of a bad reaction. The FDA must weigh the risks against the benefits when deciding to approve a new drug.

The process begins with the drug's sponsor, which is usually the manufacturer. The sponsor submits studies called new drug applications (NDAs) that show the effectiveness and safety of a drug. The NDA is supposed to tell the whole story about the drug, including what happened in the clinical trials; what components make up the drug; the results of studies on animals; how the drug behaves in the body; and how it is manufactured, processed and packaged. The clinical trials are especially important because they demonstrate how effective the drug is. (A clinical trial allows researchers to fully understand a drug—how it works, positive effects, negative side-effects, and how it is best used. People allowed to participate in drug trials usually share certain characteristics that make them appropriate for that specific trial. Furthermore, the trials usually take place under the supervision of a physician at a hospital, treatment center, or a university.) The human studies provide information that will be used for the drug's professional labeling, which is the guidance that the FDA approves for using the drug.

NDAs for drugs with the greatest potential benefit have priority over other NDAs. For example, all AIDS (acquired immunodeficiency syndrome) drugs have the highest priority, as well as drugs that of-

PMS MEDICINE

Premenstrual Syndrome (PMS) is the name given to a group of physical and emotional symptoms that women may experience prior to the start of menstruation each month. The symptoms usually begin seven to fourteen days before the onset of menstruation and can last until twenty-four hours after menstruation ceases. It is estimated that over 40 percent of women experience some symptoms of PMS.

The symptoms and their intensity can vary. Physical symptoms include headache, cramps, backache, bloating, constipation, and diarrhea. The emotional symptoms may include irritability, lethargy or tiredness, and quick mood swings. OTC drugs for PMS, such as Pamprin and Midol, treat the physical symptoms using analgesics to help relieve the pain and diuretics to reduce the bloating.

The best way for women to treat PMS is to avoid stress, exercise regularly, and watch their diets. A diet high in protein, complex carbohydrates, and vitamin B can help lessen the symptoms of PMS. It also helps to avoid salt (which helps the body retain water), coffee, tea, chocolate and cola (which contain caffeine and can contribute to headaches).

SENNA

The leaves and fruit of the senna plant, a member of the pea family, are used in herbal medicine as a potent (strong) laxative. Like other herbal remedies, people who use it should be well informed about its negative effects. Senna, also called Cassia, can cause cramps, nausea, heart palpitations, or severe diarrhea. Long-term use of senna can flush out important minerals. One of the minerals at risk is potassium, which keeps the heart beating normally. Potassium can be found in potatoes, squash, bananas and orange juice, but laxatives prevent the mineral from being absorbed. Low levels of potassium over an extended period may cause heart problems, even death. Women who are pregnant or nursing should avoid senna, since the drug passes directly through their breastmilk and can give a nursing infant diarrhea.

fer significant advances over current therapies for any disease.

When the FDA analyzes a drug, the decision to approve it is based on two questions:

- Do the studies provide enough evidence of effectiveness?

- Do the results show that the product is safe (that the benefits outweigh the risks) when used according to the proposed labeling?

The FDA's review will have one of three outcomes. The FDA may tell the sponsor that the drug is approved. The drug is then placed on the market as soon as the manufacturer has production and distribution systems in place. The FDA may also tell the sponsor that the drug will be approved if minor changes are made, or that the drug cannot be approved because of major problems. At that point, the sponsor can either amend (change) or withdraw the NDA or ask for a hearing.

The approval process can be sped up for some promising experimental drugs. These drugs can be used in unrestricted studies that not only tell researchers more about the drug but that also make treatment available to people who have exhausted all available forms of treatment. These studies are used for drugs that treat serious or life-threatening diseases for which there is currently no viable treatment.

OTC drugs used to be approved using the same standards as prescription drugs. The FDA now classifies an OTC drug by treatment category (laxative, analgesic, etc.) and evaluates the ingredients. An OTC drug does not require specific approval as long as it meets the standards that the FDA has determined for the drug's category.

YEAST INFECTION MEDICINE

over-the-counter
drugs

A yeast infection is a common infection of a woman's vagina caused by overgrowth of the yeast Candida Albicans. This yeast is naturally present in the vagina, but it multiplies rapidly when there is a change in the pH or hormone balance. This rapid growth can also be caused by antibiotics or steroid therapy. Women with diabetes often experience yeast infections because the yeast also grows quickly when their blood sugar level is high. The symptoms of a yeast infection are itching, burning, and redness in the pubic area.

OTC yeast infection drugs, such as Vagisil, treat the symptoms, while drugs such as Monistat actually kill the yeast. Available in suppository form, these drugs can cause negative interactions with oral contraceptives (birth control pills) and antacids and should not be used by pregnant women.

OTHER COMMON OTC DRUGS

There are certain OTC drugs that are somewhat controversial in nature because they are known to be addictive (habit-forming) or because they have been linked to abuse and misuse, such as sleep aids and diet pills. There are other OTC drugs that a person might not naturally recognize as being an actual "drug," such as caffeine, which is considered a drug that, when misused, can have dangerous effects.

Caffeine and Caffeine-Based Stimulants

 HOW MUCH CAFFEINE?

Doctors recommend a daily caffeine intake of no more than 200 mg (milligrams) or less. How much caffeine is in what you eat and drink?

- Chocolate cake—1 slice   30 mg
- Cola—12 oz   45 mg
- Ice tea—5 oz   100 mg
- Coffee—6 oz   175 mg

Some OTC drugs have caffeine, too:

- Anacin   64 mg
- Excedrin   130 mg
- NoDoz   200 mg

Caffeine is classified as a drug by the FDA. An organic (natural) compound, caffeine has a stimulating (speeds up or excites) effect on the central nervous system, heart, blood vessels, and kidneys. Caffeine can also make a person feel more alert and less tired. It can also cause irritability, nervousness, jitters, headaches, anxiety, and insomnia (sleeplessness). Consumed in excess, caffeine can cause heart palpitations, diarrhea, and vomiting. Some research studies have suggested that caffeine plays a role in the development of birth defects, ulcers, breast disease, diabetes, heart disease, osteoporosis, and high blood pressure. Girls, in particular, should avoid consuming caffeine if they are experiencing PMS (Pre-menstrual Syndrome) as it can make the symptoms worse.

Because caffeine is found in many common products, it can be easy to consume too much of it. Coffee, tea, many soft drinks, chocolate, and many medications, such as pain relievers and weight loss aids, all contain caffeine. To help maintain alertness and prevent sleep, people often use OTC stimulant products containing caffeine. However, because of the side effects that accompany the excessive use of caffeine or any kind of stimulant, these products are intended for short-term use only.

Why do people use OTC stimulants to stay awake if they can drink coffee or have a caffeinated soft drink? Compared to caffeinated beverages, the caffeine used in brand name products such as Vivarin and NoDoz tends to be less irritating to the stomach than that which is found in coffee.

Nicotine and Nicotine-Replacement Products

Like caffeine, nicotine is also considered a drug. Nicotine is an organic compound found in tobacco leaves. These leaves are used to make cigarettes, chewing tobacco, and other tobacco-based products. Since nicotine is addictive, regular smokers tend to become addicted to nicotine. And, in spite of the fact that many people use tobacco on a regular basis, nicotine is highly toxic (poisonous) in large doses, which can cause vomiting, nausea, headaches, stomach pains, convulsions, paralysis, and even death. In fact, nicotine is toxic enough that it is a component in some insecticides.

The nicotine in cigarettes is what makes them highly addictive to smokers. (UPI/Corbis-Bettmann. Reproduced by permission.)

The very thing that causes smokers to become addicted to smoking, however, can be used to help them quit. Smoking provides a steady supply of nicotine, which causes smokers' bodies and brains to crave nicotine when they cease smoking. Often these cravings are so strong they make smokers very likely to start smoking again after they attempt to quit. Ironically, nicotine is used in nicotine replacement therapy (NRT) products. NRT products are temporary aids that are used on a regular schedule; they provide the body with nicotine but do so without necessitating the user to smoke. Over time, these products, which are available in many forms, including the patch, pills, and chewing gum, help lessen nicotine cravings and also help smokers move away from the actual habit of lighting up a cigarette or chewing tobacco. All of this contributes to the diminishment of withdrawal symptoms. In many of the products, the dosage of nicotine is gradually decreased to help smokers wean themselves off nicotine.

Sleep Aids

When people don't get enough sleep, they often feel tired, overwhelmed, and stressed out. In fact, too much stress could even be the reason they aren't getting enough sleep.

There are several types of sleep disturbances. Sleep disturbances fall under the sleep disorder category of insomnia, which is a difficulty falling or staying asleep or a disturbance in sleep that causes individuals to feel as though they did not get an adequate amount of sleep. Transient insomnia lasts only a few days and doesn't require treatment. This is usually the result of a temporary worry or discomfort from a minor illness. If people have chronic, or long lasting, lack of sleep, they need to see doctors instead of trying to treat the problem themselves. Chronic sleeplessness could be caused by psychological (mind-related) problems, such as severe anxiety or depression, or by a physical disorder.

MANY PEOPLE THINK THAT DRINKING WARM MILK WILL HELP THEM GET TO SLEEP. IN FACT, WARM MILK CONTAINS A CHEMICAL CALLED TRYPTOPHAN THAT MAY ACTUALLY DISTURB SLEEP INSTEAD OF PROMOTING IT.

Most OTC sleep aids work by interfering with the chemical activity in the brain and nervous system by limiting communication between the nerve cells. This reduction in brain activity allows a person to fall asleep more easily. Many sleep aids use the antihistamines diphenhydramine and doxylamine to depress brain function. (Antihistamines are drugs that relieve the symptoms of allergies or colds.) With this in mind, anyone taking antihistamines should not be taking sleep aids containing the same ingredient and vice versa. Sominex and Unisom are two examples of brand name sleep aids that contain antihistamines.

Transient insomnia, which lasts less than three weeks, is treatable with OTC sleep aids, which should be used only when lack of sleep is affecting a person's general health. The purpose of the sleep aids is to reestablish the habit of sleeping, and their effectiveness is reduced rapidly after the first few nights; this means that they work best for a limited time. OTC sleep aids should not be used for more than seven to ten days or by children under the age of twelve.

GETTING TO SLEEP NATURALLY

Here are some ways to promote sleep without using medication:

- Watch caffeine intake, and avoid consuming caffeine late in the day or at night.
- Avoid strenuous exercise for two to three hours before bedtime.
- Skip bedtime snacks.
- Try to go to bed at the same time each night.
- Minimize light and noise at bedtime.
- Do something relaxing before bed—reading, lounging, or taking a bath.
- Stop worrying! Try writing worries down to clear your mind before going to bed.
- Don't use bed for studying or watching TV.

Sleep aids, by virtue of their purpose, may cause drowsiness, slowed reactions, and slurred speech. Most people who use them are asleep within an hour of taking them. However, the sleep induced by sleep aids is not the same as the sleep one experiences when falling asleep naturally. Because of this, then, people taking sleep aids often feels less rested than if they had fallen asleep naturally. One reason for this may be that these drugs suppress rapid eye movement (REM) sleep, the stage of sleep during which people have dreams. All stages of sleep are important to awakening in the morning feeling rested.

Non-antihistamine sleep aids can be addictive if taken regularly for more than a few weeks or in large doses. This is a danger, as the effects of all OTC sleep aids will diminish after a few nights' use. This may prompt a user to take more than the recommended dose. When people who exceed the recommended dose stop taking these drugs after becoming dependent upon them, they may experience sleeplessness, anxiety, seizures or hallucinations. They may also have nightmares or vivid dreams because the amount of REM sleep suddenly increases again.

Some analgesic (pain-relieving) or anti-fever drugs can also induce sleep. These are most effective if pain is keeping a person from falling asleep. People should avoid these drugs if they have are allergic to aspirin or acetaminophen.

Weight Loss Aids

OTC weight loss aids are designed to suppress (restrain) the appetite. The main ingredient in weight loss drugs such as Dexatrim or Acutrim is phenylpropanolamine (PPA). PPA disrupts the hunger signals being sent by the brain and gives people a dry mouth, which makes food taste bland and unappetizing. The effectiveness of weight loss aids, particularly PPA, is a highly debated issue. One study showed that people using PPA lost only five pounds more than those who were not using the drug at all. Furthermore, PPA has been shown to be effective for only three months.

Another factor working against PPA is that low doses of it are not very effective, and high doses can cause nervousness, nausea, insomnia, headaches, and high blood pressure. Elevated blood pressure can lead to an increased risk for stroke and other cardiac problems in individuals predisposed to these ailments. Because all of these side effects will worsen with time, PPA is not to be used for more than three months, and it should not be used by anyone under the age of eighteen or over the age of sixty. Weight loss aids containing PPA should not be used in conjunction with cold and cough medicines, as many contain PPA as well, thus putting too much PPA into the consumer's system at once.

The FDA recently banned 111 other ingredients in OTC weight loss aids because their effectiveness could not be proven. These ingredients include

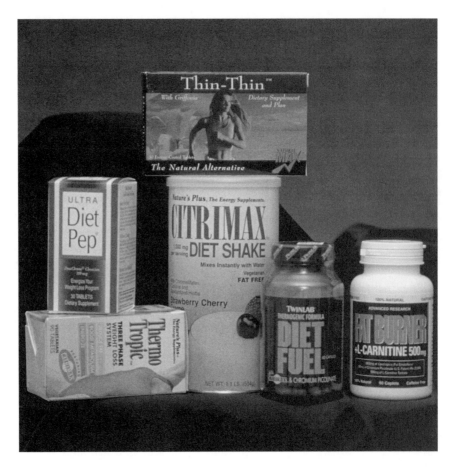

A sampling of common OTC weight loss products. (Photograph by Robert J. Huffman. Field Mark Publications. Reproduced by permission.)

alcohol, vitamin C, caffeine, sodium, and yeast. The FDA is still investigating PPA.

HERBAL MEDICINE

Many of today's drugs are derived from plants. Medicinal herbs are parts of plants that are used to treat illnesses and improve health. They have become ingredients in cosmetics, foods, teas, detergents, and even veterinary remedies. There is some controversy over the benefits of herbal medicines, and their effectiveness and safety have not been proven.

Herbal remedies are available in teas, syrups, decoctions (tough plant material that is boiled), tinctures (herbs steeped in alcohol and water), tonic wines, capsules, compresses, oils, ointments, creams, lotions, inhalants, and

An Echinacea flower. (Photograph by Robert J. Huffman. Field Mark Publications. Reproduced by permission.)

eyewashes. In general, herbal medicine is untested and unregulated. It can also have harmful interactions with similar synthetic (human-made) drugs. Always check with a physician before taking any herbal medicine.

Echinacea (Purple Coneflower)

Echinacea (pronounced ek-i-NAY-sha), known commonly as purple coneflower because of its color and shape, can be found growing on road banks, prairies, fields and dry, open woods of North America. Native Americans and early settlers used it to treat fevers, wounds, toothaches, sore throats, mumps, smallpox, measles and snakebites, which is why it is also called snakeroot. Echinacea boosts the body's immune system to help it fight off disease and has antibacterial properties as well. Early herbalists used the root of Echinacea to cleanse and heal wounds and also to treat skin disorders like boils and abscesses.

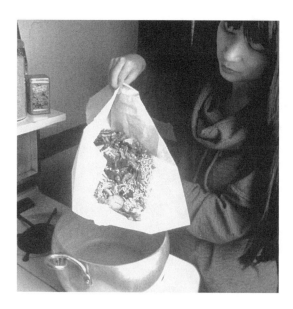

An herbalist prepares an herbal remedy. (Photograph © 1995 Eric Nelson. Custom Medical Stock Photo. Reproduced by permission.)

Studies have shown that Echinacea stimulates production of white blood cells, which fight infection, and increases the level of T-cells and other components of the immune system. Echinacea also improves the migration of white blood cells to attack foreign organisms and toxins. Furthermore, it inhibits an enzyme that destroys the natural barrier between healthy tissue and harmful organisms. Echinacea has mild antibiotic properties that are effective in treating staph and strep infections. In animal experiments, it has proven to be effective in inhibiting the growth of tumors.

Today's herbalists use this plant to treat viral, bacterial, and fungal infections such as colds, flu, and kidney infections. Echinacea helps the body defend itself against flu and may help reduce the runny nose and sore throat that accompany the flu. It can be helpful in treating tonsillitis, inflamed gums, and some forms of arthritis. Some herbalists recommend Echinacea for the treatment of chronic fatigue syndrome, indigestion, gastroenteritis, and for weight loss. It is applied externally to treat skin conditions such as burns, insect bites, ulcers, psoriasis, acne, and eczema, and there is even some evidence that it is helpful in treating allergies.

Echinacea is usually available as a tablet or tea. People who suffer from multiple sclerosis, AIDS, tuberculosis, or who are pregnant or nursing should not use Echinacea because it could trigger overactive autoimmune responses (the production of antibodies that attack the body's own cells and tissues). There are no other known side effects.

Ephedra (Ma Huang)

Ephedra (also known by its Chinese name Ma Huang) has been cultivated in China over the last 5,000 years. The dried young stems of the herb ephedra are used to treat sinusitis, colds, asthma, hay fever, and other allergies. It appears to have antibacterial properties and is the source

AROMATHERAPY

Aromatherapy is the use of fragrant, concentrated oils from parts of plants—such as their flowers, fruit, stalks, roots, and bark—for the purpose of improving a person's physical and emotional well-being. It is believed that aromatherapy has been used to increase well-being for thousands of years. The Egyptians were probably the first to use essential oils. These oils occur naturally in plants and are extracted from the flowers and leaves. They are believed to improve healing ability and have a beneficial effect on the human mind. Research has shown that they are effective in treating anxiety and depression by stimulating nerves that are linked to the parts of the brain that control emotions.

Essential oils should never be used internally. They are commonly used for massage, added to hot bath water, or used in a vaporizer.

of the synthetic (human-made) drug ephedrine, which is often used in de-congestants. However, in traditional Chinese medicine the entire plant is used, not just the isolated compound of ephedrine. The Chinese have used ephedra at the first sign of a cold or flu and to treat arthritis and fluid retention.

over-the-counter drugs

Ephedra indirectly stimulates the central nervous system. It is effective for treating asthma because it relaxes the airways. It also raises blood pressure, so people with hypertension (elevated blood pressure) or coronary thrombosis (a blockage in a vein or artery of the heart) should not use ephedra. People who are currently taking certain types of antidepressants or have glaucoma should not use ephedra either. Other possible side effects in-

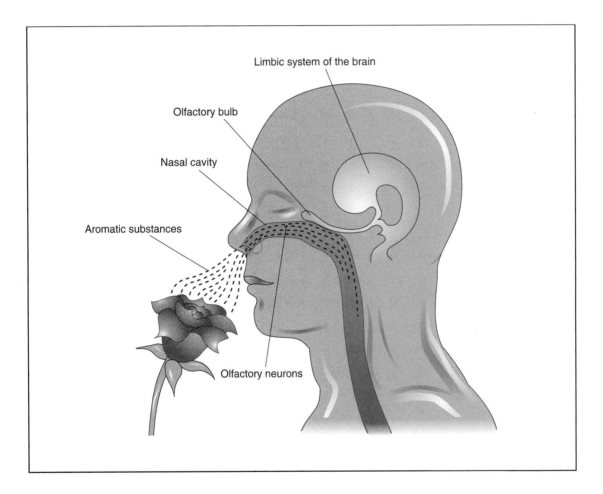

Aromatherapy is believed to benefit both the mind and body. Here, the smell from a flower stimulates the olfactory bulb and neurons (the parts of the nose and brain associated with the sense of smell). The desired emotional response (such as relaxation) is activated from the limbic system, the part of the brain thought to control emotional and behavioral patterns. (Electronic Illustrators Group. Reproduced by permission of Gale Group.)

clude headaches, irritability, restlessness, nausea, sleeplessness, and vomiting. Only adults and children over six years of age should use ephedra, and it is intended for short-term use only, because people can become dependent on it. Because of the possible side effects, ephedra is restricted in the United Kingdom, Australia and New Zealand. (Ephedra has not applied for FDA approval in the United States so its use is still unrestricted in most states.)

Feverfew

Feverfew is also known as featherfew or bachelor's buttons. It was first brought to the United States as an ornamental (decorative) plant. Clinical trials have shown that it is effective in the treatment of migraine headaches and reduces the frequency and severity of other headaches. Feverfew limits the release of the chemicals serotonin and prostaglandin in the body, which are believed to be the sources of migraine headaches. It also slows the production of histamine, so the inflammation that constricts the blood vessels in the head is reduced.

Feverfew is also known for offering relief from depression, nausea, and the pain of arthritis. Tea made from the herb is used to stimulate appetite and improve digestion and kidney function. It has been proven to lower blood pressure and cause less stomach irritation than aspirin or other pain relievers. It is believed to be helpful in treating dizziness, tinnitus (ringing in the ears), symptoms of premenstrual syndrome, asthma, and coughs.

Chewing fresh leaves of feverfew may cause mouth ulcers or loss of taste in the mouth, and pregnant women or people who are using anticlotting drugs should not take this herb.

Garlic

Although most people think of garlic as a seasoning, it is also known as nature's most versatile plant because of its medicinal uses. A member of the onion family, garlic is used to treat a wide range of health problems. It has been used for thousands of years to treat wounds, infections, tumors, and intestinal parasites. Today, clinical trials have shown that garlic lowers cholesterol and blood pressure, kills bacteria like antibiotics, and is an effective blood thinner, which reduces the risk of heart attacks and strokes. The National Cancer Institute is studying garlic as a treatment for stomach, skin, and colon cancer. Garlic is even used externally to treat corns, warts, calluses, muscle pain, and arthritis.

Garlic contains a chemical called amino acid allicin that is released when the bulb is crushed. This chemical gives garlic its strong odor and is responsible for garlic's antibacterial properties. Garlic also contains compounds of sulfur, vitamin A, and vitamin C, which combine to make it a strong antioxidant. Antioxidants protect the body at a cellular level from damage and disease.

This herb also stimulates the body's natural defenses. Garlic increases the activity of white blood cells and other components of the immune system. In fact, garlic is reported to be more effective than penicillin in the treatment of typhus disease. Garlic also helps the body fight off strep, staph bacteria, and the organisms responsible for cholera and dysentery. Many people use garlic to help prevent colds, flu, and other infectious diseases. Studies have shown that garlic stimulates the liver's production of detoxifying enzymes that the body uses to protect itself from carcinogens (cancer-causing agents) and other toxins.

Garlic may even have anti-cancer properties. It may prevent cells from turning cancerous by helping the body remove toxic substances. Many people believe garlic boosts immunity. The National Cancer Institute reported in 1992 that people who ate large amounts of garlic and onions seemed to have lower chances of getting stomach cancer.

Research has shown that garlic reduces "bad" cholesterol, or LDL, levels while raising the level of HDLs, or "good" cholesterol. Garlic is beneficial in any and all forms—raw, dried, oil, or in prepared pill form—but must be used for at least two or three months before its good effect on cholesterol becomes evident, and it may even raise cholesterol a bit at first, but it has none of the side effects of other cholesterol-lowering drugs. Garlic is also used as a blood thinner and to reduce blood clots and improve circulation. It lowers blood pressure by slowing the body's production of hormones that raise blood pressure. There have been clinical trials that show garlic can be used to effectively manage mild hypertension.

Garlic is even used to treat diabetes, urinary infections, acne, asthma, sinusitis, arthritis, ulcers, and respiratory infections like bronchitis, although its effectiveness has not been proven. It is used as a dietary supplement to maintain good circulation, reduce fat levels in blood, help resist infection, and balance out blood sugar and pressure. In large quantities, however, garlic can cause upset stomach.

Ginkgo Biloba

Ginkgo is indigenous (native) to China, Japan, and Korea. It is the oldest living tree species, and geologists (scientists who study the origin and structure of the earth) believe it has been around for 150 to 200 million years. Studies have shown that ginkgo helps prevent many health problems throughout the entire body.

Gingko increases blood flow through the network of blood vessels that carry blood and oxygen to the body's organs, including the brain. It boosts oxygen levels in the brain, which improves short- and long-term memory and increases reaction time. It is sometimes used to treat people with Alzheimer's disease and other problems with memory, absentmindedness, confusion, depression, headache, and difficulty with concentration. It is also used to treat tinnitus, dizziness and anxiety. Some people take ginkgo to combat mental fatigue and lack of energy.

The increased blood flow to other organs can improve circulation in the hands and feet, reduce swelling, and treat hemorrhoids, varicose veins, and chronic arterial blockage. It can help with complications from strokes and skull injuries. Gingko may be able to relax constricted blood vessels and reduce the amount of cholesterol that turns into plaque, which hardens the arteries. Furthermore, studies have proven that ginkgo helps improve eyesight by increasing the blood flow to the retinas, which slows their deterioration and increases vision. It also improves hearing in elderly patients. It is being tested as a potential treatment for asthma, toxic shock syndrome, and to help prevent transplanted organs from being rejected.

Ginseng (Panax)

This sweet-smelling herb is native to China, Russia, North Korea, Japan and some areas of North America. The name panax comes from the Greek word panacea, which means, "all healing." Ginseng has been used in various forms for more than seven thousand years, and it has known widespread use since the eighteenth century. Wild ginseng is rare, so the plants are cultivated (grown with the help of man). Ginseng roots are called Jin-chen, which means "like a man" because they are shaped like the human body. These roots can live for over 100 years.

Vitamins A, B6, and the mineral zinc are all found in ginseng. It also contains steroid-like ingredients that help balance and counter the effects of stress. Studies from China show that these ingredients increase production of proteins and activity of the brain's neurotransmitters. These actions help with memory and concentration, which can be impaired by inadequate amounts of blood supplied to the brain. Studies from Russia and London indicate that ginseng improves concentration and endurance.

Ginseng is often used as a tonic for people who are weakened by disease, old age, or stress. It is believed to help invigorate those who feel fatigued and are having difficulty working and concentrating. Siberian ginseng has been used since the 1930s to combat stress. It increases energy, stamina, and helps the body defend itself against infections and environmental toxins. Ginseng has both a soothing and stimulating ef-

Ginkgo in its natural form and in over-the-counter capsule form. (Photograph by Robert J. Huffman. Field Mark Publications. Reproduced by permission.)

fect on the central nervous system. Many people use this herb to improve mental performance, learning, memory, and sensory awareness. Too much ginseng, however, can cause sleeplessness.

Ginseng should not be used by people who have acute inflammatory disease or bronchitis, since the herb can actually make these problems worse. Pregnant women should not take ginseng.

St. John's Wort

St. John's Wort comes from a bushy perennial plant with yellow flowers that is native to Europe and the United States. Some people believe its name comes from early Christians who named it after St. John the Baptist and collected it on June 25, St. John's Day. Others believe its name comes from the Knights of St. John of Jerusalem, who used it to heal wounds during the Crusades (military campaigns undertaken by European Christians in the eleventh, twelfth, and thirteenth centuries). St. John's Wort has been used for centuries as a nerve tonic and has a wide range of other medicinal uses. Red extracts from the herb's blossoms are used externally as an anti-inflammatory to treat burns, wounds, and joint problems. It soothes burns by lowering the temperature of the skin. St. John's Wort is being tested to determine how effective it is in the treatment of immune deficiency problems. This herb has antiviral and antibacterial properties and is even being studied as a possible treatment for AIDS.

Today, St. John's Wort is commonly used as a mild antidepressant. Studies have shown that it can be effective in treatment of people suffering from mild to moderate depression. Reports show there was some improvement in the sadness, helplessness, hopelessness, anxiety, headaches, and exhaustion experienced by people with mild depression when taking St. John's Wort, and without any reported side effects.

The active ingredient in St. John's Wort is hypericin, which increases the theta waves in the brain. These waves usually occur while a person is asleep and are associated with meditation, pleasure, and increased creative ability. The herb also contains monoamine oxidase, which affects the brain's seratonin. Both of these chemicals act similarly to the synthetic chemicals in prescription drugs used to treat depression. St. John's Wort should never be taken with other antidepressants, and it is not effective in treating severe depression. It is best to discuss symptoms with a doctor to determine if, and at what level, one is experiencing depression.

St. John's Wort is also used to repair nerve damage and reduce pain and inflammation, such as menstrual cramps and arthritis. It also affects the secretion of bile to soothe the digestive system. In folk medicine, the blossoms of St. John's Wort are used to treat ulcers, gastritis, diarrhea, and nausea. The oil of the plant is sometimes applied to sprains, bruises, and varicose veins to relieve inflammation and promote healing.

This drug should not be used by women who are pregnant or nursing, or by people who are taking antidepressants such as Prozac. Long-term use (more than four to six weeks) of St. John's Wort may cause photosensitivity, which is an increased sensitivity to sunlight. It may also cause constipation, and fair-skinned people may be more susceptible to sunburns.

FOR MORE INFORMATION

Books

Adderley, Brenda D. *Doctor's Guide to OTC Drugs*. Warner Books, 1998.

Hill, Clare. *The Ancient and Healing Art of Aromatherapy*. Ulysses Press, 1998.

Leber, Max, et al. *Handbook of Over-The-Counter Drugs and Pharmacy Products*. Celestial Arts, 1995.

Ody, Penelope. *Home Herbal*. London: Dorling Kindersley Limited, 1995.

Sifton, David W. *The PDR Guide to Over-the-Counter Drugs*. Ballantine Books, 1998.

Web sites

Food and Drug Administration. [Online] http://www.fda.gov/ (Accessed September 10, 1999).

10

Alternative Medicine

While conventional health care is still thought by many to be the primary option for treating an illness, particularly in the United States, many people throughout the world seek alternative medical solutions to their physical ailments. In fact, alternative medicine is now becoming a widely accepted form of health care. Much of this acceptance has been prompted by a worldwide crisis in terms of quality health care, a crisis that has taken hold of the United States as well as Third World and developing nations. Prohibitively expensive conventional medical care has prompted many people to seek alternative means to cure their ailments. Often times, this decision is motivated by more than a lack of health insurance. People suffering from chronic (long-lasting or frequently recurring) conditions or life-threatening diseases will often seek out alternative treatment when they have exhausted all the possibilities that conventional care has to offer and have found those possibilities to be inadequate.

What is interesting about the growing acceptance of alternative medicine is that practices now deemed "alternative" were for thousands of years considered standard medical practices. However, as world population continues to expand and health care concerns grow, it is likely that alternative treatments will continue to expand in popularity and acceptance by lay (non-medical) persons and medical professionals alike.

Alternative medicine includes systems of medical care such as homeopathy and naturopathy, as well as acupuncture, chiropractic, massage therapy, reflexology, and yoga, all of which are explained in the sections that follow.

Homeopathy

Naturopathy

Acupuncture

Chiropractic

Massage Therapy

Reflexology

Yoga

HOMEOPATHY

Homeopathy is a system of natural remedies that centers around two basic laws. The first is the law of similars, which is built around the principle that "like cures like," meaning that a disease is cured by medicines that have the properties of producing in healthy persons some symptoms similar to those of the disease. For example, if an individual has a fever, is flushed, and has a high pulse rate, that person would be treated with an agent that would cause a healthy person to have similar symptoms. The second law is the law of infinitesimals, which states that medicines are more effective in smaller doses.

History of Homeopathy

Homeopathy grew out of a movement known as sectarian medicine. (Sectarian medicine can be compared to what today is called alternative medicine. That is, sectarian medicine was set apart from conventional medicine.) In the 1800s, sectarian medicine included Thomsonianism (the foundation for herbal medicine, based on the healing arts practiced by Native American women and popularized in mainstream society in the early nineteenth century by New Hampshire farmer Samuel Thompson, 1769–1843). Sectarian medicine also embraced Grahamism (named after Sylvester Graham (1794–1851), which advocated proper nutrition and hygiene to fight disease and sickness).

Homeopathy began its rise to popularity in America in the late 1840s, but Samuel Hahnemann (1755–1843), a German conventional physician, had created the practice in the late eighteenth century. Homeopathy grew out of

WORDS TO KNOW

Acupuncture: A form of alternative medicine that involves stimulating certain points, referred to as acupoints, on a person's body to relieve pain and promote healing and overall well-being.

Allopath: A kind of doctor who advocates the system of medical practice making use of all measures that have proved to be effective in the treatment of disease.

Alternative medicine: Medical practices that fall outside the spectrum of conventional allopathic medicine.

Artificial: Human-made; not found in nature.

Blood vessel: Vessel through which blood flows.

Chiropractic: A way of treating certain health conditions by manipulating and adjusting the spine.

Cholera: Any of several diseases of humans and domestic animals usually marked by severe gastrointestinal symptoms.

Electromagnetic: Magnetism developed by a current of electricity.

Genetic predisposition: To be susceptible to something because of genes.

Holistic: Of or relating to the whole rather than its parts; holistic medicine tries to treat both the mind and the body.

Homeopathy: A system of natural remedies.

Hormone: Substances formed in certain glands that control bodily functions.

Hypothesize: To make a tentative assumption in order to draw out and test its logical or observable consequences.

Infinitesimals: Immeasurably small quantity or variable.

Inherent: Belonging to the essential nature of something.

Iridology: The study of the iris of the eye in order to diagnose illness or disease.

Hahnemann's opposition to the medical practices of his peers, practices that were conventional but had grown from heroic medicine (see sidebar), which Hahnemann considered to be extremely crude in certain aspects.

Hahnemann's major homeopathic discovery came about while he was conducting an experiment involving cinchona, a Peruvian bark that was known to cure the disease malaria. Hahnemann had been ingesting the cinchona (he did not have malaria at the time) and found that he began to develop fevers similar to those suffered by people with malaria. When he ceased ingesting the cinchona, Hahnemann observed that the symptoms ended. This prompted Hahnemann to hypothesize (form an educated guess) that if taking a large dose of something brought on symptoms of a disease, then taking a small amount of that same substance would prompt one's body to use its defenses against that same disease. Of course, many years of experiments followed, years that led Hahnemann to form the two basic laws of homeopathy (listed above) as well as the holistic principle (emphasizing the whole of something is more important than any one of its parts) that each illness is specific to the individual.

One of Hahnemann's students, Dr. Constantine Hering, considered the father of American homeopathy, continued Hahnemann's work, bringing homeopathy to America in the early part of the nineteenth century. By 1835,

Kinesiology: The study of anatomy in relation to movement of the body.

Massage therapy: The manipulation of soft tissue in the body with the aim of relieving and preventing pain, stress, and muscle spasms.

Mortality: The number of deaths in a given time or place.

Naturopathy: A kind of alternative medicine that focuses on the body's inherent healing powers and works with those powers to restore and maintain overall health.

Neurosis: An emotional disorder that produces fear and anxiety.

Noninvasive: Not involving penetration of the skin.

Physiology: A branch of science that focuses on the functions of the body.

Plaster: A medicated or protective dressing that consists of a film (as of cloth or plastic) usually spread with a medicated substance.

Qi (or Chi): Life energy vital to an individual's well-being.

Reflexology: A type of bodywork that involves applying pressure to certain points, referred to as reflex points, on the foot.

Sectarian medicine: Medical practices not based on scientific experience; also known as alternative medicine.

Subatomic: Relating to particles smaller than atoms.

Suppress: To stop the development or growth of something.

Symptom: Something that indicates the presence of an illness or bodily disorder.

Vertebra: A bony piece of the spinal column fitting together with other vertebrae to allow flexible movement of the body. (The spinal cord runs through the middle of each vertebra.)

Yoga: A form of exercise and a system of health that involves yoga postures to promote well-being of body and mind.

Hering had opened the first homeopathic medical school in the United States. Less than ten years later, the American Institute of Homeopathy (which was the first national medical association in America) was formed.

The success of homeopathy in combating several widespread epidemics helped popularize the practice. In 1849, an outbreak of cholera in Ohio proved homeopathy's validity when only 3 percent of those treated homeopathically died from the disease; compared with a mortality rate of 40 to 70 percent for those treated with conventional, or allopathic, health care methods. Similar success was seen in New Orleans, Louisiana, in 1879 when homeopaths (as practitioners of homeopathy are called) treated 1,945 people with yellow fever with a mortality rate of only 5.6 percent; conventional treatment used during the same epidemic yielded a 16 percent mortality rate.

Benjamin Rush. (Library of Congress)

HEROIC MEDICINE

When one thinks of going to the doctor, it is most likely a conventional, or allopathic, physician that the individual will be seeing. However, up until the late eighteenth century, most medicine could be considered sectarian, or alternative. Thereafter, however, allopathic medicine, or conventional health care, which stems from heroic medicine, began to rise in popularity.

Heroic medicine was an inexact branch of medicine practiced in the early nineteenth century, the forerunner to today's conventional medicine. Heroic medicine was called such because heroic measures were taken to cure a patient. The foundation of heroic medicine was that all diseases resulted from an excess of fluids in the body, and the cure was to relieve the body of the excesses through bloodletting (the letting of someone's blood in the [false] belief that it was a remedy for fever, inflammation, and other disorders) and purging. In heroic medical practices, doctors did not hesitate to add to a patient's pain in the name of a cure; furthermore, natural causes and treatments were completely discounted. Many people believed heroic methods worked as the treatments did provide visible and predictable effects (though not necessarily cures).

For example, Dr. Benjamin Rush (also a signer of the Declaration of Independence), a major figure in heroic medical practices, advocated the use of bloodletting on women in the throes of childbirth as he viewed childbirth as a disease. Rush also utilized techniques such as blistering the skin with camphor and tartar plasters on a patient's chest (when blisters or second-degree burns appeared, Rush concluded that the infection had been drawn out because of the appearance of pus in the blisters).

Another factor lending itself to the popularity of homeopathy is that there long existed in the traditional medical practice community a prejudice and misunderstanding toward women and ailments particular to their bodies. Women's frustration with traditional health care, coupled with the fact that women, as the primary child-rearing force in the home, typically made the health care choices within their families, led many to seek out homeopathic solutions for their children's ailments. Thus, this too led to the surge in homeopathy.

Homeopathy soon became so popular that books on the practice appeared in several languages, some of which even offered up cures for animals' ailments. By the turn of the twentieth century, there were almost one hundred homeopathic hospitals and twenty-two homeopathic medical schools in the United States. It is also estimated that nearly 15 percent of American physicians were engaging in homeopathic practices at the time.

By the 1930s, homeopathy's popularity had begun to decline due to competition from conventional medicine and the American Medical Association (see sidebar on page 274). However, in the 1990s, homeopathy, like many other age-old alternative health care practices, enjoyed a growing resurgence in the United States and around the world.

Principles of Homeopathy

LAW OF SIMILARS. Hahnemann's law of similars actually stems from the observations and studies of another great medical mind, Hippocrates (c. 460–377 B.C.), who observed the law of similars in the fourth century B.C. The notion that "like treats like" has been proven again and again, specifically by scientific minds of the twentieth century, such as Jonas Salk (1914–1995) with his invention of the vaccine against polio. Salk and others who have developed similar vaccines use small amounts of the actual disease to help an individual's body "immunize" itself against the disease. For example, individuals who receive allergy shots today often receive small amounts of an allergen (the allergy-causing substance) to boost their bodies' tolerance to that allergen.

LAW OF INFINITESIMALS. The law of infinitesimals states that medicines are more effective in smaller doses and involves using trace amounts of a substance. A mixture is prepared by using one part of a particular substance that brings on the symptoms of a disease and mixing

Samuel Hahnemann. (UPI/Corbis-Bettmann. Reproduced by permission.)

it with ninety-nine parts of either pure water or alcohol. This procedure is then repeated anywhere from twenty-four to thirty times to further dilute the mixture. The process also involves shaking the substance vigorously, something Hahnemann believed imbued the mixture with energy.

Critics of homeopathy have wondered how homeopathy actually works, if after twenty-four successive dilutions of a remedy are performed, there is virtually no trace of the original substance remaining in the remedy; therefore, the so-called remedy is actually only water and/or alcohol. Advocates of homeopathy have proposed theories that center on subatomic activity that takes place within the remedies themselves. Specifically, it has been suggested that structures form in the remedies that are capable of holding electromagnetic signals that may carry a message to the body, prompting the body's immune system to respond appropriately.

HOLISTIC DIAGNOSES. The holistic principle that is also employed by homeopathy centers around the fact that not all illnesses are alike even though they may fall into similar categories. For example, one person's headache should not be treated in the same manner as another person's headache as their symptoms will never be identical. In fact, according to homeopathic theory, there are more than two hundred diverse patterns of symptoms for headaches alone, with different remedies for each pattern.

HERING'S LAWS OF CURES. Dr. Hering introduced yet another principle to the practice of homeopathy with Hering's laws of cures. These laws of

THE ALLOPATHS VS. THE HOMEOPATHS

The American Institute of Homeopathy, founded in 1844, was the first formal medical association in the United States. It wasn't until 1847 that the American Medical Association (AMA) was founded, some say in large part to combat the popularity of homeopathy. In fact, by examining historical records, it appears that the primary mission of the AMA at its inception was to abolish the practice of homeopathy. The zeal with which the AMA attacked homeopathic medicine was due, in large part, to financial considerations. The homeopaths were taking business away from conventional allopathic physicians. Still, many allopathic physicians did embrace homeopathic solutions to illness.

By the early twentieth century, however, competition between medical schools, hospitals, and practitioners was on the rise. The AMA discouraged allopaths from associating professionally with homeopaths. And to compound matters, the AMA forged a bond with many major pharmaceutical companies. This bond centered on a mutually beneficial financial relationship; doctors received free samples of drugs and endorsed certain pharmaceuticals while the pharmaceutical companies purchased advertisements in the *Journal of the American Medical Association.* These advertisements gave the AMA the financial power it needed to improve its medical schools.

Soon, rating systems for medical colleges were created. These ratings contributed to the closing of the less financially stable homeopathic medical schools and organizations. By the 1930s, homeopathy had faded from the American medical field.

cures upheld that healing begins from the deepest part of the body and then moves toward the extremities. Likewise, healing originates with emotional and mental aspects before moving to physical aspects; and finally, healing begins at the head and works its way down to the feet.

Another element of these laws includes Hering's assertion that the body will begin to heal its most recent disorder before moving to an older, preexisting condition. All of this means, then, that a homeopath will treat a condition in layers (from the inside to the outside, from the new to the old, from the top to the bottom, etc.). Yet, Hering also postulated that, as healing begins (new and old), a patient's condition might worsen before it gets better. This is what is known as the "healing crisis."

Homeopathy Helps Many Conditions

Homeopathy has been touted as being effective in treating a variety of diseases, from skin disorders to asthma to arthritis to diabetes. Practitioners believe this is so because it cures a disease at its deepest level. Many conditions, however, upon which homeopathic remedies have proven effective center around colds, influenza, or the flu, headaches, digestive disorders, and hay fever.

Other research indicates success in using homeopathic remedies to treat Parkinson's disease, bronchitis, sinusitis, pain, and rheumatoid arthritis.

Homeopathy Today

Currently, more than 500 million people in the world have received or are seeking homeopathic treatment for their illnesses. The World Health Organization has recommended that homeopathy be integrated into conventional medical practices so that health care demands worldwide will be met by the early twenty-first century.

Homeopathy is widespread in Europe, particularly in Germany, France, and Britain. Britain has a national health care system that includes homeopathic hospitals and clinics. India, too, has long advocated homeopathy; the country has more than 25,000 homeopaths. Homeopathy is also popular in Mexico and parts of South America.

In the United States, homeopathy, although its popularity is growing, still faces challenges. The Food and Drug Administration's lengthy approval process (*see* Chapter 9: Over-the-Counter Drugs) requires a great deal of funding. Many homeopathic remedies are extremely inexpensive (thus, unprofitable for a manufacturer) so the likelihood of homeopathic remedies appearing on pharmacy shelves is less than that of traditional over-the-counter or prescription drugs. As health care reform continues to be a topic of discussion in the United States, and individuals continue to explore and embrace alternative medicine, homeopathy may once again become an integral part of American health care practices.

Naturopathic medicine, or naturopathy, is another alternative form of medicine that differs from allopathic medicine. Naturopathy, like most alternative medicine, has been around for thousands of years and is one of the oldest types of medical practices. In fact, naturopathy is more a combination of various healing practices than a single method; it encompasses homeopathy as well as other alternative health care practices, such as acupuncture (see section below) and therapeutic exercises, such as yoga (see section below). Naturopathy focuses on the body's inherent (natural) healing powers and works with those powers to restore and maintain overall health.

Six Principles of Naturopathy

Naturopathic doctors, or N.D.s, do not use artificial drugs or perform surgery. Rather, the practice of naturopathy is based on six main principles that take into account many different aspects of a person's body and lifestyle.

NATURE'S HEALING POWER. Naturopathic physicians believe that the body has the power to heal itself by using its own life force. The role of the naturopathic physician, however, is very important to help the body in its healing process. The naturopathic physician tries to uncover any factors preventing good health or recovery from an illness and tries to combat those factors. In addition, the physician helps a person create a lifestyle and an environment that promotes good health.

IDENTIFY AND TREAT THE CAUSE OF ILLNESS. Naturopathic physicians know that an illness does not occur without a cause. Causes, however, must not be confused with symptoms. Symptoms are signs that the body is trying to heal itself. For example, when an illness is present in the body, a symptom will appear, such as a fever, stuffed-up nose, or a cough. These symptoms are signs that the body is trying to fight the illness. The philosophy behind conventional medicine is to suppress and, therefore, relieve symptoms, but an important doctrine of naturopathic medicine is that symptoms should be left alone so that the causes of an illness can be uncovered. Causes may be rooted in physical, spiritual, or emotional problems. By identifying the cause and then treating it, proper healing and recovery can occur.

FIRST DO NO HARM. Because naturopathic physicians believe that the body will heal itself once the cause of the illness is identified and treated, trying to suppress symptoms is considered harmful. Physicians are committed to treating a person in a way that is complementary with the body's own healing process. Any practice that does not support the body's natural healing process is avoided at all times by naturopathic physicians.

TREAT THE WHOLE PERSON. Naturopathic physicians aim to treat the whole of a person, not just the part that is ailing. For this reason, healing involves the examination of many different factors in a person's life. These factors can be environmental, social, genetic, spiritual, mental, and/or physical in nature. The physician must address each of these factors to heal an illness. It is not until all these factors are working together in harmony that a person can be assured good health.

DOCTOR AS TEACHER. While naturopathic physicians are important in promoting good health, they have a responsibility to their patients to educate them in the practices of maintaining health. The role of the patient is equally as important in achieving good health because it is the patient who ultimately must accomplish the healing. As a result, the relationship between physician and patient must be caring, understanding, and respectful. Through education and encouragement, the naturopathic physician can give the patient the wisdom and hope he or she needs to embrace and practice good health.

HISTORY OF NATUROPATHIC MEDICINE

Benedict Lust (1872–1945) is considered the father of naturopathic medicine. Even though the practice has been around for thousands of years, it was Lust who established the first official school of naturopathic medicine in the United States. In fact, he coined the term naturopathy in 1902.

Lust learned about naturopathic medicine by studying in Europe under Father Sebastian Kneipp. Kneipp had pioneered a philosophy of health, which was referred to as the "nature cure." This philosophy believed that good nutrition, exercise, and regular exposure to sun and air were essential to good health. These factors later became the basis of Lust's naturopathic medicine. In fact, Lust recovered from a bout of tuberculosis by following Kneipp's philosophy of hot- and cold-water treatments. When the cured Lust returned to America, he and his wife started the Yungborn Nature Cure Health Resort in New York. The resort was very successful, and three years later Lust opened the first school to teach others naturopathic medicine.

The popularity of naturopathic medicine grew in the next few years and more than twenty schools opened by 1925. The outbreak of World War II (1939–45), though, contributed to a reliance on medicine based more on science and technology. Prescription drugs, such as antibiotics, and surgical procedures became the preferred method of medical treatment in part because of their effectiveness in treating the soldiers who were wounded or fell ill during the war. Many believed at the time that medical science would soon find cures for most known diseases. As a result of these developments, naturopathic medicine suffered, and its popularity declined sharply as the American Medical Association (AMA) worked to establish itself as the main authority of medicine.

A resurgence in naturopathic medicine occurred in the late 1970s. At this time, many people became discontented by science and technology and more interested in all things natural and organic. As a result, more conventional medical schools began to offer courses in alternative medicine and naturopathy. In the 1990s, Americans spent billions of dollars on alternative health care, believing that good health involves one's diet and lifestyle and that one should take an active role in maintaining good health. Currently, there are approximately one thousand practicing naturopaths in the United States.

PREVENTION IS THE BEST CURE. The final principle focuses on prevention (preventing illness before it strikes), which is at the root of naturopathic medicine. By promoting health through prevention, instead of working to combat disease and illness after the fact, naturopathic physicians can help their patients achieve good health. The naturopathic physician helps the patient identify any risk factors, such as genetic predisposition to disease or environmental hazards, that can be avoided. With the proper steps, a physician can help a patient avoid these risk factors and prevent illness and disease.

SPECIALTIES OF NATUROPATHY

Naturopathic medicine has many different specialties which include:

- Clinical nutrition: Uses food and nutritional supplements to treat illness.

- Physical medicine: Focuses on the muscles, bones, and spine, using massage, exercise, heat, water, and cold to heal.

- Homeopathy: Works to strengthen the body's immune system by giving natural medicine that produces similar symptoms to what the body is already feeling in order to treat an illness.

- Botanical medicine: Uses plants as medicines to treat illness.

- Naturopathic obstetrics: Offers natural alternatives before, during, and after childbirth that do not involve any drugs and take place outside of a hospital.

- Chinese medicine: Follows ancient beliefs that unify the body and the mind and restore balance to the body's energy force, referred to as Qi. Includes acupuncture and acupressure.

- Psychological medicine: Uses counseling and different types of therapies to achieve mental and emotional health.

- Environmental medicine: Focuses on helping people deal with the toxic elements that are part of their environment and may be causing certain illnesses.

What Happens During a Naturopathic Doctor Visit?

Naturopathic doctors handle their patients differently from allopathic doctors. When a person makes an appointment with a naturopathic doctor, the N.D. will spend a few hours with the patient, during which time the N.D. takes a complete medical history. The N.D. will also discuss the details of the patient's symptoms and then proceed with a physical examination.

The N.D. will also conduct what is called a constitutional intake. This is a series of in-depth questions that explore the patient's lifestyle and diet. The constitutional intake will allow the N.D. to better understand the patient in order to recommend the right treatment for that person.

Once the questioning is complete and the physical examination has taken place, the N.D. will discuss treatment and a course of recovery. The patient is encouraged to take an active role in promoting good health. The N.D.'s responsibility is to make sure the patient has the information needed to heal. It is also normal for future visits to be scheduled so that the N.D. can monitor the patient's progress.

The Benefits and Limitations of Naturopathy

Naturopathy has many different benefits, from physical and mental to financial. Sometimes, patients find that conventional medicine isn't providing them with the care they need or that conventional therapies are failing as treatment. For these patients, naturopaths can offer a different type of treatment—one that is nontoxic and noninvasive. Because naturopaths focus on prevention and a holistic approach to treatment, patients may find better results with naturopathic methods. Naturopathic treatments are less expensive than conventional treatments because natural drugs do not cost as much as prescription medicines, which are manufactured by pharmaceutical companies, and because naturopaths do not rely on high-technology medical equipment to treat their patients.

Because naturopaths must learn a great deal about their patients' lives, they tend to be more involved with their patients. Part of their training involves counseling and communications skills, which enables them to develop a strong relationship with patients and, therefore, be in a better position to help them.

JOHN AND WILL KELLOGG WERE EARLY ADVOCATES OF NATUROPATHY. THE KELLOGGS, ALONG WITH C. W. POST, A FORMER EMPLOYEE, WENT ON TO START COMPANIES THAT PRODUCED BREAKFAST CEREALS THAT REFLECTED NATUROPATHIC PRINCIPLES.

Naturopaths do have their limits, however. Sometimes naturopaths must refer their patients to allopathic doctors, especially when patients need surgery. Naturopaths are not licensed or trained to perform surgery. For example, if a patient breaks a bone, an allopathic doctor has to set the bone, while the naturopath doctor can assist with the recovery process.

ACUPUNCTURE

Acupuncture is a form of alternative medicine that involves stimulating certain points, referred to as acupoints, on a person's body to relieve pain and promote healing and overall well-being. These points are most often stimulated by thin needles and are found along twelve pathways in the body, called meridians. According to acupuncturists, these pathways have energy, called Qi (or Chi; both pronounced chee), flowing through them. For the body to be healthy, it is important for the flow of Qi to be balanced, and needling of acupoints helps to balance the flow of energy. Acupuncture also aids in balancing yin and yang, opposite forces that make up all things, including the human body.

Acupuncture has become popular in the United States in recent years. It has been found to help relieve pain and restore and maintain health. Many people use acupuncture in combination with other forms of treatment and have found it helps them recover from their conditions at a faster rate. Acupuncture has been found to help include headaches, drug addictions, asthma, tonsillitis, nausea, paralysis, stomach ailments, and even the common cold. In a few cases, it has even been used to control pain during surgeries performed in Asian countries. Mental conditions, such as depression and anxiety, have also been treated with acupuncture.

Yin and Yang

Chinese medicine has been influenced by the Chinese philosophy Taoism. In Taoism, it is believed that everything is made up of yin and yang. Yin is all things dark, negative, and feminine. Yang is all things light, positive, and masculine. One cannot exist without the other. However, one may overpower the other and create an imbalance. Acupuncturists believe if yin and yang are not balanced within a person, he or she will be more prone to illness or disease. Acupuncture helps to restore yin and yang balance.

Qi: Life Energy

As well as having balanced yin and yang, a person should be concerned with having balanced Qi, or life energy. In English, Qi has been called "life

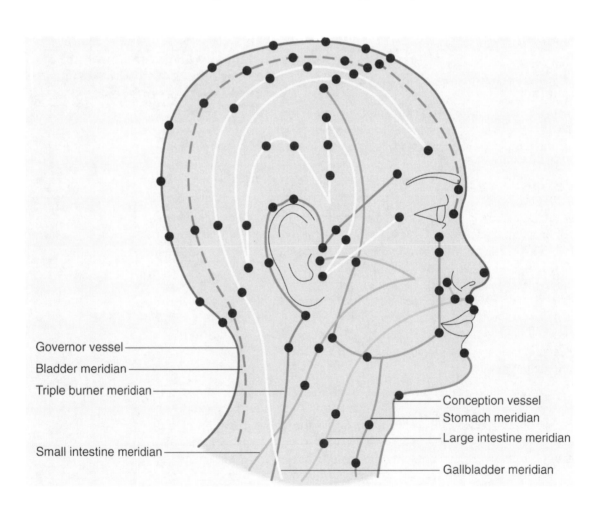

Acupuncture sites and meridians on the face and neck. (Electronic Illustrators Group. Reproduced by permission of Gale Group.)

energy," "vital life energy," "life force energy," or "life activity." This energy is invisible and is considered vital to each person. Acupuncturists believe that a balanced flow of this energy is important to a person's health. If the flow is interrupted at any point, some parts of the body are going to be affected and not function at their best. This may lead to illness or disease. In order to restore health, Qi must be rebalanced. The practice of acupuncture, then, works to rebalance the flow of Qi and allow the body to naturally heal itself.

The Ancient History of Acupuncture

Acupuncture goes as far back as five thousand years and was developed by the ancient Chinese as a form of medicine. Ancient Chinese practitioners mapped out acupoints, the places on the body to be stimulated. Researchers have found that these points have more nerve endings than other areas of the skin. These acupoints total more than 365; some say there are as many as one thousand points. Acupuncture was developed and used in China for many years before it spread to neighboring countries and eventually to Europe and the United States. The first introduction of acupuncture in the United States occurred during the 1700s, but it wasn't until the twentieth century that it became a popular form of medical treatment.

Stimulating Acupoints: Needles and Other Ways

Acupuncturists most often stimulate points on a person's body with needles that are as thin as a hair. Early needles were made of stone, bamboo, iron, silver, or even gold. Today, acupuncture needles are made of stainless steel and are typically used only once and then thrown away. Not all of the needles are straight. One type, called a staple, is round with a small needle and can be attached to the ear so the patient can wear it out of the office. This type of needle can be worn for about two weeks and is used often with patients who suffer from addictions, such as nicotine addiction.

Other ways of stimulating the points include using pressure with hands (acupressure), electrical stimulation, lasers, magnet therapy, drug needling, and moxibustion. In electrical stimulation, a weak electric current is sent into the acupoint to stimulate it. In laser acupuncture a laser is used instead of a needle to stimulate a point. Magnet therapy has the acupuncturist placing magnets over the acupoints for stimulation. Drug needling is when herbal medicine or vitamins are injected into the acupoints, and moxibustion is when the mugwort herb is burned and placed on the head of the needle in order to send heat into the acupoint.

A PRESIDENT'S SEAL OF APPROVAL

Acupuncture sharply increased in popularity in the United States following President Richard Nixon's (1913–1994) trip to China in 1970. During this trip, one of the people from the Nixon group needed to have an appendectomy, a procedure in which the appendix is removed. During the operation, pain was controlled by the use of acupuncture. After seeing the effects of acupuncture on his colleague, Nixon returned to America and made an effort to increase public awareness of acupuncture.

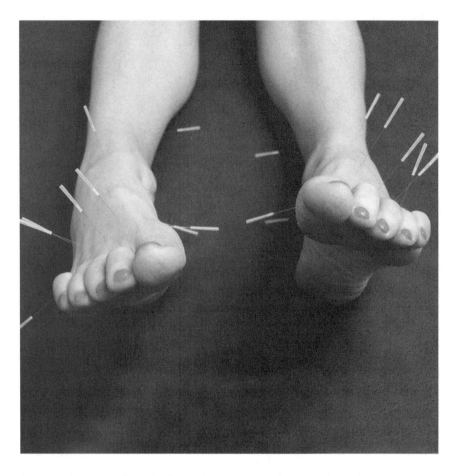

Acupuncturists most often stimulate points on a person's body with needles that are as thin as a hair. (UPI/Corbis-Bettmann. Reproduced by permission.)

What Does Acupuncture Feel Like?

Surprisingly, acupuncture is not painful. Acupuncturists are trained in the proper insertion of the needles so they don't cause pain. However, patients will feel a tingling sensation and possibly some cramping or heaviness in the area of the needle. Typically, the needles are inserted about one-quarter to one inch deep into the skin. The acupuncturist will usually insert only about twelve needles during one session. The placement of the needles depends upon a patient's condition. For example, if a patient is suffering from back pain, the needles may be placed in the leg. Once the needles are placed in their appropriate acupoints, the acupuncturist may twirl them to stimulate the acupoints even more. The idea of having needles inserted into a person's body may not sound appealing, but it is not as scary as it looks, and it is thought to offer great benefits to the body.

[*See also* Acupuncturist section in Chapter 7: Health Care Careers.]

CHIROPRACTIC

Chiropractors, practitioners of chiropractic medicine, are commonly known to help patients with back problems. While many clients of chiropractors are people with back problems, chiropractors claim to be able to ease all kinds of health conditions. They do this by manipulating and adjusting the spine. Chiropractors believe that if the spinal column is in the correct position then the nerves in the spine may function at their best, which in turn allows other bodily systems to function at their best. Therefore, chiropractors may treat a variety of conditions, including back, shoulder, and neck pain, as well as headaches, sports injuries, heart disease, allergies, and epilepsy.

alternative
medicine

What Is Chiropractic?

Chiropractic is a way of treating certain health conditions. The word chiropractic comes from Greek origins and means "done by hand." This is a good description of how chiropractors treat their patients. They use their hands to manipulate and adjust the spinal columns of their patients. According to chiropractors, vertebrae (the bones forming the spinal column) can become slightly misaligned and cause problems with nerve function since the spinal cord (which carries nerve impulses to and from the brain) runs through the vertebrae of the spinal column. Chiropractors call these misaligned vertebrae that affect the flow of nerves subluxations. It is believed that subluxations block some messages from the brain as they are routed through the nerves in the spine. This means that, depending on where the subluxation is located, certain organs are not receiving all of their vital messages from the brain. When this happens, the organs are not functioning at their best and may start to have problems. These problems can, in turn, result in illness or disease.

Chiropractors try to fix subluxations by using quick thrusts with their hands or applying pressure to the problem area on the spine. Once the spine is in the correct position, chiropractors believe nerve function will improve and the body will be able to fight illness and disease better. Thus, chiropractors do not heal the illness or disease; they work to have a person's body functioning at its best so it can naturally heal itself.

The History of Chiropractic

Chiropractic got its start in 1895 by Daniel David Palmer (1845–1913). A faith healer (a person who treats patients using prayer and faith

ACUPUNCTURE AND YOUR EAR

One form of acupuncture, called auricular acupuncture, focuses on stimulating the ear instead of the whole body. French neurophysiologist Paul Nogier, M.D., mapped out certain points on the ear. He founded auricular acupuncture after he noticed that by stimulating certain points on the ear different parts of the body received a benefit of increased energy flow. This increase in energy flow is thought to improve health. A similar type of therapy to auricular acupuncture is reflexology. In this practice, reflexologists stimulate certain areas on the feet in order to provide benefits to the whole body. (See the Reflexology section in this chapter.)

in God) from Davenport, Iowa, Palmer founded chiropractic after he restored hearing in a man, Harvey Lillard, by realigning part of his spinal column. Lillard had suffered a work injury many years before that resulted in his hearing loss. When Palmer examined him, he found a painful area on Lillard's spine. By thrusting on the area with his hands, Palmer was able to adjust the spine and Lillard's hearing returned. From this experience Palmer formed his beliefs that would become the foundation for the practice of chiropractic. He even started the first chiropractic school in the United States in 1897.

Part of Palmer's chiropractic beliefs were spiritual. He believed that every human has a life force that flows through the nervous system. He called it "innate intelligence." According to Palmer, a balanced flow of this life force is important for good health. Since innate intelligence flows through the nervous system, it can be affected if the spinal column is not aligned properly. Thus Palmer believed that by realigning the spine, chiropractors would be improving nerve function as well as rebalancing the innate intelligence.

After Palmer founded chiropractic, his son, B. J. Palmer, carried on his father's beliefs and heavily promoted the practice. However, he did not work to create a relationship with practitioners of conventional medicine. Instead, he spoke out against medical doctors and their use of drugs to heal illnesses and disease. Chiropractors' rocky relationship with medical professionals was further shaken when, in the 1960s, the AMA deemed it unethical for their members to work with any chiropractors and sought to expose problems in chiropractic beliefs. A lawsuit was eventually filed by five chiropractors against the AMA and other similar associations for violating their rights. The chiropractors won the lawsuit and chiropractic has since established itself as the most popular form of alternative medicine in the United States. There are now more than 50,000 chiropractors in the United States, the third largest group of health care practitioners in the nation.

EARLY HEALING THROUGH THE SPINE

Treating health conditions by working with the spine occurred before the founding of chiropractic. It has been documented that people of ancient Egypt and ancient Greece manipulated the spine to promote healing, as did Europeans during the Middle Ages (c. 500–1450). Native Americans were also known to manipulate the spine before chiropractic practices were formalized in 1895 by Daniel David Palmer.

What Happens During Treatment?

Treatment by a chiropractor includes manipulation and adjustment of the spinal column and other joints and muscles as well as counseling in nutrition and other areas to promote healthy living. Chiropractors are trained to provide painless treatments. Before working on the patient's spine, a chiropractor will ask the patient about his or her medical history and perform a physical examination. A chiropractor will also create a treatment plan for each patient.

As well as feeling for displaced vertebrae with their hands, chiropractors often rely on

X rays to locate misalignments in the spine. After locating problem areas, a chiropractor will have a patient lie on his or her stomach; the practitioner will then try to reposition the spine. Chiropractors may also use other forms of treatment in addition to manipulation with their hands. These may include massage, electrical stimulation, traction (a pulling force applied to a part of the body), ice, heat, or ultrasound.

[See also Chiropractor section in Chapter 7: Health Care Careers.]

MASSAGE THERAPY

Massage therapy is defined as the manipulation of soft tissue in the body with the aim of relieving and preventing pain, stress, and muscle spasms. In addition, massage therapy works to improve blood circulation and the body's ability to recover from illness and injury. There are many physical as well as psychological benefits to massage therapy, which will be discussed later in this section.

The practice of massage therapy has been around for thousands of years. Even ancient Greek and Roman civilizations recognized the many benefits of massage and often participated in massage after exercising or competing in athletic games. While massage therapy is considered an alternative treatment, many conventional physicians now encourage patients to seek out massage therapy for illness and injury. According to a survey in the *Journal of Alternative and Complementary Medicine,* there are forty-nine conventional medical schools that offer courses in massage therapy. Furthermore, conventional doctors refer patients to massage therapists for a wide variety of problems, including allergies, asthma, arthritis, carpal tunnel syndrome, headaches, insomnia, stress, bronchitis, chronic pain, and constipation.

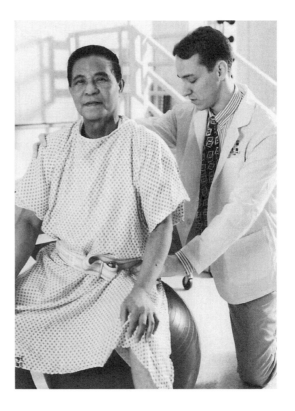

The use of a balance ball can help strengthen a patient's back muscles, which help support the spine. (Custom Medical Stock Photo. Reproduced by permission.)

The Different Types of Massage

There are many types of massage therapy, and each one uses a different technique to achieve a similar result. These include, but are not limited to, Swedish massage, reflexology, shiatsu and acupressure, and sports massage. Swedish massage, perhaps the most well known and popular type of massage, combines knead-

Boxer Evander Holyfield receives a pre-event massage from one of his trainers. (UPI/Corbis Bettmann. Reproduced by permission.)

ing and stroking of the muscles with movement of the joints. Reflexology focuses on certain points on the hands and feet that are connected to other areas on the body. Shiatsu and acupressure are Asian techniques that apply pressure to certain points on the body that correspond with acupuncture meridians. Meridians are the channels through which the body's energy, or Qi, flows. Finally, sports massage focuses on improving an athlete's performance, preparing an athlete for a specific event, and helping the particular muscles that are used in a certain sport.

The Physical Benefits of Massage Therapy

There are many physical benefits to massage therapy. Massage therapy's rhythmic movements and applied pressure help increase one's blood circulation. It also helps blood vessels to expand, allowing more blood to pass through them. In addition to increased blood circulation, massage therapy works to increase lymph (a white substance that carries the body's toxins away) flow. Since lymph, unlike blood, does not move on its own, it must be stimulated through muscle movement, or exercise and massage. The increased flow of blood and lymph has a positive effect on the body's cells, which contribute to a person's overall health. More blood means more oxygen and more lymph means less waste and toxins.

Massage can be particularly important when a person is involved in an exercise regimen or participates in a sport on a regular basis. When muscles are being used more often, there is an increase in certain acids that build up in the tissue if the muscles do not get the oxygen they need. If these acids remain in the muscle tissue, cramping, soreness, and fatigue generally follow. Massage can help to drain the muscle tissues of these acids and thus help muscles recover more quickly.

 ## THE INS AND OUTS OF SPORTS MASSAGE

As professional and amateur athletes strive to reach their peak performance, sports massage therapy works to keep their bodies in top shape. Massage helps athletes perform better, avoid injuries, and recover more quickly from minor injuries. The three main areas of sports massage therapy are maintenance massage, event massage, and rehabilitation massage.

Maintenance massage is used to improve an athlete's flexibility and range of motion. A trained therapist knows how to focus on the particular muscle groups that different types of athletes use most often. This allows athletes to train more effectively and prevent possible injuries.

Event massage includes two categories: Pre-event massage and post-event massage. Pre-event massage helps athletes prepare for a big event by increasing their blood circulation and releasing any muscle tension that may be present before a big event. Post-event massage reduces muscle spasms that may occur and helps athletes' muscle tissues recover from the event. This allows athletes to be ready to compete in the next event. Both pre-event and post-event massage enable athletes to compete at their best while reducing the risk of injury.

Rehabilitation massage is used when athletes suffer from injuries, such as muscle tears, cramps, bruises, and aches. Even the best athletes have injuries, and it is a sports massage therapist's job to help athletes recover quickly. Massage is used simultaneously with proper medical care and helps the muscle tissue heal by removing lymph fluid (a white substance that carries the body's toxins away). Finally, rehabilitation massage can make the recovery process less painful for the athlete, which helps to restore the mental edge that athletes need in order to perform their best.

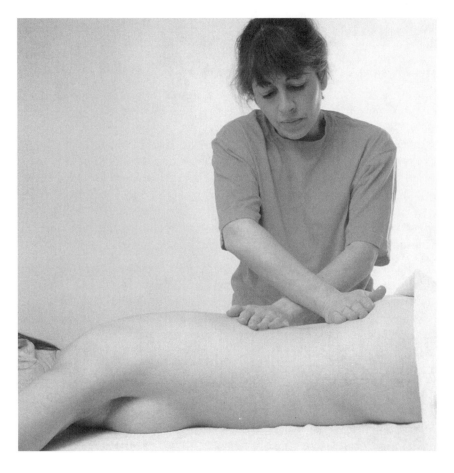

A massage therapist works a client's lower body. (Photograph by Paul Biddle. Custom Medical Stock Photo. Reproduced by permission.)

Another important aspect of overall health is good nutrition. Giving the body the proper vitamins and nutrients will help it function properly. Massage therapy can increase the benefits of good nutrition by helping the nutrients reach their destination: the cells. As mentioned, massage expands the blood vessels, which increases circulation. By having a clear and open path, nutrients have an easier time finding the cells that work to keep the body healthy.

The Psychological Benefits of Massage Therapy

In addition to physical benefits, there are many psychological, or mental, benefits to massage therapy. The most obvious benefit is stress relief. Stress affects everyone, young and old alike. Frustrations can build in many aspects of a person's life, whether it be job, family, friends, or school. Stress prompts the release of certain hormones that cause blood vessels to shrink. The shrinking of blood vessels results in poor circulation, which can greatly harm a person's overall health. Research has indicated that stress is a main cause of certain illnesses, such as migraine headaches, depression, high blood pressure, constipation, and other digestive disorders. Massage therapy can help to reduce the risk of these illnesses. Massage therapy also helps people release repressed, or built-up, emotions, which can result in an overall sense of relaxation and peace.

REFLEXOLOGY

Reflexology is a type of body therapy that involves applying pressure to certain points, referred to as reflex points, on the foot. Many people seek reflexology for relaxation and to improve their health and well-being. It is thought that by pressing points on the feet, impulses are sent through pathways to certain areas of the body, increasing energy and health in those areas. During treatments, patients may even feel tingling sensations in the parts of the body to which the impulses are being sent. Reflexology is thought to help anxiety, asthma and allergies, chronic pain, diarrhea and constipation, high blood pressure, migraine headaches, premenstrual syndrome (PMS), skin problems, and stress.

The Roots of Reflexology

Reflexology is approximately as old as acupuncture, which has been around for the past five thousand years. Like acupuncture, reflexology has its roots in China, but evidence has been found indicating that reflexology was also used in Egypt as far back as 2330 B.C. Reflexology was first devel-

WHAT HAPPENS DURING A MASSAGE?

Massage therapists work hard to make sure their clients feel comfortable when receiving a massage. Clients usually are asked to remove most of their clothing during the massage. However, if this makes clients feel uneasy, therapists can provide a towel or sheet to cover up their clients, leaving only the body part being massaged exposed. Some clients like to have complete quiet during a massage while others enjoy music. Therapists will accommodate their clients in every way possible, providing soft music or total silence. Oils and lotions may also be used if the client wants, but these things are not necessary to a good massage.

While some clients prefer not to talk during a massage, a successful session often relies on good communication between the client and the therapist. A good therapist should answer any questions a client has and lay to rest any anxiety the client may have.

Overall, the most important thing for a good massage is for the therapist to be well trained in the areas of anatomy (study of the human body), physiology (study of bodily functions and processes), and kinesiology (study of human movement). Also, the therapist should be sensitive to a client's needs and open to feedback to promote overall health for the client.

oped in the United States by William Fitzgerald, M.D., in 1913. Fitzgerald had begun to realize that his patients would feel less pain when pressure was applied to certain areas of the body, such as the hands or feet, before surgery. Deciding to research this further, Fitzgerald conducted some experiments and concluded that pressing points on certain areas of the body produced beneficial effects in other areas of the body. Fitzgerald called this "zone therapy."

Physiotherapist Eunice Ingham further developed Fitzgerald's zone therapy into the practice that is known today as reflexology. During the 1930s, Ingham used zone therapy and concluded that applying pressure to the feet yields the best results to the body. She also asserted that it is better to vary the amount of pressure applied and that greater benefits than just pain relief occurred from applying pressure to the feet. Ingham then mapped out the reflex points on the feet to be pressed and the specific areas of the body that relate to the points on the feet. Thus reflexology was officially born in the United States.

How Does Reflexology Work?

Students of reflexology are trained to know the correct points to press on the foot. They may refer to foot reflexology charts that show which areas of the foot should be pressed and which organs will be affected if a certain area of the foot is pressed. The reflex points on the feet are located on the bottom as well as the top and sides of the feet. Reflexologists are taught that pressing points on the right foot affects organs on the right side of the body and pressing points on the left foot affects organs on the left side of the body. They also learn that different points on a foot relate to different organs in the body. For

THE BENEFITS OF MASSAGE FOR BABIES

Massage therapy for premature babies (babies that weigh less than five pounds at birth) is a relatively new phenomenon, pioneered by Dr. Tiffany Field, a child psychologist who founded the Touch Research Institute at the University of Miami Medical School. Its mission is to research the medical benefits of touch and further its role in the treatment of illness and disease. Field's thinking, however, has quickly caught on with both parents and the medical community. Although doctors believed for many years that premature babies were so fragile that it would be harmful to touch them at all, this belief has been challenged by the tremendous benefits massage has produced with such babies. According to the Touch Research Institute, premature babies who are massaged three times a day develop more quickly by gaining weight faster than those preemies who are not massaged. Babies who receive massage also develop better mental and motor skills just months after their births.

Massage not only benefits premature babies, but it also aids all babies by helping them sleep better and generally be more relaxed. While the benefits of massage therapy for babies seem to be evident, many hospitals still do not have programs that incorporate this therapy, and even if they do, many insurance companies won't cover the costs. As a result, many new parents are taking classes to learn how to massage their babies at home.

example, if a reflexologist presses an area just below the three middle toes, the eyes and ears may be affected, and if the tips of the big toes are pressed, the head and brain are affected. Sending impulses to these areas is thought to allow the organs to perform better and thus contribute to healing or maintaining the health of the body.

According to reflexologists, other benefits of reflexology include the reduction of lactic acid in the feet. Lactic acid is a waste product produced from using muscles and too much of it can cause problems, such as stiffness. Reflexologists also believe there are tiny calcium crystals that build up at the nerve endings of the feet and cause problems in energy flow. They claim reflexology helps to break up these crystals and restore healthy energy flow.

OTHER MAPS TO THE BODY

Reflexology is not the only practice that sees one part of the body as a map for the entire body. In Chinese and Indian medicine, many practitioners examine the tongue as a way to determine the health of the rest of the body. In iridology, practitioners use the iris of the eye to diagnose disease in other parts of the body. The colon has also been thought to show signs if another part of the body is suffering from an illness. Auriculur acupuncture (see Acupuncture section) focuses on the ear in order to restore or maintain health in the entire body.

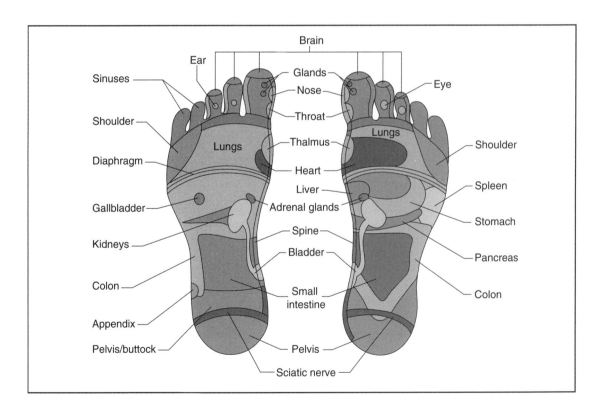

Reflexology charts show the areas of the foot that should be pressed in order to affect certain organs. (Electronic Illustrators Group. Reproduced by permission of Gale Group.)

Although many people today are embracing yoga solely as a form of exercise, yoga is actually considered to be a system of health, such as homeopathy or reflexology. In the United States, yoga has slowly grown in popularity; however, in Eastern cultures, such as India, yoga has always been a common practice.

The term yoga means "union" in the Sanskrit language, and it refers to the relationship of physical, mental, and spiritual energies that enhance all facets of an individual's well-being. Dating back to the second century B.C., when a writer named Patanjali wrote the *Yoga Sutras,* one of yoga's primary philosophies is that the health of the mind and the body are linked together and that one cannot function properly if the other does not. Proponents of yoga claim, then, that its practices can restore this balance between body and mind and promote overall health.

Yoga Postures

Yoga postures are known as asanas (often categorized as Hatha yoga). In Sanskrit, the word asana means "ease." Asana refers not only to postures but also to exercises that revolve around these postures to promote positive change in the body. Asanas often entail a limited amount of movement from participants, but at all times the body and the mind remain engaged, working together to achieve a state of simultaneous energy and relaxation.

When an asana is done correctly, it is designed to create a perfect balance between movement and stillness. Two types of asanas used today are meditative and therapeutic.

MEDITATIVE ASANAS. Meditative asanas are used to properly align the head and the spine. In turn, they also promote a state of relaxation that may be influenced by the improved circulation these postures elicit. This means that while the mind is at rest, the body's major organs and glands are enjoying a great deal of energy.

THERAPEUTIC ASANAS. Initially used to introduce the body into a relaxed state prior to meditation, therapeutic asanas (which include the popular shoulder stand and lotus positions) can also be used to ease pain in the back, joints, and neck. In fact, holistic practitioners often prescribe these positions to their patients as a way of alleviating such pain. Therapeutic asanas were originally referred to as cultural asanas; however, their applicability to pain reduction has contributed to the change in their name.

Breathe Easy

Controlling one's breathing in yoga is called pranayama, which refers to the control of prana, or the life force/life energy. Breath control is practiced in yoga to help yogis (experienced practitioners of yoga) regulate their autonomic

Meditation is best done in a quiet place where a person can feel comfortable and relaxed. (Photograph by Robert J. Huffman. Field Mark Publications. Reproduced by permission.)

physical functions (heart rate, for example). Yoga philosophy suggests that controlling one's breathing to make it slow and steady results in having a relaxed mind. Therefore, yogis try to perfect their breathing using smooth motions that promote an evenness of breath. It is believed that this, in turn, promotes a serenity (calmness) of the mind and raises concentration and energy at the same time. This is why breath control is integral to the practice of meditation.

Meditation is Concentration

Once a yogi has mastered his or her breathing and the appropriate postures, the yogi can move on to meditation. Meditation refers to a state of heightened concentration in which many practitioners enjoy feelings of peace and awareness. Meditation creates a state in which yogis can focus fully on the balance between the mind and the body.

Expert yogis strive to achieve the final stage of yoga, known as samadhi. In this stage, the yogi is believed to realize a state of awareness (consciousness) that is above those states of dreaming, sleeping, and wakefulness. Samadhi is the fourth stage of consciousness.

Yoga's Benefits to the Body

Yoga's benefits to the body are numerous, according to proponents of the practice. Like any type of physical activity, yoga promotes a certain degree of muscle strength. Even more so, yogis enjoy a great deal of flexibility, and flexible muscles lead to improved posture. In fact, a common trait in yogis is their exceptional posture that resonates from the top of their heads down to their feet. While yoga is not considered to be an aerobic (cardiovascular) exercise, people engaging in yoga often break a sweat and, like any activity, yoga does burn calories, which further promotes fitness.

Yoga has also been credited with diminishing symptoms of and suffering from certain physical conditions. Specifically, many studies have been built around yoga's positive effects on reducing the blood pressure in those suffering from hypertension. Other physical conditions thought to be improved by yoga, according to the Yoga Biomedical Trust survey (1983–1984), include back pain, arthritis and rheumatism, migraines, menstrual disorders, premenstrual syndrome (PMS), asthma and bronchitis, hemorrhoids, cessation of smoking, and obesity.

Yoga's Benefits to the Mind

It is only natural that yoga has direct benefits to a person's mental health and well-being since the practice centers around unity between the body and the mind. Because it employs breathing techniques and meditation, yoga helps reduce people's overall stress, anxiety, and insomnia. Furthermore, advocates of yoga claim that it improves concentration as well, allowing individuals to focus clearly and easily on a thought or a task at hand.

FOR MORE INFORMATION

Books

The Burton Goldberg Group. *Alternative Medicine: The Definitive Guide.* Tiburon, Calif.: Future Medicine Publishing, Inc., 1997.

Cargill, Marie. *Acupuncture: A Viable Medical Alternative.* Westport, CT: Praeger, 1994.

Cassileth, Barrie. *The Alternative Medicine Handbook: The Complete Reference Guide to Alternative and Complementary Therapies.* New York: W.W. Norton, 1998.

Facklam, Howard. *Alternative Medicine: Cures and Myths.* New York: Twenty-First Century Books, 1996.

Kastner, Mark and Hugh Burroughs. *Alternative Healing: The Complete A-Z Guide to More than 150 Alternative Therapies.* New York: Henry Holt, 1996.

Murray, Michael T. and Joseph E. Pizzorno. *Encyclopedia of Natural Medicine,* 2nd ed. New York: Prima Publishing, 1997.

Wolfson, Evelyn. *From the Earth to Beyond the Sky: Native American Medicine.* New York: Houghton-Mifflin, 1993.

Web sites

American Association of Naturopathic Physicians. [Online] www.naturopathic .org (Accessed October 1, 1999).

American Massage Therapy Association. [Online] http://www.amtamassage .org (Accessed October 1, 1999).

American Yoga Association. [Online] http://users.aol.com/amyogaassn/ (Accessed October 1, 1999).

Homeopathy Online. [Online] http://www.lyghtforce.com/HomeopathyOnline/ (Accessed October 1, 1999).

Office of Alternative Medicine at the National Institutes of Medicine. [Online] http://altmed.od.nih.gov/oam (Accessed October 1, 1999).

Reflexology Association of America. [Online] http://members.xoom .com/_XOOM/reflexusa (Accessed October 1, 1999).

Bibliography

BOOKS

General

Adderholt-Elliot, Miriam and Jan Goldberg. *Perfectionism: What's Bad About Being Too Good.* Minneapolis, MN: Free Spirit Publishing, 1999.

Davitz, Lois Jean, Joel R. Davitz, Lois Leiderman Davitz, and Jo Davitz. *20 Tough Questions Teenagers Ask: And 20 Tough Answers.* Minneapolis, MN: Paulist Press, 1998.

Holm, Sharon Lane (Illustrator) and Faith Hickman Brynie. *101 Questions Your Brain Has Asked About Itself but Couldn't Answer. . .Until Now.* Brookfield, CT: Millbrook Press, 1998.

Kalergis, Mary Motley. *Seen and Heard: Teenagers Talk About Their Lives.* New York: Stewart Tabori & Chang, 1998.

McCoy, Ph.D., Kathy, and Charles Wibbelsman, M.D.(Contributor). *Life Happens: A Teenager's Guide to Friends, Failure, Sexuality, Love, Rejection, Addiction, Peer Pressure, Families, Loss, Depression, Change and Other Challenges of Living.* Perigee Paperbacks, 1996.

Parsley, Bonnie M., Scott Peck. *The Choice Is Yours: A Teenager's Guide to Self Discovery, Relationships, Values, and Spiritual Growth.* New York: Fireside, 1992.

Roehm, Michelle (Editor) and Marci Doane Roth (Illustrator). *Girls Know Best: Advice for Girls from Girls on Just About Everything.* Beyond Words Pub. Co., 1997.

Roehm, Michelle (Editor) and Marianne Monson-Burton (Editor). *Boys Know It All: Wise Thoughts and Wacky Ideas From Guys Just Like You.* Beyond Words Pub. Co., 1998.

Turner, Priscilla (Editor), and Susan Pohlmann (Editor). *A Boy's Guide to Life: The Complete Instructions.* New York: Penguin USA, 1997.

Eating Disorders

Chiu, Christina. *Eating Disorder Survivors Tell Their Stories.* (The Teen Health Library of Eating Disorder Prevention). Minneapolis, MN: Hazelden Information Education, 1999.

Davis, Brangien. *What's Real, What's Ideal: Overcoming a Negative Body Image.* (The Teen Health Library of Eating Disorder Prevention). Minneapolis, MN: Hazelden Information Education, 1999.

Erlanger, Ellen. *Eating Disorders: A Question and Answer Book About Anorexia Nervosa and Bulima Nervosa.* Minneapolis, MN: Lerner Publications Company, 1988.

Frissell, Susan and Paula Harney. *Eating Disorders and Weight Control.* (Issues in Focus). Springfield, NJ: Enslow Publishers, Inc., 1998.

Harmon, Dan and Carol C. Nadelson. *Anorexia Nervosa: Starving for Attention.* (Encyclopedia of Psychological Disorders). New York: Chelsea House Publishers, 1998.

Kaminker, Laura. *Exercise Addiction: When Fitness Becomes an Obsession.* (The Teen Health Library of Eating Disorder Prevention). Minneapolis, MN: Hazelden Information Education, 1999.

Kolodny, Nancy J. *When Food's a Foe: How You Can Confront and Conquer Your Eating Disorder.* Boston, MA: Little Brown & Co., 1998.

Moe, Barbara. *Understanding the Causes of a Negative Body Image.* Hazelden Information Education. Minneapolis, MN: Hazelden Information Education, 1999.

Monroe, Judy. *Understanding Weight-Loss Programs: A Teen Eating Disorder Prevention Book.* Minneapolis, MN: Hazelden Information Education, 1999.

Patterson, Charles. *Eating Disorders (Teen Hot Line).* Chatham, NJ: Raintree/Steck Vaughn, 1995.

Smith, Erica. *Anorexia Nervosa: When Food is the Enemy.* Minneapolis, MN: Hazelden Information Education, 1999.

Sneddon, Pamela Shires. *Body Image: A Reality Check.* (Issues in Focus.) Springfield, NJ: Enslow Publishers, Inc., 1999.

Stanley, Debbie. *Understanding Anorexia Nervosa.* Minneapolis, MN: Hazelden Information Education, 1999.

Stanley, Debbie. *Understanding Bulimia Nervosa.* Minneapolis, MN: Hazelden Information Education, 1999.

Habits and Behaviors

Connelly, Elizabeth Russell, Beth Connolly, and Carol C. Nadelson. *Through a Glass Darkly: The Psychological Effects of Marijuana and Hashish.* (Encyclopedia of Psychological Disorders). New York: Chelsea House Publishers, 1999.

Holmes, Ann, Carol C. Nadelson (Editor), and Claire E. Reinburg (Editor). *Cutting the Pain Away: Understanding Self-Mutilation.* (Encyclopedia of Psychological Disorders). New York: Chelsea House Publishers, 1999.

Klein, Wendy. *Drugs and Denial.* (Drug Abuse Prevention Library). New York: The Rosen Publishing Group, 1998.

Peacock, Nancy, Carol C. Nadelson (Editor), and Claire E. Reinburg. *Drowning Our Sorrows: Psychological Effects of Alcohol Abuse.* New York: Chelsea House Publishers, 1999.

Snyder, Solomon H. (Editor) and P. Mick Richardson. *Flowering Plants: Magic in Bloom.* (Encyclopedia of Psychoactive Drugs, Series 1.) New York: Chelsea House Publishers, 1992.

Wilkinson, Beth. *Drugs and Depression.* Minneapolis, MN: Hazelden Information Education, 1997.

Mental Health

Adler, Joe Ann. *Stress: Just Chill Out!* (Teen Issues). Springfield, NJ: Enslow Publishers, 1997.

Barrett, Susan L., Pamela Espeland (Editor), and J. Urbanovic (Translator). *It's All in Your Head: A Guide to Understanding Your Brain and Boosting Your Brain Power.* Minneapolis, MN: Free Spirit Publishing, 1992.

Carlson, Dale Bick, Carol Nicklaus (Illustrator), and R. E. Mark Lee. *Stop the Pain: Teen Meditations.* Madison, CT: Bick Pub House, 1999.

Carlson, Dale Bick, Hannah Carlson, and Carol Nicklaus (Illustrator). *Where's Your Head?: Psychology for Teenagers.* Madison, CT: Bick Publishing House, 1998.

Espeland, Pamela and Elizabeth Verdick. *Making Every Day Count: Daily Readings for Young People on Solving Problems, Setting Goals, and Feeling Good About Yourself.* Minneapolis, MN: Free Spirit Publishing, 1998.

Hipp, Earl, Pamela Espeland, and Michael Fleishman (Illustrator). *Fighting Invisible Tigers: A Stress Management Guide for Teens.* Minneapolis, MN: Free Spirit Publishing, 1995.

Kincher, Jonni and Pamela Espeland (Editor). *Psychology for Kids II: 40 Fun Experiments That Help You Learn About Others.* Minneapolis, MN: Free Spirit Publishing, 1998.

Kincher, Jonni, Bach, Julie S. (Editor), and Steve Michaels (Illustrator). *Psychology for Kids: 40 Fun Tests That Help You Learn About Yourself.* Minneapolis, MN: Free Spirit Publishing, 1995.

Krulik, Nancy E. *Don't Stress! How To Keep Life's Problems Little.* New York: Scholastic Trade, 1998.

Miller, Shannon (Introduction), Nancy Ann Richardson (Contributor). *Winning Every Day: Gold Medal Advice for a Happy, Healthy Life!* New York: Bantam Doubleday Dell, 1998.

Packard, Gwen K. *Coping With Stress.* Minneapolis, MN: Hazelden Information Education, 1997.

Policoff, Stephen Phillip. *The Dreamer's Companion: A Young Person's Guide to Understanding Dreams and Using Them Creatively.* Chicago: Chicago Review Press, 1997.

Romain, Trevor and Elizabeth Verdick. *What on Earth Do You Do When Someone Dies?* Minneapolis, MN: Free Spirit Publishing, 1999.

Mental Illness

Connelly, Elizabeth Russell and Carol C. Nadelson. *Conduct Unbecoming: Hyperactivity, Attention Deficit, and Disruptive Behavior Disorders.* (Encyclopedia of Psychological Disorders). New York: Chelsea House Publishers, 1998.

Garland, E. Jane. *Depression Is the Pits, But I'm Getting Better: A Guide for Adolescents.* Washington, D.C.: Magination Press, 1998.

Gellman, Marc, Thomas Hartman, and Deborah Tilley (Illustrator). *Lost and Found: A Kid's Book for Living Through Loss.* New York: Morrow Junior, 1999.

Holmes, Ann, Dan Harmon, and Carol C. Nadelson (Editor). *The Tortured Mind: The Many Faces of Manic Depression.* (Encylopedia of Psychological Disorders). New York: Chelsea House Publishers, 1998.

Kaminker, Laura. *Exercise Addiction: When Fitness Becomes an Obsession.* (The Teen Health Library of Eating Disorder Prevention). Minneapolis, MN: Hazelden Information Education, 1999.

Moe, Barbara. *Understanding the Causes of a Negative Body Image.* Minneapolis, MN: Hazelden Information Education, 1999.

Monroe, Judy. *Phobias: Everything You Wanted to Know, but Were Afraid to Ask.* (Issues in Focus). Springfield, NJ: Enslow Publishers, Inc., 1996.

Nardo, Don. *Anxiety and Phobias.* (Encyclopedia of Psychological Disorders). New York: Chelsea House Publishers, 1992.

Porterfield, Kay Marie. *Straight Talk About Post-Traumatic Stress Disorder: Coping With the Aftermath of Trauma.* Checkmark Books, 1996.

Silverstein, Alvin, Virginia Silverstein, and Laura Silverstein Nunn. *Depression.* (Diseases and People.) Springfield, NJ: Enslow Publishers, Inc., 1997.

Wilkinson, Beth. *Drugs and Depression.* Minneapolis, MN: Hazelden Information Education, 1997.

Sexuality

Baer, Judy. *Dear Judy, Did You Ever Like a Boy (Who Didn't Like You?).* Minneapolis, MN: Bethany House, 1993.

Basso, Michael J. *The Underground Guide to Teenage Sexuality: An Essential Handbook for Today's Teens & Parents.* Minneapolis, MN: Fairview Press, 1997.

Carlson, Dale Bick, Hannah Carlson, and Carol Nicklaus (Illustrator). *Girls Are Equal Too: How to Survive Guide for Teenage Girls.* Madison, CT: Bick Pub House, 1998.

Fenwick, Elizabeth and Robert Walker. *How Sex Works: A Clear, Comprehensive Guide for Teenagers to Emotional, Physical, and Sexual Maturity.* DK Publishing, 1994.

Gravelle, Karen, Nick Castro (Contributor), Chava Castro, and Robert Leighton (Illustrator). *What's Going on Down There: Answers to Questions Boys Find Hard to Ask.* New York: Walker & Co., 1998.

Harris, Robie H. *It's Perfectly Normal: Changing Bodies, Growing Up, Sex, and Sexual Health.* Candlewick Press, 1994.

Pogany, Susan Browning. *Sex Smart: 501 Reasons to Hold Off on Sex.* Minneapolis, MN: Fairview Press, 1998.

WEB SITES

ADOL: Adolescence Directory On-Line. http://education.indiana.edu/cas/adol/adol.html

The American Dietetic Association. http://www.eatright.org

Better Health. http://www.betterhealth.com

Centers for Disease Control and Prevention. http://www.cdc.com

Channel One. http://channelone.com/

The Children's Health Center. http://www.mediconsult.com/mc/mcsite.nsf/conditionnav/kids~sectionintroduction

Club Drugs (National Institute on Drug Abuse). http://www.clubdrugs.org

CyberDiet. http://www/cyberdiet.com

Drug-Free Resource Net (Partnership for a Drug-Free America). http://drugfreeamerica.org

bibliography

Healthfinder. http://www.healthfinder.gov

InteliHealth: Home to Johns Hopkins Health Information. http://www.intelihealth.com

Mayo Clinic Health Oasis. http://mayohealth.org

On Health. http://www.onhealth.com

Prevention Online (National Clearinghouse for Alcohol and Drug Information). http://www.health.org

The Vegetarian Resource Group. http://www.vrg.org

Index

Italic type indicates volume number; **boldface** type indicates main entries and their page numbers; (ill.) indicates photos and illustrations.

A

AA. *See* Alcoholics Anonymous
AAPCC. *See* American Association of Poison Control Centers
ABMS. *See* American Board of Medical Specialists
Abnormalities, from endocrine disrupters *1:* 133–34
Abortion *1:* 77–78
Abscess
    defined *1:* 32
    tooth *1:* 44
Abstinence. *See* Sexual abstinence
Abstract thinking, Alzheimer's disease and *3:* 311
Abuse
    sexual (*See* Sexual abuse)
    substance (*See* Substance abuse)
Accidents, sleep deprivation and *2:* 216
Accreditation, defined *2:* 166
Acetaminophen *2:* 244
    defined *2:* 240
Acetylsalicylic acid. *See* Aspirin
Acid (Drug). *See* LSD (Drug)
Acid rain *1:* 119–20
    defined *1:* 112
Acne
    medication for *2:* 240–42
    in puberty *1:* 34–36, 36 (ill.)
Acquaintance rape. *See* Date rape
Acquired immunodeficiency syndrome. *See* AIDS

Acrophobia *3:* 344 (ill.), 345
Activity, physical. *See* Physical activity
Actors and actresses, substance abuse and *3:* 385
Acupoints *2:* 279, 280 (ill.), 281, 282
Acupressure *2:* 281, 285, 286. *See also* Massage therapy
Acupuncture *2:* 167 (ill.), 279–82, 280 (ill.), 282 (ill.), 282 (ill.), 283
    defined *2:* 270
    history of *2:* 281
    managed care and *2:* 160, 160 (ill.)
    naturopathy and *2:* 276
    in recovery from drug addiction *3:* 401
Acupuncture points. *See* Acupoints
Acupuncturists *2:* 165–68, 167 (ill.)
Adaptive behavior, defined *3:* 324
ADD. *See* Attention-deficit disorder
Addams, Jane *2:* 199
Addiction *3:* 381–83
    defined *3:* 382
    to exercise (*See* Exercise addiction)
ADHD. *See* Attention-deficit/hyperactivity disorder
Adler, Alfred *3:* 416–17
Adlerian psychology *3:* 416–17
Adolescence. *See also* Puberty
    breakfast and *1:* 27–28
    calcium and *1:* 10
    dating in *1:* 69–70
    eating during *1:* 24, 28
    nicotine in *3:* 397–98
    nutrients and *1:* 3–4, 7